As I started to move, the barrel of an AK-47 stuck itself out of the bunker's second opening. Knowing that I'd already killed the soldier with the rocket, I wondered how many more were down there. Not wanting to stick my head over to see, I reached over, grabbed the front wooden grip of the assault rifle and jerked it out of the soldier's hands.

With no real plan other than survival, I popped the pin on a grenade, yelled "Fire in the hole!" for the other Blues, released the spoon, and counted to a quick three before rolling it into the opening. Covering my head and ears, I turned away. Seconds later a violent explosion rocked the bunker turning it into a volcano, first throwing dirt and debris skyward and then falling into itself. Suddenly, I found myself in a depression, my ears bleeding and trying to keep from passing out. . . .

ACCEPTABLE LOSS

Kregg P.J. Jorgenson

IVY BOOKS • NEW YORK

Ivy Books
Published by Ballantine Books
Copyright © 1991 by Kregg P.J. Jorgenson

Library of Congress Catalog Card Number: 91-92122

ISBN 0-8041-0792-0

Manufactured in the United States of America

First Edition: November 1991

Cover photo by Art Dockter: all other photos by the author, except where credited.
UPI photo used by permission of the Bettmann Archive.
Map by Thomas E. Hitchins.

"It's not the critic who counts, not the man who points out how the strong man stumbled, or where the doer of deeds could have done better. The credit belongs to the man who is actually in the arena . . ."

—from the creed of Hotel Company Rangers, 75th Infantry, 1st Air Cav Division, Phuoc Vinh, Vietnam

ACKNOWLEDGMENTS

I'd like to thank everyone involved in this project: Phyllis Kristjanson, Mary Reilly, Carla Stone, and my family and friends for their support. Without it I might've just as easily given up writing for something more profitable, like collecting aluminum cans alongside of the expressway.

I'd also like to take the time to acknowledge Charles Edward Eaton, author of *The Girl from Ipanema*, and many other award-winning books, for encouraging me to take my writing seriously back when I thought it would be little more than a hobby.

Portions of this book first appeared in *Soldier of Fortune* magazine, and though it's easy to wince at its ads, SOF was one of the first publications ever to have something good to say about those caught up in the Vietnam War. Robert K. Brown, Dale Dye (the technical director for the movie, *Platoon*), Jim Graves, Don McLean, Tom Slizewski, and the rest gave us a chance to tell our stories long before it became popular.

As a sometime personal technical advisor to Terrence Knox on the television series, *Tour of Duty*, I may have offered some small advice on the war while Knox, in turn, provided some helpful nudging, reminding me to hang in there and keep writing whenever it got bogged down. It was appreciated then and now.

Finally, I'd like to thank my editor, Owen Lock, at Ivy Books for his valuable assistance, the likes of which produced this book . . .

. . .which is dedicated to my daughters: Kelli, Kristen, and Katie.

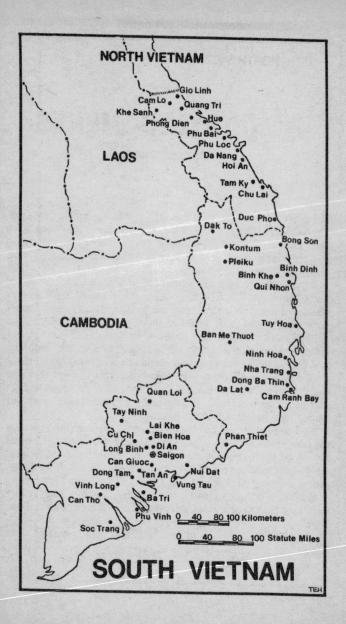

NORTH VIETNAM

Gio Linh
Cam Lo • • Quang Tri
Khe Sanh • • Hue
Phong Dien • Phu Bai
• Phu Loc
Da Nang
Hoi An

LAOS

Tam Ky • Chu Lai

Dak To • Duc Pho

• Kontum Bong Son

• Pleiku Binh Dinh
Binh Khe • • Binh Dinh
Qui Nhon

Tuy Hoa •

CAMBODIA

Ban Me Thuot •

Ninh Hoa•
Nha Trang•
Dong Ba Thin•
Da Lat • Cam Ranh Bay

Quan Loi •

Tay Ninh •

Lai Khe•
Cu Chi • • Bien Hoa Phan Thiet•
Long Binh • • Di An
⊛ Saigon
Can Giuoc •
Dong Tam • Tan An • Nui Dat
Vinh Long • Vung Tau
Can Tho • • Ba Tri

Phu Vinh 0   40   80 100 Kilometers

0   40   80 100 Statute Miles

Soc Trang •

SOUTH VIETNAM

TEH

NORTH VIETNAM

LAOS

Quang Tri

Hue

Thua Thien

Da Nang

Quang Nam

Chu Lai

Quang Tin

Quang Ngai

Kontum

Binh Dinh

An Khe

Pleiku

Qui Nhon

Pleiku

Phu Bon

Phu Yen

CAMBODIA

Darlac

Khanh Hoa

Nha Trang

Quang Duc

Tuyen Duc

Ninh Thuan

Cam Ranh Bay

Phuoc Long

Lam Dong

Binh Long

Binh Thuan

Tay Ninh

Long Khanh

Binh Tuy

1   Binh Duong
2   Bien Hoa
3   Gia Dinh
4   Hau Nghia
5   Long An
6   Go Cong
7   Kien Tuong
8   Dinh Tuong
9   An Giang
10   Sa Dec
11   Vinh Long
12   Phong Dinh
13   Sa Xuyen
14   Chuong Thien

Chau Doc

Kien Phong

Saigon

Phuoc Tuy

Kien Giang

Sac Lieu

An Xuyen

Can Tho

Vinh Binh

Kien Hoa

0   40   80   100 Kilometers

0   40   80   100 Statute Miles

SOUTH VIETNAM

TEH

PROLOGUE

SEPTEMBER 17, 1969

Rumor had it that the war would soon be over and that the Paris Peace Talks would hurriedly bring about its negotiated end.

Of course, that was only one of the rumors we heard on the long flight and maybe the only one we really gave any credence to because for myself and the two hundred or so other GIs heading toward Vietnam the war was just beginning.

I was a sergeant E-5, a buck sergeant, which was the lowest rung on the sergeant grading ladder. What's worse was that I was a nineteen-year-old "shake 'n' bake," the Vietnam War's version of the ninety-day wonder. Only in this case instead of becoming lieutenants after the ninety days of training, those of us who entered and successfully completed the Noncommissioned Officer's Candidate Course became sergeants. The theory was the same—to produce combat leaders in a short period of time and rush them into battle where they were sorely needed.

The trouble was, because of the brevity of the course and our ages, we were often viewed by the more experienced soldiers as less than well seasoned. Hence, the nickname shake 'n' bake. We were also known by a few other names as well, not that it mattered since the disdain still tasted the same.

But then, like everyone else who had shuttled into the war, we'd have to prove ourselves. To be honest, for the most part we did look like somebody's little brothers playing soldier. That couldn't be helped. We *were* young, but we were well-trained, enthusiastic if inexperienced, and ready to do whatever was expected of us.

All we wanted was the chance; digging ourselves into the proverbial pile of horse manure, we were certain there had to be a pony under there somewhere.

CHAPTER ONE

BIEN HOA, VIETNAM

As I stepped from the plane, it wasn't the sudden rush of heat or humidity that immediately caught my attention. It was the applause! Off to one side of the airbase terminal, several hundred gaunt, tanned, and laughing GIs wildly applauded our arrival. That is, the loosely assembled audience was applauding the arrival of our plane—a plane that when refueled would take them out and away from the Vietnam War. We were simply an added attraction.

Grabbing my duffel bag from the cargo area, I followed the other new arrivals to the terminal, running the gauntlet of catcalls and comments from the soldiers who'd soon be shuttling out of the war zone.

"Fucking new guys! Cherries!" howled a veteran, a thin, sharp-faced soldier who then pointed to our new, dark green jungle fatigues that still smelled of the mothballs they'd been stored in only a few days before. Pinching two fingers against his nose he added, "Shew! They even smell new!" Finally, there was one ringing editorial from another soldier that caused many to laugh and shake their heads knowingly. "Good luck, assholes!" he said. "You're gonna need it!"

Luck? Sure, why not? Hadn't the drill sergeants and training officers back in the States said we'd need training and luck "in the Nam" and that all of the training in the world wouldn't mean a thing unless Lady Luck was on our side? God, too, for that matter? Then didn't they smile, saying there was no such thing as luck and that God probably didn't really want to get involved in this nasty little mess anyway?

To many veterans, the war seemed to be an inside joke, and we new guys always seemed to be part of the punchline. After all, we

3

were the latest source of entertainment. So, with sweat beading our foreheads and spreading out at our armpits and lower backs, we grinned as though we really understood the jokes—or simply realized there was nothing to laugh about.

Facing the Viet Cong I knew would be easier; they'd only try to kill us. However, unlike our welcoming party, they'd probably leave us a little more dignity.

Shrugging off the insults, I followed the other "new meat," under the ushering of a bored and mildly agitated master sergeant, into the cool shadows of the terminal holding area, where we were told to sit and wait for the transportation that would take us to the replacement station to begin our in-processing orientation. At nineteen, I was anxious to begin fighting. Like the others, I was also tired and surprised by the surroundings; the eighteen-hour flight with its stopovers in Alaska and Japan had taken its toll. Any momentary surge of adrenaline at finally being "in the Nam" gave way to protracted weariness. All I really wanted to do was get processed in, get assigned to a unit, and begin saving a people and a country, both of which I knew little about. Not that it mattered. I'd save them in spite of myself.

The tour of duty for the average army infantryman was exactly 365 days—one calendar year—and the clock was officially ticking, but for now, like so many other times in my brief army career, I'd have to hurry up and wait. Even in the war zone this army maxim seemed to hold true. Taking a seat, I waited and watched what was going on around me, taking in the limited view of Vietnam from the busy air force facility.

From where I was sitting, it wasn't anything like I'd expected. There were no "Hit the beach" landings or cigar-chomping Sergeant Rocks, or John Wayne types telling us why we were there or what we'd have to do. Maybe that had been an earlier war. This one in the summerlike fall of 1969 had been going on officially for six years and unofficially for well over one thousand.

Any sense of urgency gave way to boredom and common everyday matters. On a nearby bench a GI, indifferent to our arrival, was lost in a comic book. Waves of ninety-plus heat, along with the lingering smell of jet fuel, exhaust, and mothballs, mixed with a slight breeze from the opening doors and tasted of dust. With the exception of the heat, Bien Hoa wasn't much different from McChord Air Force Base in Tacoma, Washington, which we'd left from the day before. If anything, Bien Hoa seemed more laid back.

Like most other military travel facilities, the Southeast Asian,

American air base was lean and Spartan at first glance; on second inspection it reflected the clean and responsible comfortable attitude of the air force. Something not lost on either the airmen who lived and worked there or on the army soldiers, like us new arrivals, who were only passing though.

A sign on a nearby wall pointed to a snack bar and said that it was open between the hours of nine and five. If war was hell, then here the extra heat melted the cheese and kept the side orders of fries warm.

Around the terminal soldiers and airmen, dressed in sun-bleached, faded jungle fatigues or clean, neatly pressed khakis, came and went. Some reading dog-eared paperbacks or old letters, while still others managed to sleep, even as a loudspeaker droned out manifest numbers to such distant and remote destinations as Nha Trang, Tay Ninh, or Vung Tau.

There were also salesmen in makeshift booths or at tables vying for the attention of the servicemen. Car salesmen showing brochures instead of actual products in a "pay now, drive later" plan. In this case the "later" came when the GI returned home after his monthly installment payments that made the down payment and more during his tour in Vietnam. Korean and Hong Kong vendors competed for attention as did a host of others. They had a captive audience, and they knew it.

One who was doing brisk business was a Bible salesman who hawked the large, family-size, vinyl-covered books that were complete with gold leaf and trim. At seventy-five dollars each—with a convenient installment plan—the salesman was getting his share of takers, especially the new arrivals. One, a tall, stoop-shouldered soldier, a new PFC, said the Book was a good investment, adding that he'd probably sell it at a profit the closer we actually got to the fighting. With prospective buyers around him taking a look, the PFC showed off his new purchase while the Bible salesman went back to his pitch. The carnival was still open for business, and he still had commissions to make.

"You can get one free from your chaplain," a vet said from a nearby chair. His tanned face was three days into a beard. Both the comment and the attention seemed to be an afterthought, since his attention was focused on another activity across the airstrip. An olive drab forklift was lifting large metal crates into the hold of a transport plane.

"What?"

"I said you can get a Bible free from your chaplain's office. A small one you can carry in your rucksack. Ain't no way you're gonna be able to carry that thing in the jungle," he said, turning his attention to a large white Bible.

"Thanks," I said. Then, wanting to make conversation, I added, "You been here long?"

"If you mean here as in Bien Hoa, maybe four hours or so. If you mean in-country, I'm going on five months."

I turned to see what he was watching but didn't see anything other than the loading operation. Turning back to the soldier, I noticed that he seemed beat for only five months. My face must have revealed what I was thinking because he smiled and shook his head. "I know it doesn't seem like all that long, but for some, new guy, five months is a lifetime. Like for those guys," he said, pointing to the transport plane.

"Which guys? You mean the ones who applauded out there?"

"No," he said quietly. "The ones in the boxes. Those are aluminum caskets. One day, five months, whatever. A lifetime, you know?"

Jeeps rolled in from time to time to pick up and escort officers and high-ranking noncommissioned officers (NCOs) to their units while the rest of us awaited less personal transportation. They had received their orders Stateside, assigning them to specific units, while the rest of us fell into a general replacement pool.

When our transportation finally arrived, it was in the form of olive drab, army school buses with mesh-screen windows, "to keep out grenades," someone said. Once again grabbing our baggage, we climbed aboard, some clamoring to sit near the windows while others fearfully avoided them. It was a short, bumpy ride across the divided base to the army's side of the large, fortified installation and the division's replacement station, and as we rode along, we craned our necks trying to get a better look at the country that would be our home for the next 364 days.

Besides the airfield and terminal complex, Bien Hoa was home to fighter planes, helicopters of various sizes and functions, sand-bagged hangars and retaining walls to house them all, and a variety of maintenance shops. Farther on lay a bookshop, snack bar, gift shops, a base exchange, troop barracks, enlisted, NCO, and officers clubs, a chapel, and a number of air force support units and single-story offices, each with its own sign bearing unit mottos and legends in large, bold print, and each claiming a history of prompt and efficient service. I guess every unit had to have a motto, and each tried to outdo the others with slogans like "THE BEST ABOVE THE REST!" and "CAN DO, SIR!" along with more that few actually believed. Farther on down the road and off to one side of the Special Forces compound stood a steam bath and massage center that, the bus driver informed us, doubled as a pretty decent whorehouse, which, of course everyone believed. Hormones were easier to convince than common sense.

"You can get steamed and creamed in there for twenty dollars MPC," the driver said, grinning, while we filed it away for future reference. MPCs were the Military Payment Certificates that we'd be paid with while we were in Vietnam. "Play money," added the driver, "but it spends like the real thing. Uncle Sam don't want you black-marketing any greenbacks while you're here, so they issue you MPC to keep you from getting any ideas."

I wanted to ask him just what kind of ideas about money he thought we'd have in the jungle and maybe remind him that it didn't seem to be Tarzan's primary concern, especially when he had a million screaming fuckers trying to spear his butt. Instead I let it ride.

For a while we rode along in silence, taking in the airstrip and adjacent countryside.

Surrounding the base perimeter were waist-high rows of barbed wire, ankle-high wire barriers known as tanglefoot, the sand-bagged bunkers, and periodic guard towers that marked the boundaries of the encampment. Signs in Vietnamese and English told of minefields and other dangers, while day guards, cradling M-16s or draped over machine guns, reminded us that in spite of its physical comforts, Bien Hoa was still in a war zone.

The paved road and an MP checkpoint gave way to a dirt road that led into the army's section of the base. Though unlike the reasonably comfortable side that was disappearing behind us in a swirl of orange dust, the army section had a bearing that was uniquely its own, a shabby boomtown version of the one we'd just left behind. "Shit! And I joined the army to get away from the ghetto," a tall, black GI said to no one in particular.

While the air force side hinted at war, the army's made it painfully clear. Fighting positions were more evident, and instead of barracks to house the soldiers, the army erected "hootches," single-story wooden huts set on concrete foundations and sporting corrugated sheet metal roofs. Circling each were waist-high walls of sandbags. Protection against the mortar or rocket attacks from the Viet Cong, providing the rounds were not direct hits and fell short of their objectives.

Besides the hootches, there were community showers and out-houses. Empty rocket tubes covered with wire mesh screens and set in the ground at angles served as urinals. There were also quartermaster buildings, logistic centers, command posts, mess hall tents, aid stations, and motor pools. There were storage sheds and warehouses, ammunition bunkers, and all the amenities the air force had but on a lesser scale, an army scale. When someone on the bus said as much, the driver piped in, "You bet. The air force has the attitude that hey, we gotta live here, so let's make the best of it. So they build in all the comfortable stuff to surround their pilots with. The army, well they have an attitude problem. They figure, 'Screw it, we'll probably be moving again soon anyway.' There it is," he said using a catch phrase the we'd later use ourselves. There it is.

It had a certain finality to it, as well as a sense of cynicism. It would take a while before we began to appreciate its meaning.

Everything about the army's side of Bien Hoa seemed temporary, a frontier town on the edge of nowhere, with no industry or business other than the war to keep it going. Business then was good, and like the boom towns that had grown in other times and situations, there was little to give it any sense of permanence or future development or growth. The war had been going on too long for that, and now even the settings looked weary.

"This ain't nothing!" the bus driver said, knowing what we were thinking. "The fire support bases are the pits! There are rats, snakes, bugs, mosquitoes, ankle-deep mud, and all kinds of weird shit. What are you guys anyway?" he asked, referring to our army job classifications, our MOSs (an acronym for Military Occupational Specialties).

"Infantry," shouted several replies.

"Too bad. Compared to a fire support base, this place is uptown, but you'll see soon enough."

From time to time we'd pass Vietnamese day workers hired and brought in each morning to perform many of the mundane tasks that otherwise might have been assigned to the soldiers—everything from filling sandbags, washing clothes, and cleaning offices and hootches to serving as barmaids, bartenders, or go-go dancers for the on-base service clubs. For many of us, it was our first real opportunity to get a look at the Vietnamese we'd come to save.

"So those are the gooks, huh?" said the soldier who'd bought the white-vinyl Bible at the airport terminal. "They don't look so tough."

"New guy, those are pussy cats compared to the VC or NVA

regulars,'' the bus driver said. Most of us knew that the initials VC meant Viet Cong but NVA was something new; yet another of the many buzzwords and acronyms we'd have to get to know.

"What are NVA?"

"North Vietnamese Army regulars. They're pretty hardcore little bastards.''

"So we'll kick their asses!'' the PFC said, more for the riders' approval than that of the driver.

"Uh-huh, sure you will, hotshot.''

"What do you know anyway, you're just a bus driver,'' said the cocky PFC.

At that, any trace of smile on the driver's face disappeared. He pulled the bus over, came to an abrupt stop, and turned around to face the critic. "All I know is that I've been here for ten months and fourteen days, and three times a day I drive by the airfield, and too many times I see them loading the metal coffins on the planes that fly outta here. This war has been going on for some time now, and it ain't the kind you win. It's the kind you survive. You kick ass, and you get your ass kicked, and if you're good enough, maybe smart enough to know that luck has a lot to do with it, then maybe you survive. A lot of good people are in those metal boxes, but like you said, what do I know? I'm just a bus driver.'' Turning back around in his seat he released the brake, put it in gear and drove on dismissing us all as "fucking new guys.''

It was a few minutes before some mumbling and the conversation turned back to the base and what we might come to find in it. Later, as we wheeled into the 1st Cavalry Division's replacement stations, we got a look at an NCO leadership academy with a cadence-singing training class going through drill-and-ceremony formations. Next to it lay a sniper school, complete with practice range where division snipers could work on the techniques that would make them highly appreciated in their units. There were other training units as well, with cadre and students coming and going with purpose, though the course names didn't ring any bells with us, and since we'd alienated the bus driver, we couldn't expect any more help from him. A large sign reading KIT CARSON SCOUT AREA was one of them. A vet explained it was where they trained former enemy soldiers to work for us. We eyed them suspiciously as we passed. Inside the replacement station, we received more smiles and cheers from the soldiers there. This time though it wasn't from veteran soldiers, just new arrivals and replacements who had arrived a few days before. Finally they had someone they could laugh at, someone newer than they were.

When the bus finally stopped, a master sergeant holding a clip-board yelled for us to fall out of the buses and into formation, while a black buck sergeant collected copies of our assignment orders. In formation we were given a quick briefing and introduction on what would be expected from us while we were there. He said there'd be indoctrination and training classes to attend as well as everyday chores and duties, such as perimeter guard, KP, and "Bar-B-Q."

"We gotta cook?" a voice asked from the rear of the formation.

"Not quite," the master sergeant said. A slight smile caught the corner of his mouth, while the buck sergeant smothered a laugh. "The Bar-B-Q is latrine duty. Every morning three or four of you will be assigned the task of pulling the cutaway barrels from the crappers, adding kerosene to the contents, and then lighting it. Over here we don't dump our waste, we burn it. For those of you with weak stomachs, keep upwind. Others will be detailed to fill water barrels for the showers."

He went on to say that over the next few days we'd be issued our rifles and equipment and have our division patches sewn on our jungle fatigue uniforms. He said the last item was to help make us feel like part of the Team. The Team that he was referring to was the First Team, the 1st Air Cavalry Division, the Cav, with its air mobility concept that utilized the spectrum of helicopters and gunships to achieve objectives. What began as a familiarization formation was turning into a kind of pep rally, complete with veteran cheerleader and enthusiast to help make us feel welcome and useful. None of us were cheering, but we were scared enough to listen.

There was a certain amount of divisional pride in the Cav, something that could easily be seen in the large shoulder patch that made it stand out over the others in the army. It was the army's largest patch and designed to be noticed. Initially, it had been designed for the old horse cavalry, and the modern division carried many of the old traditions and designations. For the dress uniform, the patch was a black and gold shield design, but in the war zone the patch was a subdued olive drab and black. Later in the training courses we'd be given an historical perspective on the division as well as updates from this war where the Cav had played major roles in routing the enemy forces, such as in the battles of War Zone C, Operation Pegasus that helped break the siege against the Marines in Khe Sanh, and the other many distant places with names that were hard to pronounce or spell—like Plei Mei, Pleiku, Tay Ninh, or Hong Kong Mountain in An Khe.

"These names don't mean much to you now," the sergeant said, "but they will."

An advantage of being in the Cav, we were told, had to do with the many helicopters the division had at its disposal. While grunts in other divisions had to hump it out to the boonies, the Skytroopers, as we would be known, would be ferried out by helicopter.

The trouble is, one cynic said in a low whisper, the Viet Cong are getting pretty good at setting landing-zone traps and shooting the helicopters down, and when the helicopters fell in a ball of twisting flames and debris, so did the Skytroopers who rode in them. "Crispy critters," the cynic said. "The name's Beal. Ed Beal, Greensboro, North Carolina," he said, holding out his hand.

"Kregg Jorgenson, Seattle," I said, shaking it. At twenty-one, Ed Beal was a veteran on his second tour of duty in Nam, this time with the Cav. His first tour had been as a dog handler/scout up north in '67. When it was up, he had been sent to Germany.

"So what are you doing back here?" asked the PFC who'd purchased the Bible.

"Too much bullshit," he said. "Too many people trying to prove something. Since they're not in the war, they try to make it miserable for those of us who have been, so I reenlisted and came back here. Look," he added, knowing that his reasoning didn't make much sense to the PFC, "for all that's wrong with this place, it's still not all that bad. The scary part is that it grows on you, and even though you hate it, you'll find that you'll never let it go." Staring into the PFC's blank, expressionless eyes, Beal smiled and shook his head. "There it is."

When we weren't on detail or attending classes in patrolling, rappelling from helicopters, studying Viet Cong ambush and booby-trap techniques, or attending one of the three daily mandatory formations, we were on our own. We could get drunk at the NCO or enlisted clubs, take in a movie at a makeshift outdoor theater, or visit the immediate areas for informal inspections or observations. After the last formation in the early afternoon, few GIs took to wandering, while many opted for the enlisted club, and still others took to the Quonset-hut-like barracks-hootches that were unique to the replacement station. There they wrote letters home. Lying back on a thin mattress in the late afternoon heat, I drifted off into a deep, warm sleep. The first few days of indoctrination and travel had taken their toll, and though I wouldn't know it at the time, it would be the last real comfortable sleep I would get.

I awoke several hours later, slapping at the circling drone of a mosquito that flew in rhythm to a USO band playing rock music on a nearby outdoor stage. As I walked out toward the bandstand, a parachute flare off in the distance drew my attention away from the music. "A Viet Cong ground probe or attack," a voice said from behind me. It was Beal. The ghostlike white flare against the black velvet backdrop of the Vietnamese evening set the stage for another kind of show, one punctuated and splintered with green and red machine-gun tracer rounds accenting the pyrotechnic display.

The flare slowly floated to the jungle floor, swinging back and forth before it disappeared into the evening.

"Too far away to matter," Beal said, "at least for us. For now anyway."

I knew we'd soon be the ones off in that distance, while other new-guy grunts would be watching the fragments of our private piece of the war, and perhaps they too would turn back to the bandstand, trying not to think about it and not having much luck, either.

CHAPTER TWO

For every soldier in Vietnam who was actually fighting in the field, there were five support personnel in large, reasonably comfortable, rear-area bases or camps to service them. Besides the infantrymen there were the military police, medical specialists, supply and transportation soldiers, administration personnel, communication, intelligence, laundry, and maintenance units, along with various other companies or detachments who the infantry or grunts referred to less lovingly as REMFs.

This acronym, said with a certain amount of disdain, meant that these people were rear-echelon motherfuckers. How close you were to the actual fighting and what you did whenever it began set the REMF boundary. Combat medics were okay, as were some artillery people, tankers, various pilots and crew, and certain other select personnel. Any and everyone else who didn't fall into those classifications were REMFs and despised and maybe secretly envied because of their safe jobs.

"You see, it has to do with war stories and the folks back home," Beal said in a late-night rap session. "Everyone back home thinks we're all over here doing hand-to-hand combat with Uncle Ho and the boys. They have no real idea or notion what's going on over here, let alone where to find Vietnam on a map or globe. As for the villages, well to most of them these places sound like little more than dropped silverware—Bong Song Bing or whatever—while to us the names have their own special meaning. The trouble is, they all think we're doing the same dirty job over here."

"So?"

At that the veteran grunt just stared at me with a quizzical expression and shook his head in disgust. Maybe he was wasting his time with me and the others.

13

"Boy, you are new, aren't you? Let me put it another way. It's like the Great San Francisco Earthquake of 1905—"

"Of '06," I said, correcting him. His quizzical expression changed to an annoyed glare.

"Whenever," he replied curtly. "The point is that the residents in the city at the time knew what was really going on, while the folks across the bay said they heard a terrible noise and were frightened for their own safety. For the REMFs it's the same thing. They hear the noise, see the smoke in the distance, and go home and tell everyone that war is hell and they don't want to talk about it; they share in our shit but don't want to step in it like we do. It has to do with front lines and proximity."

Sitting around the bare bulb that lighted the hootch, sipping cans of warm beer, we huddled around Beal, hoping to get a better understanding of the war and how it would affect us.

"I read somewhere there weren't any front lines over here," the PFC said, still having not learned his place in the scheme of things. For now, I was off the hook. I had only made a minor correction about something other than the war, while the PFC had stepped on it, the *it* being the male organ and the phrase applying to a GI's social faux pas. The PFC had a name now, not that it mattered anyway. His, he said, was Breeze. Not really a religious man, Breeze was covering his bet with the purchase of the Bible at the airport, like the ten-spot he'd put in the church collection plate on Sundays instead of going to confession on the Saturday evening before.

"What?"

"I said, I read where there ain't no front line over here, so what does it really matter where you are or what you're doing?"

Even though Beal knew the PFC's nickname, he wasn't about to recognize him in that way.

"New guy, new guy, new guy," Beal said rubbing his eyes. "In a week or so, when you're assigned to a line unit and you're out in the bush on patrol and when you hit the shit, I mean, when Charlie ambushes you and you're lying on your stomach in the dirt, hoping your rifle won't jam while thirty or forty of them are rushing at you yelling and screaming and firing their B-40 rockets and AK-47 assault rifles and thinking seriously about bayoneting your butt, I want you to think about the pizza stands back here, the go-go bars, steam baths, nightly movies, beer halls, and all the other fancy comfortable things like toilet seats and showers. Then, I want you to think about the REMFs here enjoying them and that dumb-ass thing you just said about there being no front line.''

"So how come you're going to be a grunt again, I mean, if you know better? Why aren't you a REMF?"

"Pride maybe, a sense of satisfaction of being in the infantry," Beal replied, "and the fact I couldn't lie, whine, or bribe my way into a comfortable REMF job. They may seem like dumb fucks to us, but they're smart enough to know just how good they got it.''

Like most of the other young soldiers in the replacement station, I had no real idea why I was there or what, if anything, I'd accomplish. At nineteen years of age, I didn't really believe we were saving the world from Communism or Vietnam for the Vietnamese. I knew little of their language or culture, let alone the history of their thousand-year struggle against the Chinese, Khmers, French, Japanese, the French again, or the Americans and our allies.

Also, I didn't really think we were winning the war, either, since I'd overheard others with more age, education, rank, and experience say that it had already been going on longer than it should have. After all, Vietnam was a small country and not exactly a major power, so perhaps, as some had suggested, we were just testing new weapons, battle strategies, or even seasoning the troops using the "it's the only war we have, so let's make the most of it" policy.

So why was I there? Like some of my friends back home in Seattle, I suppose I could probably have maneuvered myself into college and out of the army, only I didn't want to because college didn't interest me as much as the war did. As any Saturday matinee moviegoer knew, war was exciting. It served as a rite of passage and test of manhood in too many popular films and books of fiction. The war in Vietnam already had been going on for nearly six years, and there were rumors that it would soon be over, so I wasn't so much afraid of going to the war as much as I was afraid of missing it! I had some friends back home who felt the war was wrong, while others said it was a matter of patriotism and of helping decent people who desperately needed help. All I knew was that I had to find out for myself. Action seemed better than inaction, so with all the bravado of any boy still in his teens, I enlisted in the army and volunteered for the infantry and Vietnam.

I had a certain fascination with war because I couldn't yet comprehend its consequences. I was too young and dumb to appreciate fear or the aftermath of hard-fought combat. It hadn't occurred to me that I might be filling the position of another, earlier, replacement who, just as cocky, just as foolish, had been killed by an equally young Vietnamese who was fighting for the liberation of his homeland, the freedom of his people and country, rather than worrying about his social status or any grand notion of vaulting into manhood. He would have a purpose while I would only have the war.

But then, I was still a new guy, an "FNG"—and not a "Funny New Guy," either, the way a writer in *Reader's Digest* had suggested—but rather a Fucking New Guy. The difference was that of cynicism as opposed to humor. Like other FNGs, I was still filled with illusions of petty glory and comic book heroics.

I signed for my rifle at the division's quartermaster supply shop. Like most rear-area supply storage depots, it was run like a general store, a tropical 7-11 for all the staples of war.

A sign on one of its two doors displayed its hours of operation. For those who worked there, the war was a nine to five workday.

A staff sergeant, watching our truck drive us and drop us off, eyed us with disdain. In a short, staccato speech he told us that we'd enter alphabetically through the door marked IN, pick up our gear, sign for our rifles, and exit through the door marked OUT. We were also told to keep the noise and grab-ass down inside and once we got out he didn't give a damn what we did.

One by one we shuffled in and received our combat gear, which we loaded in a duffel bag and cloth laundry bag. Along with the rifle came all the necessary equipment needed by an infantryman to do his job, all that is, with one major exception—no ammunition. The quartermaster didn't want any overanxious young GIs bringing the war, or anything that remotely resembled it, closer to his safe and quiet shop. Too many of the new young hot dogs thought of themselves as tigers, and he preferred his tigers without teeth.

When it was my turn to sign for my rifle in the shop's large property book, I noticed the bold print letters KIA penciled in red across several signatures whose last names started with the letter J. The three letters, KIA, meant that the soldiers had been killed in action. An ominous note for an otherwise ordinary transaction.

"Take care of your rifles," the staff Sergeant said as we exited the shop. "Otherwise, you'll pay for 'em!"

Thinking about the penciled letters KIA, yet another acronym we'd become familiar with, I knew that in one way or another, we certainly would pay for those rifles.

*   *   *

The staff sergeant was a black grunt from Chicago, a veteran on emergency leave and staying the night at the replacement station before he returned to his unit in the field. Several new arrivals were pushing to find out what the jungle was like and the war. He laughed at the questions; Beal only smiled. They knew the score, while the rest of us didn't, as yet, understand the game plan.

"You seen anyone get shot and killed?" a new arrival asked.

The sergeant smirked. "Shot and killed, huh? Well, man, if you only got shot at over here, then that wouldn't be so bad," the black sergeant replied.

"What do you mean?"

"I mean, there are a thousand and one other ways you can die over here as well. Besides getting shot, you can get rocketed, mortared, bombed, or bayoneted. Your helicopter can crash, your bunker can cave in, your jeep turn over, or a tank can accidentally grind you into ravioli. And before you ask, yes, the North Vietnamese Army has tanks down here. What else? You can get malaria, plague, dysentery, jungle rot, or die from a simple runaway infection."

Beal, sitting up in his bed, nodded to the vet. "Or you can get rabies from a dog or rat bite, gored or stomped on by a pissed-off water buffalo or elephant, or bitten by any number of poisonous snakes, like the bamboo viper or king cobra."

The staff sergeant laughed. "Or you can die from heatstroke, heat exhaustion, or from being napalmed—accidentally. You can overdose on heroin or any combination of pills. You can step on a land mine, trip a trip wire to a booby trap, drink battery acid or ground glass that the Viet Cong had been known to put in GIs' beers. You can be cut, slashed, or flayed."

"What's more," Beal chimed in, "your pecker can fall off from any number of strains of VD, so whoever said a coward dies a thousand deaths while a brave man only dies once didn't take into consideration an active imagination."

"Or a keen grasp of the situation," the black veteran sergeant said, walking over to Beal and giving him the dap, the intricate handshake that originated with the black soldiers and had crossed over to many of the other veterans in the field. Meanwhile, the rest of us were laughing.

"Now, before you bust a gut, keep in mind that every one of these ways of dying we just mentioned, along with others we haven't even though about, is ridiculously possible."

The black sergeant nodded somberly and then broke into a wide grin. "You see, war ain't only hell. It's a motherfucker."

CHAPTER THREE

Social scientists say that environment plays a major role in the development of behavioral patterns, and perhaps included somewhere in that theory is the effect of audio stimulation on the imagination. I knew the war stories I'd heard were beginning to have an effect on the way I viewed the war and the people around me.

For instance, the two most common war stories seemed to be the one about the old Vietnamese barber who later turned out to be a Viet Cong officer, and depending upon which version you believed, was (A) killed in a ground attack on the base one early morning, or (B) was caught after cutting the throats of unsuspecting GIs.

The second most commonly told and retold war story was the one about the GI who shot the little shoeshine boy after the kid produced a grenade and killed several more unsuspecting GIs.

Even in just my few days in-country, I'd personally heard those two stories at least five times, which of course, were added to the number of times I'd heard them in basic and advanced infantry training prior to coming to Vietnam. Each story became suspect, leaving me to believe that if they had happened as many times as I'd been told, then there couldn't be a decent haircut or pair of polished shoes in the entire country!

Still, the stores shaded the way I viewed the Vietnamese because like most stories there was probably a trace of truth in each.

Like most grown or nearly grown adults, I was rational enough not to believe in ghost stories, while wondering—and, maybe, shaking—whenever something unseen went bump in the night.

I'd also come to learn that everyone had his war stories, even if they were sometimes bullshit, borrowed, slightly embellished, or flat-out major productions. Everyone had or wanted his piece of the war, and sometimes the stories served as little more than object lessons or entertainment for the new guys.

There were war-story critics who said that the only difference between a fairy tale and a war story is that the fairy tale begins "Once upon a time . . ." while the war story starts off with "This is no shit."

While some were told and retold, there were still a few floating around that were unusual or different, like the one the black sergeant told later that evening at the replacement station.

"So there we were, spread out around this small dust-blown dink village just outside of Quan Loi. Anyway, we're waiting for the lieutenant to come up with something interesting to say to the troop commander, who's flying around overhead," he said, twirling the first finger of his right hand in small circles.

"See, the TC is flying round and round, waiting for the action to begin, only after sweeping through this village it doesn't look like anything's gonna happen.

"I mean this big-time operations is supposed to uncover a Viet Cong hideout—only after maybe two or three hours of searching, we ain't found shit. Not one damn Victor Fucking Charlie. However, what we did find was a bunch of old people and children along with maybe one run-down, raggedy-ass-looking water buffalo.

"So we're all standing around watching these folks, while the platoon sergeant and the louie are tossing around a few ideas and things to tell the old man. Now most of the villagers are standing outside their hootches, looking like scared poodles caught out on the freeway by the lights of an oncoming Buick.

"Like the poodles, they don't know whether to shit or run, and their feet are about as heavy as a pile of bricks. That is, all except for this real old woman and a young boy.

"This old woman just waddles out and smiles at us like we're long-lost friends. I tell you, this old woman had to be one hundred if she was a day! She was bent, wrinkled, and looked like a banana left out in the sun too long. And all the time she's smiling through these ancient gums, drooling across three or so chipped, green nubs that were trying to pass for teeth. To make things worse, it was hot, so hot that there wasn't really anything for her to smile about. One-oh-two in the shade—but there ain't any—only here's this woman and kid, smiling all moon-faced and happy.

"A few minutes of this goes by until the kid walks over to Henderson and says:

" 'You not French?'

"So Henny, cradling his M-16, looks down at him, smiling, and says, 'Neither are you, sport. So I'd say we're even.'

"The kid, smiling bigger than before, says in broken Pidgin English that his grandmother—the old woman—thought that we might be French, but he told her he didn't think so, so she sends him over just to make sure.

Henderson explains to him that we're Americans, and at that the kid nodded.

" 'Why you here?' the boy asked, holding one hand in front of his eyes to cut the glare from the noonday sun.

" 'Well, my boy,' Morgan, the smart ass says, opening a can of C-ration peaches. 'We Americans are champions of justice, able to leap tall buildings in a single bound while struggling against social injustice to help you little fish-head eaters fend off those boys from Hanoi who are trying to keep you from your meager squalor.'

"At that the kid slowly shook his head and stared. 'No understand,' he said all wide-eyed and confused.

" 'That makes two of us,' Morgan says, looking the kid and the old woman over. 'Here. Take these for you and your grandmother,' he says, tossing the kid two boxes of C rations. The kid makes an O.J. Simpson catch and breaks for daylight back to the old woman who, by the way, is still smiling. After a minute or so of exchanging words with the old lady, the kid turns and hauls ass back toward Morgan screaming at the top of his lungs about the booby traps.

"Can you believe this shit? I mean, we search the whole village and don't find diddly, and the boy is talking about booby traps. Then he explains to Morgan that the village isn't booby-trapped, but the trail that leads out of the far side of the village is. The kid says that the Viet Minh came in the night and booby-trapped the trail we'd use on our way out.

"Viet Minh! Can you actually believe that? This old woman has got her wars messed up! Anyhow, the lieutenant, being so college smart and all, doesn't want to believe the kid because during his ROTC training he was taught to be an officer and a gentleman and a dumb ass.

"So the kid, giving the louie a badass look, walks to the far side of the village, picks up a few good size rocks, and starts tossing them down the trail. After a few misses, he triggers an explosion which drops him to the ground, only to have him get back up smiling, which shuts the lieutenant up, and maybe takes care of the platoon sergeant's case of constipation.

"The louie calls in to the troop commander that we just blew a VC ambush, while everyone else wildly digs through their rucksacks for any excess C rations to give to the old woman and the kid. After a while she's got enough food to last her the rest of her natural life, provided she dies the following Thursday, which is something she just might do with her being so cobwebbed and all.

"Now, the thing is, before we moved out, Morgan asked the kid to ask the old woman why she wanted to know if we were French. So the kid asks, and the old woman flashes a neon smile, and in a screen-door-closing says, '*Xin loi.*' Just like that '*Xin loi.*' "

"So what does that mean, *Xin Loi*, I mean?" I asked while the two vets both smiled.

"Well, new guy," Beal said, "technically, it means 'sorry about that' but lately it seems to mean about the same as tough shit."

CHAPTER FOUR

It was during my fifth day in-country, when a lanky, red-haired PFC stuck his head in the door of our transient barracks and yelled: "Anybody here wanna be a Ranger?"

Heads turned as a barrage of questions and insults flew at him too fast to counter or avoid.

"Whoa! Wait a minute!" the PFC said. "I'm just delivering the message. There are a few of them who can answer questions better than I can out near the training area looking for people."

"Come on, Jorgy," Beal said. Breeze and a few others who were serious about what they had to offer followed us out. Taking a seat on long, flat benches, we waited for the sales pitch.

Airborne Rangers. The stuff of Jody songs that had been drilled into us throughout basic and advanced training and during any formation that required troop movement and feet. Dressed in starched and faded jungle fatigues, the two Ranger recruits, a small, wiry staff sergeant and a spec-four, who could've easily been a college football fullback, made an impressive sight. Black berets crowned their heads, while the large red, white, and black 75th Infantry Ranger scroll overshadowed the subdued division patch below it. The spec-four cradled a CAR-15 automatic rifle while the staff sergeant carried a holstered .45 slung low on his hip. Both wore the highly polished Cochran jump boots with the heel and toe sections of the boots displaying a black-mirror finish.

"We're from Hotel Company Rangers, 75th Infantry Airborne, and we're here to find qualified personnel to serve as replacements in our unit. Unofficially we're here to look for volunteers," the staff sergeant, whose name was Mitchell, said matter of factly.

"Yeah, well if we're not Airborne qualified? Does that mean maybe you'll send us back to the States if you want us?" Breeze asked. The staff sergeant only smiled. "I mean, for Ranger training and all?"

"Maybe if a frog had wings he wouldn't bump his butt everytime he jumped," the Ranger spec-four said.

"You don't have to be Airborne qualified," the staff sergeant added. "Whether you know it or not, this is the 1st Cavalry Division, and here we do everything with helicopters. There's no need to be dropped by parachute when the helicopter can take you where you want and need to go."

"What about Ranger training?" a new "shake 'n' bake" E-6 staff sergeant asked. A small black OD Ranger tab was sewn in place over the oblong Cav patch. His bearing was Fort Benning, while his drawl and twang said he was from Texas or Oklahoma. As a shake 'n' bake he was a graduate of the thirteen-week NCO course that the army introduced during the war to produce the sergeants needed to fill out the ranks of the infantry units.

"We have a two-week, in-country training program that will teach you the basics of everything you'll need to know to function as part of a Ranger team."

The new E-6 replacement looked over the small audience. "A few of us here are already Ranger qualified," he said.

"Everyone who volunteers will go through our training. If you make it to graduation, you'll receive a training certificate, a Ranger scroll patch and be assigned to one of our teams."

"But you won't be a Ranger. I mean, not a real one—"

It was the wrong thing to say, and judging by the look on the face of the two LRRPs, they were about to let him know it.

"The shake 'n' bake stepped on his dick," Beal said.

"Real Rangers?" sneered Staff Sergeant Mitchell. There was a noticeable edge to his voice. "What's a real Ranger? Someone who goes through an eight-week course back in the States, where they parade around showing their Ranger tabs and posing, or someone who earns the title here doing the job? The two-week training course we offer deals with what it takes to do the job as a LRRP—"

"What's a LRRP?" someone asked.

The spec-four fielded the question. "A LRRP is a member of a long range recon patrol team. It's an acronym for who we are and what we do."

"We pull long range patrols in Charlie's backyard," added Mitchell, "so that's why we have our own training program. We have to be certain you can cut it before we assign you to a team."

"What kind of training?" asked the new E-6 with the drawl, trying to make up for his blunder.

"Map reading, rappelling from helicopters, radio maintenance and operations, aerial-rocket and gunship coordination, medic training, ambush techniques, enemy weapons familiarization, enemy unit identification, and anything else we can think of. There'll also be a lot of physical training and harassment because we want to be sure you're in shape and that you won't fall apart at the first sign of trouble. It won't be easy, but even if you don't make it on a team and you decide to drop out, you'll at least have picked up enough to maybe survive it as a grunt in the bush."

"But in just two weeks? What can you possibly learn in two weeks?" It was the new E-6 again.

"This time he jumped on it with track shoes." Beal laughed. Mitchell shook his head, as the spec-four lit into the E-6. "Two weeks ain't shit, new guy!" he said. "But it's all the time we have to try to whip your cherry ass into some sort of reasonable shape. I'm a team leader, and I can't afford to have anyone on my team that can't do the job. The two weeks of training are designed to show you new guys just how much you don't know, in spite of your rank or any schools you might've graduated from.

"We have to know that when you get assigned to a team you'll know enough to keep your mouth shut and your eyes and minds open. Patches, tabs, and certificates don't mean shit. You prove to us you can do the job, and then and only then will we recognize you as Rangers. What's more, we'll recognize you as LRRPs."

"Gentlemen," added Staff Sergeant Mitchell, "Nam ain't no picnic. But for those of you that want to learn how to survive it, we'll show you what you need to know. You'll be working with good people who'll watch out for you. Keep in mind, most of you people will be going to grunt companies, and no matter how good you are or how good you think you are," he said, looking directly at the new E-6, "you'll have others around you, not all, but a few, who'll get you blown away for any one of a hundred silly reasons. Someone may fall asleep on guard or call in the wrong artillery coordinates or anything else just as dumb—and you'll be dead. Shipped home in a metal box with a folded flag for your family."

He paused to let that take effect.

"If you don't believe us, then ask the vets around you. Some of you with CIBs know what I'm saying." Heads turned and the veteran soldiers reluctantly agreed.

"Another thing to keep in mind," Mitchell added. "The grunts may be out in the bush for a month at a time, but we pull five-day patrols. Then, we usually come back in for two before going back out."

"How big's the company?" a veteran asked.

"We have two platoons and a number of support personnel. We operate out of the division's headquarters in Phuoc Vinh at Camp Gorvad though our patrols work everything from Tay Ninh to Quan Loi. For most of you those names don't mean anything yet. But they will," the Ranger staff sergeant said pointedly.

"The platoons go out for five days at a time?" Breeze asked.

The company recruiter shook his head. "No platoons. The teams go out for five days at a time."

"So how many men on a team?"

"Five," the staff sergeant replied. The answer hit the crowd of GIs like a hard slap, and maybe the recruiters from the LRRP company expected as much. I imagine the answer always elicited the same response—stunned silence and nervous fidgeting.

"But that's five people who know what they're doing. Most of the time we're inserted into an area, and the NVA and VC don't even know we're there. We do our thing and get out before they've even caught on," Mitchell said, clarifying the point. It was a soothing tactic, one not lost on us potential recruits.

"Our unit's not for everyone," he added, "in fact, more than half of the people who volunteer won't make it through the training. Of those that do, a few won't make it past their second mission. They won't be able to handle it, and they'll want out. But for those who hang in there, it'll be well worth it. Now, if there are no more questions, then that's all we have. Those of you who want to give it a try stick around, while the rest of you are free to go. Dismissed." He turned away to discuss something with the spec-four.

"What do you think, Ed?"

"I think it's not bad. Some of what they said is pep talk, but most of it makes sense. Besides, I saw our names posted in the orderly room. It seems we're going to be sent to the 7th Cav so it's either the LRRPs or General Custer's old unit."

"Any Little Big Horn valleys over here?" I asked.

"Kid, let's not take any chances."

Of the twenty or so soldiers assembled, eight of us hung around to join the company. Among our group was the Fort Benning Ranger from Texas. Training, we were told, would begin in a week. First, they'd take our names and social security numbers and get our orders changed. Perhaps the next day we'd receive new orders assigning us to H Company, where we'd join other volunteers who were waiting to begin training as well. They'd been recruited from the various units within the division.

"Congratulations," the spec-four said to us before turning towards the replacement station's orderly room. "Whether you know it or not, you made one of the best decisions you'll ever make over here."

As predicted, the next morning we received our revised orders. Turning in our bedding, we reported to the orderly room and were trucked back to the airfield where we caught a Chinook helicopter for Phuoc Vinh. After a jerky forty-five-minute flight, we lumbered into the division headquarters in Phuoc Vinh. Stepping from the helicopter, duffel bags and rifles in hand, we were greeted by Staff Sergeant Mitchell and a driver who ferried us into the company area. The official name for the division's headquarters base camp was Camp Gorvad, named after a division soldier killed in action. Like the army side of Bien Hoa we'd left that morning, Camp Gorvad was a step down from our previous stop. Smaller than Bien Hoa, it was better defended but it had reason to be. In the middle of the III Corps infiltration routes, it was the operations center for the smaller fire support bases within its region.

Home for the next three weeks would be a platoon-size training tent in the surprisingly small company area that was the LRRP enclave. Two platoon hootches housed the company, while an orderly room, training room, radio room, and briefing hootches lay off to one side. A weapons-cleaning area, along with protected bunkers, lay on the other. In the far reaches of the area were the outhouse and shower area. And, of course, between them all, the training tent. A volleyball game was going on when we arrived, and we received catcalls and sullen stares from the players as we came through the main gate, which displayed the company name, along with 75th Ranger scrolls and logos. One sign announced that the company commander was a captain named Richard F. Griffiths, while below it read "Ronald Guerin, First Sergeant." We'd find empty cots in the tent and make ourselves as comfortable as possible. And comfort was rough, defined by pallet-floors, open flaps, and a constant flow of orange dust. Bare bulbs powered by company generators provided night lighting; from dawn to dusk the open tent flaps offered light from bright to gloom. Surrounding the tent was a waist-high wall of sandbags, "to keep down the shrapnel spray from exploding rocket and mortar rounds," Beal explained. When it rained, small leaks in the tent made themselves evident, but then the training offered little in the way of comfort. Why should our living conditions be any better? The company was trying to prepare us for the war going on in Vietnam and not the one of our imaginations. Even the rats that scurried beneath the slat flooring had the satisfaction of knowing that they'd been there longer than we had and would probably be there long after we left.

Faces began to take names. There was Frank Duggan from Boston, Johnny Rodriguez from California, Gene Sprague, Dennis Smith, and a host of others whom we'd get to know over the course of the two-week training—which, we were later informed, would actually take three weeks. The class, along with the training tent, was filled.

Of those who'd be going through the training, several were on their second tours of duty, but the majority of us were on our first. Ranks varied from the lowly, private first class (E3) to staff sergeants (E6) with enough time in grade to be promoted to sergeant first class (E7). While we were in training, our ranks wouldn't mean a thing, nor would they when we graduated and were assigned to a team.

"Team leader ranks range from spec-four to staff sergeants," Gene Sprague, a staff sergeant with twelve years of service, explained. "Anyone who joins a team takes on the medic or RTO role, which means, besides his own equipment, he's responsible for either the medic bag or the radio. The team leader has the final say on matters, and our input doesn't mean a whole hell of a lot, but then maybe that's the way it has to be."

"Why's that?" Breeze asked.

"Because they have the experience in the field. They have the time logged in on missions, which gives them the edge. We're entitled to a voice when we have our time logged in."

"Yeah, but you're a staff sergeant. It doesn't seem right."

Surprisingly, it was the Ranger staff sergeant from Fort Benning who responded to the question. "Maybe they know how things really are while the rest of us only have an idea."

"Just because I was a squad leader in a line unit on my last tour doesn't mean I know how to do this job. I'm not too thrilled about having to take a back seat to someone else in a lower rank, but I like to think I'm smart enough to know I don't know their game plan yet," Sprague added.

As for priority, we were last on the list. Members in the company were entitled to use the showers first, while we had any water that was left. We also had the shit-burning detail as part of our daily routine. So much for glamor.

The first day of our actual training began with a popping click of a CS riot-gas grenade igniting in our tent, courtesy of the training NCO, who—upwind and poised—yelled for us to get our "nasty asses" out of his tent and out to the company formation area where we'd begin with physical training—stationary exercises, mostly, followed by a predawn run. At 4:30 in the morning, it was time for us to be introduced to the uncertainties of Vietnam.

We began with a one-mile run and added a mile each day until we reached the five-mile goal. On the second day we were supplied with rucksacks in which we'd carry a thirty-pound sandbag. That, and the weight from our rifles and web gear, provided the weight we needed to get used to carrying in the jungle. All totaled, it weighed nearly sixty pounds, which Staff Sergeant Mitchell said would only be part of the weight we'd have to carry.

The run began in front of the company area on a road that took us to the camp perimeter road. The course would take us down the perimeter road and often between the strands and lines of barbed wire and the bunkers that watched over that wire and the camp.

As we ran, we occasionally received words of encouragement from the grunts who were housed in the bunkers. Proud of their Rangers they greeted us with enthusiasm.

"Keep the noise down, you assholes!" one would yell while others would laugh, adding insults of their own. "John Wayne dumb fucks! Gonna die!" and more, with the jeering and laughter diminishing in the distance as we kept up our run. Then, too, there were other obstacles to overcome on the morning runs such as snakes, monsoon streams, and of course, incoming rocket or mortar rounds.

"Down! Down! Get your dumb asses down!" Mitchell yelled one morning when a few of us heard the explosions and then turned to view the brief displays of bright, orange-white light. "This ain't the Fourth of July, and those ain't sparklers! That's shrapnel, so get the hell down! NOW!"

After the predawn physical training, we were given time to shower, shave, and then walk over to the mess tent that we shared with an engineer unit across the camp. In return for use of their mess facilities, we pulled their perimeter guard.

After a morning formation, our official training day would begin—a course that was split between classroom training and hands-on outdoor training and application.

The small, one-room building served as our school room. Captured flags and equipment lined its walls as did other training aids such as maps, medical equipment, and a variety of radios. Hours were spent going over what we needed to know, while even more were spent on the walking drills, the formation the LRRP teams used while on patrol, all under the watchful eye of Staff Sergeant Mitchell.

"Not good enough!" he'd say. "Do it again." And we would, over and over again until he gave us a nod. That was as good as it would get by way of praise.

"Contact front!" he'd yell. "Front scout, fire one eighty and fall back. Second man, fire and move," and so on down the line, working and then reworking us in the jungle formation drills.

Nods were sometimes replaced by slow shakes of his head, coupled with insults. "Before you folks arrived our kill ratio was forty-four to one. You dumb shits just made surviving a fifty-fifty proposition!"

During the training, team leaders and company officers would stop by to view our progress, and they, too, would harass us for good measure. Push-ups were the standard punishment for minor infractions, while low crawling through pools of orange mud left by a sudden monsoon shower became the sentence for more serious infractions like frowning.

"You miserable son of a bitch!" Fabian whispered after we'd completed PT, showered, and changed into clean jungle fatigues, and then were ordered to low crawl through the mud again.

"What did you say?" an officer yelled. Fabian, not one to run from a challenge, repeated his comment.

"You forgot to add 'Ranger' to the end of it. Crawl back through again."

Meanwhile LRRP teams came and went. Quiet when ready to go, they performed a final weapons' check and test-fired in a barrel designed for that purpose. Then, they lined up for a team picture and boarded the small flatbed mules that would drive them to the airfield and their insertion helicopter.

Not all the missions went the scheduled five days. Many involved contact—a sudden confrontation when the teams blew an ambush, retrieved any intelligence, or captured any enemy soldiers who somehow managed to survive the ambush, and then got lifted out. In theory, the teams were designed to serve as intelligence-gatherers, to spy on enemy actions and report that information back to division intelligence (G-2), who'd analyze it and make recommendations to the strategists and tacticians who played out this dangerous human chess match. Theory often left a great deal to the imagination, and any sneaking and spying by the

LRRP teams was careful enough. But it was impossible for them to remain as invisible as they'd like.

While the teams slowly moved through the jungle in camouflaged uniforms and painted faces, looking for signs of enemy activity, fresh footprints, dropped equipment, listening for unusual sounds (like the sound of metal clinking) or talk or even catching a whiff of a small cooking fire, the teams themselves were subject to the same tactical faults as their enemy. Even the best have their off days, and in Vietnam it only took an off instant to make a deadly error, so the training and experience of those on the patrol often determined the outcome of a mission.

"We keep off of trails when we find them!" Staff Sergeant Mitchell said. "They'll booby-trap them or lead you into trouble, so whenever you come across one in the jungle, you mark it on your map and then parallel it if you have to."

Movement was deliberate, usually at a slow walk. Metal objects were taped, there would be no talking. Whispering was okay at times, but hand signals became the usual method of communication. Radio contact would be maintained between the Ranger radio-relay stations set up throughout the region. Team coordinates would be relayed during the day and at the night position. Whenever possible, the night position would be in an inaccessible area, an unlikely place for the enemy to use. At night, when the light disappeared and the rain forest grew black and heavy, guard duty would be every two and a half hours, leaving time for a light rest or sleep.

"If you hear or notice movement at night, something out of the ordinary, then you squeeze the arm or leg of the nearest person to you to get his attention. You don't open up, giving your team position away, unless you're absolutely sure you have to," Mitchell added.

"For the most part the Viet Cong and North Vietnamese soldiers are just like us, they don't move so well at night without making sounds or giving their positions away. Adhere to these principles and things should go okay. Of course," he added knowingly, "there may be times when they'll find your trail and begin stalking you. One of their tactics is to leave one of their people in probable landing zones, waiting for a team to be inserted. Then they'll inform their superiors, and you hunters will become the hunted.

"It's more than a game of hide-and-seek, because they'll kill you if they find you out. It's that simple."

The five-man teams would be made up of a team leader, who

was usually the front scout, an assistant team leader, a rear scout, a radioman, and a medic. In theory each man could do the others' jobs, if he had to. The team leader's word or whisper was law on patrol. There was no room for dissension on patrol, nor were mistakes taken lightly.

Some patrols were "picnics," five-day walks through the woods where little or no sign of enemy movement would be noted. Precautions were still taken, but there was a general feeling of guarded ease. It was the other patrols—the ones where fresh boot prints would be found on a newly discovered trail—that would keep the adrenaline running and the team extra cautious.

"Keep in mind that the purpose of these missions is to gather intelligence on enemy movement and activity. Say it to yourselves a few times until you get the message. Stealth and concealment are a LRRP's two best weapons. The gooks are human, just like the rest of us. They make their mistakes, too, and though the popular rumor is that they're invisible or regular Tarzans in the jungle, the truth will surprise you. We've had patrols spot NVA units walking down the trails smoking grass, listening to transistors, or using flashlights to find their way around, so you look and listen for these things, and in the dark jungle at night, if they're there, you'll notice them," he said.

Beal's hand shot up and Mitchell acknowledged it.

"You said the NVA or VC will sometimes leave someone to watch potential landing zones for insertions, so what's to keep them from compromising the mission then and there?"

"It could happen, but more than likely they'll report the insertion, note the direction you took, and then follow you with the others." It was a sobering thought at best, one which the veteran team leader expanded on. "Standard operating procedure for any team upon insertion is to sit and listen for ten to fifteen minutes, looking out for one of these spotters. Even if they don't see one, they'll move out and change course a few times to throw anyone who might be tracking them off the scent.

"It's not unusual for a team to be spotted and then followed, only to have the followers walk into a LRRP ambush, which leads us to another thing—though the mission is to gather intelligence, the taking of a POW would be better. In fact, the company has a policy that for every enemy prisoner of war you bring in, you get a three-day, in-country R&R."

Mitchell then went on to tell us about a team leader in the company, who after detonating an ambush on a Viet Cong patrol, chased a lone survivor a mile or so down the trail, tackled him, and with the aid of a .45 pistol escorted him back to the stunned team.

"So if I bring in 117 POW's on my first mission, then I can spend the rest of my tour getting tanned on the beach?" Breeze asked.

"If you get a chance, don't take it," Mitchell replied. "We had one team working along the border who found a trail, set out their claymores only to have three hundred NVA soldiers walk in front of them at night. In the dim light the team leader and the others said they could see the enemy soldiers walking three abreast, while an officer ran up and down the formation yelling at them to keep moving. The team didn't move a muscle, even when the officer tripped over the claymore wires thinking they were vines, so if you think you want to try to bring in 117 of them, let your team leader know first so he can get the rest of the team out of there before you try out your Sergeant York impression."

"York got his in-country R&R, right?"

"What?"

"Sergeant York, he got the R&R for chasing the gook and catching him, didn't he?"

Mitchell studied the thin-faced New Yorker, slowly shaking his head as the snickering built into open laughter.

"Breeze," he said, "be thankful we don't have an IQ test as part of the acceptance requirements."

By the end of the third week, four people had quit the training, each saying the training wasn't difficult but the harassment was bullshit. By the end of the second week, five more had resigned, opting for the infantry, where at least you didn't have to do push-ups at five in the morning. By the final day of training, Mitchell seemed less like a training NCO than he did a concerned instructor. He was responsible for our knowing our jobs, and if we failed, then he knew he had failed.

"For the most part the training's over. General Roberts will be down tomorrow to shake your hands and give you your patches and certificates. The Ranger's black berets you'll have to buy, but you'll get a chance to do that on pass after the graduation ceremony.

"The team leaders will be around tomorrow, kicking your tires to see if you're any good, determining if they really need you or not. If they accept you, you'll still have to prove yourselves the first few missions. But hang in there because I know you can do it. If you couldn't, then you would've left by now."

"So we're real Rangers, now?" The Fort Benning Ranger asked, thinking maybe it was time to ask the question again.

"Not quite," Mitchell said smiling, "All you have to do now is survive the war, but welcome to the company anyhow." He held out his hand and the lanky Texan shook it, smiling back.

CHAPTER FIVE

Of the half dozen or so graduates in our training class, Tony Fabian was the first to be placed on a team for a mission, the first to break the ice as a LRRP. After the short graduation ceremony, we were busy congratulating ourselves and looking forward to the day pass we'd been promised as a graduation present. The pass would entitle us to go into the nearby village to celebrate and applied to all the new graduates until Staff Sergeant Mitchell, the training NCO, came out of the orderly room and pulled the new Ranger/LRRP aside.

"Fabian, you won't be going on pass with the others. You're going out with 3-3 at 1600. Report to Lieutenant Rice in the 1st Platoon, and he'll introduce you to your team leader." Rice was Lieutenant Arthur A. Rice, the 1st Platoon leader and Company XO (executive officer). Fabian looked surprised as the rest of us. We knew sooner or later we'd be assigned to teams for patrols. Later seemed the certainty, but then we'd come to learn that nothing was certain in Vietnam, and certainly not a day pass.

"Take it easy out there, Tony," I said, shaking his hand and wishing him luck. In a way I wished it were me going out and in another instant glad that it wasn't. I still hadn't found the war I came searching for so eagerly, and it was a source of naive frustration. At nineteen I was more gung-ho than I should've been, a pain in the ass to some, I was sure, but maybe too eager to get involved with something I knew little of. I had programmed myself to be a soldier, accepting it after it seemed a certainty when my draft board changed my status from the student deferment of 2-S to 1-A—immediately available. Resigned to my fate, I decided to make the most of it. Since I was there, I wanted to do the best I could and as a result always managed to graduate in the upper percentages of my formal training programs. I even managed to become the Ranger class honor graduate, but I knew I became the honor graduate because of my enthusiasm. I wasn't really a better soldier than any of the others in the training cycle, certainly not more intelligent, just maybe more gung ho. I yelled louder when we performed the harassment push-ups in the mud, up—and up to our wrists in a monsoon mud puddle—and down, *splash,* face first into the orange-brown mud ooze. "One!" repeating the count after the instructor.

When it came to the five-mile running competition, I'd finished first. We were told we'd run it in the predawn when it was cooler. But when dawn came and passed, we knew that all was not what it seemed. By late morning we were told to get ready. Shouldering our thirty-pound rucksacks, we began the five-mile course. Unlike the previous runs, this was monitored along the route by Rangers from the company who'd insure we wouldn't stop or cheat. Stopping meant quitting, and they wouldn't tolerate a team member quitting on them in the jungle. I completed the run in forty-three minutes, first in the competition, sweat-soaked, legs wobbly, and lungs burning, while those LRRPs in the company at the finish line applauded and then threw me into a giant water-and-ice-filled cooler that held soft drinks and beer.

So it was my enthusiasm and that schoolkid need to be accepted as one of them that made me the honor graduate. But that was the icing on the cake.

Watching the rest of us head out of the company area towards town, Fabian waved, saying, "Don't get the clap!" and then disappeared inside the 1st Platoon's barracks to join his new team, take part in the mission briefing, and make the necessary weapons and equipment preparations. While we were celebrating in town, he and the others on team 3-3 would be inserted into the jungle by helicopter, quickly slip into the rain forest, and begin the deadly game of hide-and-seek.

"What do you think about Fabian?" I asked Rodriguez.

He shrugged. "That's the luck of the draw. Meanwhile, life goes on and, Mr. hotshot honor graduate, it's time to round out the rest of your education, you and the other first-timers. Gentlemen," he said, addressing the group, "Ranger training, phase two. Contrary to popular belief, Vietnamese pussy is not slanted or filled with razor blades to slice, cut, and dice your peckers like some of the stories you've heard, so I suggest the first thing we do is find ourselves a steam bath and get laid!"

Others, on limited budgets, opted to go find the nearest bar. I decided to take a look around the village/town of Phuoc Vinh, promising to find them later at the bar. I wasn't ready for the steam baths as I was still under the influence of too many years of conditioning from nuns of various orders. Besides, I knew I owed a letter to my girlfriend and didn't want to write: "Honey, finished training, scored high, celebrated by getting laid. All my love or at least part of it." With still less than a month in-country, I didn't feel up to it yet.

Phuoc Vinh was a paradox of sorts; on the surface it appeared to be little more than a sleepy little town that catered to the nearby army base camp. Dust swept down the dirt streets and bounced off the walls of the various structures that made up the few streets and blocks. Unlike Vietnam's stereotypical thatched-hut villages, Phuoc Vinh had a boomtown and carnival flavor. Bars gave way to steam baths, laundries, and small cafes, while street vendors listlessly waited for GI customers. Jeeps, trucks, and mopeds came and went, and the pale blue exhausts mingled with the smell of frying vegetables, spiced meats, and the stench of open sewers that ran the length of the streets, paralleling the buildings. Left over from an earlier occupation, the village first served the French rubber plantation and now survived on the business from the base camp.

Each of the bars seemed to cater to specific clientele. Soul music roared out of one, while country-western music came from another. Somewhere down the street Mick Jagger was screaming that he couldn't get no satisfaction, while a bar girl, sitting on the porch of the tavern, wearing a bright colored dress and bored expression, sang back, "No, no, no."

Vietnamese and U.S. MPs patrolled the streets, checking passes and ID cards and looking bored in their jeeps, legs propped up and aviator sunglasses set in place. They were small country-town sheriffs without speed traps.

I walked the length of the small village, not really knowing what I was looking for, the casual sightseer and tourist taking everything in on the surface and wondering what lay underneath. The depth, I knew, was there. I was just getting my feet wet.

"You buy watch!"

"What?" I said, turning to find a small, shoeless orphan, clad only in old and faded olive drab boxer shorts, holding something in his hand while using his other to block out the glare of the afternoon sun.

"I say, you buy watch. Good watch. You like, you buy." He seemed annoyed that I'd missed part of his salespitch.

"No, that's okay," I said. "I already have one," I added, turning my wrist over to show him that I didn't really need another.

At twelve years of age, with the majority of them probably spent on the streets of the dust-blown village adjacent to the nearby army base camp, the kid was hustling to survive.

"What kine watch you have? Timex! Shit. Numbah ten. Bess watch is Seiko. Twenny dollar, you buy. Numbah one watch. You buy!" the boy said, thrusting the watch up into my view. It wasn't a request as much as it was an order, but then in war the hard-sell approach was probably the only one he knew.

"You look! Take. Look!" he said putting it in my hands for my inspection. The face bore the Seiko brand name and a promise of seventeen jewels in the movement. It was used to be sure, and other than a few minor scratches on the face, it looked like a good watch and even a good buy.

"How much?" I asked, pretending I was in Mexico and trying to barter the kid down to a lower asking price. What I'd overlooked was that the kid was a *bui doi*, one of the street children that even their own countrymen described as "the dust of life." He had never known anything other than a life of hardship and war. Hustling and prostitution were a way of life for many of the *bui doi*, and while I pretended to be a seasoned buyer, the boy was the marketing professional. In Vietnam small businesses like his didn't go bankrupt; they crawled into urine-smelling corners of rat-infested back alleys and laid down and died.

"Twenny-five dollar, numbah one watch."

"I thought you said it was twenty dollars?"

"Then why you ask again?"

Staring at the kid I laughed. "I'll give you fifteen dollars." The small, moonfaced child shook his head. "Twenny dollah."

"Seventeen dollars," I countered.

"You buku dinky dow," he said, telling me in bastard French and Vietnamese I was crazy. "Numbah ten crazy," he added. "You new to Vietnam so you bring cheap Timex watch. Watch no lass, you no lass. Seiko good watch. GI with buku new-guy time need Seiko watch to lass. Twenny dollah."

"Okay, champ, twenty dollars," I said, uncertain why I wanted to buy the watch but maybe learning something in the process. Pulling out a twenty-dollar MPC note from my wallet I handed it to the kid, who in turn, handed me the watch.

"Steam bath juss down the block. You get laid there. Number one boom-boom," the boy said, pointing to a building down the block, just past a bar that fed loud country-western music out its opened doors and into the afternoon.

Money in hand the kid took off running, disappearing around a corner as I put the watch in my pocket and turned my attention back to the village, unaware that my new watch, minus the jewels and many of the inner workings, had already quit working.

It was nothing personal. It was just business.

CHAPTER SIX

As new graduates we were assigned to one of the two platoon hootches and to the teams that needed the latest cherries to round out their patrols. While some teams remained constant and intact, most changed personnel for reasons of illness, injuries, R&Rs, or emergency leaves. You name it, and it sometimes was enough to cannibalize teams in order to make new ones.

Assigned to the 2d Platoon hootch, I was in Lt. Michael Brennan's platoon. Brennan, a West Pointer, was rumored to be—and several brief encounters confirmed—a decent sort, smart enough to leave his team leaders alone to do their jobs. In fact, he had gained that insight from taking part in several patrols as an observer. Company policy was that the team leader's word was law on patrol, regardless of who came along for the ride. Brennan did his part and for that earned the respect of many of those in the platoon.

He also had the honor of being personally responsible for redesigning the company's Ranger scroll to read RANGER above the AIRBORNE, instead of the other way around as with most of the other 75th Infantry Ranger companies assigned to the other combat divisions in Vietnam. Brennan reasoned that, while not everyone in the company was Airborne or paratrooper qualified, each of the members of the unit was Ranger qualified on completion of the training. His idea made sense, and the patch was altered.

Assigned to his platoon, I'd soon be placed with a team. The cannibalization process was going on, and it looked as though I'd be a medic or radioman on one of several teams. Since all LRRPs were cross-trained as medics and RTOs the cherries were usually given the honor of humping the extra weight of the aid bag or the

39

PRC-25 radio. But that, too, would come later. For the time being, I was given a bunk and an area to call my own. In spite of the leeway the Ranger/LRRPs were given by Captain Griffiths and his officers, there were still the daily army rituals to go through: duty rosters to be assigned to, daily inspections to pass, guard details to round out, and formations to announce pertinent matters.

At the conclusion of morning formations, Lurp, a mixed breed, medium-size, honey-colored dog (the unit's mascot), would eagerly await his own unique mission. Since the base and company areas were plagued with rats, traps were set to catch the rodents, and every morning the rats would be released for Lurp to eagerly race after and kill with a quick snap of the spine in the dog's powerful jaws.

Lurp's kill ratio was extraordinary, and the dog seemed to bask in the applause of the Rangers who watched the display with loud admiration. Sure, we were prejudiced. The rats weren't the cute, little lab variety, and since their bites could often lead to serious complications, Lurp's skill was greatly appreciated if for no other reason than it prevented our having to stare down the fanged cat-size rodents that occupied the wall braces just inches away from our pillows.

A favorite joke had it that a Ranger awoke one early morning to find two forty-pound rats talking at the foot of his bunk.

"Should we eat the Ranger here or take him back to the nest?" the first rat asked the second.

"Eat him here," said the second rat. "If we drag him back, the big ones will take him away from us!"

Of course, there were always the snakes and lizards to worry about, but the rats took priority because of their numbers and danger.

After morning formations and Lurp's performance, the platoons were dismissed to go about platoon business. Much of a platoon's morning routine was learning more about the company through the rumor mill.

The company's call sign was Slashing Talon; the platoons were broken up into teams with double-digit designators. For example, the 1st Platoon's teams began with a three designator, with teams running from 3-1 up to 3-9, if need be. Second Platoon's teams began with four. On patrol the teams would be Talon 3-2 or Talon 4-whatever. Griffiths the CO, was Talon 6, but probably the most notable Talon 6, according to the stories, was Capt. George Paccerelli.

Paccerelli's name was usually whispered in awe, but then his combat record had a great deal to do with it. "He earned his Combat Infantryman Badge (CIB) in Laos with the Special Forces in '62," a veteran LRRP explained.

"Yeah, an A Team leader, too, who took out an NVA soldier who bayoneted him," piped in another.

A mustang officer, Paccerelli came up through the ranks the hard way with some equally hard assignments. He was a professional soldier, and he demanded professionalism from those who served him and something more.

It seems that once an MP jeep pulled up to the company orderly room carrying two handcuffed LRRPs who'd been caught when the MPs raided a whorehouse.

When the MP in charge brought out the arrest report, Paccerelli, was said to have ripped it up and then ordered the MPs out of his company area. With the military police fuming just outside the gate, Paccerelli locked the veteran LRRPs' heels together and chewed them out. The trouble was he didn't chew them out for being in an off-limits area, but instead chewed them out for getting caught by the MPs! "After all, you're Rangers, and Rangers are not supposed to get caught!"

There were other stories too about how the former Green Beret took several of his men out one evening as a three-man, quick-reaction force when a helicopter was shot down and no one else wanted to go out until sunlight. But then, everyone said or seemed to anyway, that was Paccerelli.

I felt sorry for Captain Griffiths. As cherries, little was expected of us. As Talon 6 he had some big shoes to fill. But even the little that was expected of us cherries wasn't easy when it came to the company and its responsibilities. The stakes were always high. The game always deadly. Even the easy missions or patrols were uncomfortable: there were no hot meals, no changes of clothes, and little or no time to relax. In the bush, the uniforms were usually buttoned to the neck, with the sleeves rolled down and buttoned at the wrists. Camouflage paint covered any exposed areas of the body. The rucksacks were often up to one hundred pounds, and in the tropical, sometimes staggering heat, even the uniforms and equipment became opponents to contend with.

At night the teams slept in short thirty-minute to one-hour shifts, sitting up and facing out so that each compass direction was covered and protected. There was no speaking allowed, and any communication was done in hushed whispers or hand signals.

There were no air mattresses, ponchoes, or shelter halves, and when it rained, which was frequently, the team members simply took it in stride—wet, uncomfortable, and always keeping an eye on the surrounding jungle. At night, when the heat from the Vietnamese sun could no longer work its way through the layer after layer of intertwined jungle vegetation, the rain-soaked Rangers would shiver, knowing that at least the rain and cold were keeping away the swarms of mosquitoes.

On patrol, the teams walked in a prescribed style and manner, with the first LRRP or point man covering 180 degrees to his front while the second watched and covered the right side. The third man protected the left flank, the fourth man again covering the right, with the last Ranger or rear scout watching for any movement behind the team. Careful to avoid detection, the teams avoided trails and worked to cover their own direction of movement. Over the course of the five-day mission, the team would cover a five-thousand-meter area—five "klicks"—searching for the enemy or signs of his recent activity.

Since the odds were usually against the small teams, contact with the enemy was to be avoided. Reconnaissance patrols were supposed to be just that, and it was much easier determining strategy when the opposition didn't know it was being monitored. However, if contact was made with an enemy unit, the teams went into a well-rehearsed and practiced escape-and-evasion drill, with the first man initiating contact firing a complete twenty-round magazine then turning to run. Followed by the second man in line, who did the same, and so on until the team was out of the contact area. With five-man teams, the hunters could quickly become the hunted.

In theory, all was supposed to go well, while in fact, the war left much to chance. If strategies were a gamble, then combat could sometimes become a crapshoot. What improved the odds was the quick thinking or action of its participants.

A blown ambush one moment might lead to a retreating scramble where a a second more successful ambush might occur. A sudden encounter with a lone NVA point man might be the difference between life and death for a quick-thinking Ranger point man or rear scout who could take him out quietly. Or just the opposite could happen, where Ranger/LRRPs could just as easily become the victims. The war seemed to be a matter of inches to live or seconds to die.

Out of those numbers came some remarkable people whose

stories were the stuff of Saturday matinees. And at times, even though their war stories were sometimes embellished, they usually had their core centered on truth. Any heroism or glory came at a considerable price; a price most of us new cherries had yet to comprehend.

CHAPTER SEVEN

CONTACT!

"Jorgy, wake up! Fabian's in contact. Come on!" Beal said, shaking me out of a light sleep. I rolled over and stared through the mosquito netting and dim light of the darkened platoon barracks. "3-3's in contact. Fabian's team, come on!"

I followed him to the end of the platoon bay, where a group of LRRPs was listening in on the team's radio frequency with the platoon radio. Someone started to say something and was immediately hushed by the crowd, who strained to pick up the details from the flurry of voices, code names, and yelling coming over the frequency.

Someone was directing gunship support while the team leader yelled he had two wounded. The company commander bounced a medevac helicopter, sending one out to recover the wounded after extracting the team.

Taking heavy automatic gunfire, 3-3 had managed to hold on until the gunships arrived on station and, in the difficult night engagement, managed to secure a bullet perimeter with minigun automatic gunfire around the team. The team had been compromised on the insertion, "an LZ watcher," a veteran team leader said, while others nodded in response. A fairly common occurrence in this line of business, where a lone enemy soldier would watch a potential landing zone for insertions, note the directions of movement of the LRRP team, and then retreat to inform his superiors. Then the game of cat and mouse would begin, and the North Vietnamese Army soldiers had spent the day and most of the night trying to locate the five American Rangers.

"Six is pulling them out," another vet said.

A long moment later there was a collective sigh of relief when the team had managed to escape and evade (E&E) to an alternate pickup zone, running and firing as they did.

The "line twos" (wounded LRRPs) were not seriously injured and would be treated at the battalion aid station. Following the others down to the landing strip, we waited in the too quiet, dark October evening for the helicopter to arrive. When it finally did, the haggard team emerged from the pit of the aircraft. Taking some of their equipment, we walked them over to the aid station.

"Congratulations, new guy. You just got your first Purple Heart!" a vet said to Fabian, who quietly nodded.

"You okay, Tony?" I asked.

"Yeah, a piece of shrapnel cut across my back. I didn't feel a thing then, and it's not so bad now, really! It's a bleeder, but it isn't that bad," he said, showing the hastily bandaged, blood-soaked wound caused by a fragment from an exploding RPG-7 rocket. "I'm okay, really! I'm fine."

Animated and anxious, he was smiling as he seemed a little uncertain about what to do next.

"Fabian, I want the medics to look at your wound," the team leader said. He was limping from a leg wound, a grazed right thigh from a bullet during the night attack. It was a flesh wound, one that sliced up a good portion of the muscle and would leave him feeling like the leg was cramped and just needed loosening up.

"It scared the piss outta me," Fabian said, sporting a ridiculous grin before turning toward the aid station. "A hell of a way to begin a tour. Could you take my rucksack back to the company for me?"

I said I would, lifting the heavy rucksack and heading back to the company area. Beside me, Beal carried Fabian's web gear. "It's not what he expected it to be, but he's hooked anyway."

"What do you mean?"

"I mean it's never what anyone expects it to be."

"So, how do you get used to it?"

"You don't, you just plan for and expect the worst, and you won't be disappointed."

There was too much I didn't understand, too many pieces of the puzzle missing to make any sense of it.

"Why did you come back? To Nam, I mean? You did a tour, so why are you back? Germany couldn't have been all that bad."

Beal shrugged. "I don't know. Maybe it's because it's the only war we have, and maybe it's the only place that matters anymore. Nam's the place you'll love to hate, kid, the nightmare that leaves you in a cold sweat, making your heart seem as though it'll push through your chest, and leaving you afraid to close your eyes until after a while you look forward to it. It's a rush you find you can't live without. The war feeds on you, and you end up feeding on it. No matter what happens after this, you'll never be the same, kinda like that old saying from World War I when folks sang, 'How you gonna keep 'em down on the farm after they've seen Paree?' ''

I nodded as though I understood, and as we walked back to the company compound, I wondered if maybe the emphasis on curbing the use of drugs over here was overstated and that maybe the real addiction might be the war and that maybe going cold turkey wasn't the way you treated it.

Jesus, why didn't they issue us handbooks when we arrived so we'd have something to answer all of the questions that seemed to jump out at us from everywhere?

Who knows, maybe the powers that be knew that if we had such a book and if we read it then we wouldn't stay. Maybe it would frighten the hell out of us, or maybe we wouldn't believe it anyway.

Assigned to a team, I'd have my answers soon enough. Or more questions.

My first few missions were picnics, five-day outings that began and ended quietly. Other teams weren't as lucky. Contact had been sporadic and random encounters, such as front scouts slowly turning a jungle branch only to find a North Vietnamese soldier turning one only feet away from the Ranger. Screaming and scrambling for his weapon, the soldier fell to the LRRP who was fortunate enough to have his rifle pointed at the man. There were ambushes, captured Viet Cong and materials, but few significant injuries to the LRRPs. All around me, Rangers I'd graduated with had been in contact, but I hadn't been involved in anything other than long-drawn-out patrols. My only real battles were with the endless swarms of mosquitoes, leeches, and termites that owned the jungle and demanded payment for our time in it, nature's Shylocks exacting their pound of flesh in tiny increments.

Initially, I found I couldn't sleep in the jungle at night, a result of fear, anticipation, the constant drone of mosquitoes, and the strain of looking too hard to find an enemy who wasn't there. The nocturnal noises fed the fear until, by the third night, I learned to cope, learning how to sleep lightly like the others, never really falling into a deep, satisfying sleep but getting by day after day.

A new training cycle had begun, and I suppose I was viewed by the others as a vet, still wet behind the ears but wet because of the sweat from the missions.

In late October, while on a mission out of Tay Ninh, a western province that bordered Cambodia, our front scout came across fresh bootprints and bicycle tire tracks on a jungle trail. The edges of the prints were crisp and sharp, showing that the VC or NVA had left earlier that morning. A raised hand froze us in place as he read the trail and slowly scanned the surrounding jungle, looking to see if they were still around. In dense vegetation or vine-locked rain forest, a man could be hiding only a few feet away, and you'd never see him unless he moved or coughed or made some other noise that drew your attention to his location. Fortunately, the jungle worked for us as well, and that's what the team leader/front scout was counting on.

Team 4-3 was a cannibalized team. Sgt. Henry Morris was team leader and Charlie Steel the assistant team leader, the ATL. Another Ranger veteran, Howard Shute, added to the team's experience, while a recent LRRP graduate, Julius Zaporozec, and I rounded out the team.

Zap humped the radio while Morris and Steel gave me the job as the team medic with an additional responsibility as the rear scout. Walking backward slowly on patrol became a chore, but Shute was doing his best to school me and having reasonable success. Reasonable meant I didn't get lost too often. When I came to the team, Steel seemed to have his share of reservations about me, the new guy, but then so did the others on the team. After all, I was a potential liability until I proved myself.

By the second day Morris seemed satisfied with our performance. But then he and Steel had more urgent matters on their minds, fresh signs of NVA activity. Campsites were new, and footprints and tracks were everywhere. Even occasional pieces of equipment that had been dropped or left behind told us we were close. Morris motioned for the rest of us to keep an eye open, and then stepping over the trail, he signaled for us to follow as he paralleled the trail, moving in slow, deliberate steps. A few minutes later he came across a fighting position that guarded a nearby bunker complex. Backing away he had us set up our claymore antipersonnel mines, linking or "daisy-chaining" them together with the explosive det cord and blasting caps, each interlocked and connected to a single wire that led back to Morris who controlled the detonating device, the clacker.

Zap threw on the long whip antenna for the radio and established contact with our relay station, and on Morris's orders called in what we'd found.

"Roger, Talon 4-3. Talon 6 says monitor the Bravo Charlie and see if anyone shows up. We'll have support standing by. Talon Relay out."

The message was clear. Watch the bunker complex, the Bravo Charlie, and set up an ambush. Morris had anticipated the order and acted accordingly. With a defensive perimeter established, we waited.

The time passed with no significant activity, the picnic taking on the flavor of a guarded watch. When no one showed after the first few hours, we began to relax our guard. From the tense, nervous stage—the stage of heightened awareness—when we initially found the bunker complex, we eased into a phase where noises rather than movements became suspicious.

The sun's light filtered down through the thick foliage giving the floor below a twilight gloom that slowly diminished as the day wore on.

"Let's see if they're night owls," Morris said to Steel, who nodded in agreement.

Then, throughout most of the long night, the waiting continued. We finally set up a one-man guard rotation so we'd be ready for whatever happened in the morning. Morris and Steel seemed certain that something would happen.

In the predawn darkness I saw myself sleeping, using the small piece of camouflage liner to cover my face from the mosquitoes. I heard him first, eyes open beneath the towellike liner, slowly pulling it from my face, I saw the North Vietnamese soldier deftly creep around the trail to our front, sidestepping the claymore mines and lowering his AK-47 assault rifle to bayonet me. I try to reach for my rifle, but it isn't close by, and as the thin, needlelike blade pushes into my stomach, I wonder why the others don't react. I sat up, startling the Ranger on guard. The dream had been too real, and after he settled back to his duty, I stayed awake, rifle ready, watching the bend in the trail. Had the soldier really been there after all? I felt my stomach and found no wound. It was only a nightmare, but still I remained awake covering the trail.

The following morning, just as were readying to move out, we heard the first voice laughing in the near distance, maybe twenty yards away—a laugh that froze us in place, a small laugh, quickly muffled by a sharp command. To our left the sounds of someone chopping wood rang through the twilight of the jungle. More voices to our rear told us we had managed to slip into an NVA unit, a platoon- or even a company-size element.

"Call in a Pink Team," Morris's whisper seemed like a shout as I relayed the message.

Within twenty minutes the small observation helicopter flew at treetop level over the carpet of thick rain forest we occupied, knowing our position and looking for the enemy we said were in the immediate area. Sporadic bursts of machine-gun fire from the small helicopter's doorgunner produced no return fire. The Vietnamese wanted to stay hidden. They knew the machine-gun fire was intended to draw them out so that when they came out of their fighting positions and bunkers to return the fire, the small helicopter would pull pitch and quickly veer away, while the more deadly Cobra gunships that circled thousands of feet above the region could swoop in with their automatic miniguns, the multibarreled machine gun that fired thousands of rounds a minute, along with the just-as-deadly, automatic grenade launcher and rockets it carried as well.

It was a tactic the Pink Teams used effectively and the Vietnamese knew it. If the "recon by fire" tactic didn't work, they knew the helicopter would withdraw. After the helicopters broke station, pulling away for further instructions, we waited and listened. For what seemed like forever nothing stirred, not the many birds, reptiles, jungle animals, or Vietnamese until finally a few voices were heard barking orders. A lone North Vietnamese soldier cleared the bend of the trail, carrying a shoulder weapon in one arm and his boots in another. Steel was the first to see him and then, when the Vietnamese was only a few feet from us, he saw the green-and-black-covered face of the assistant team leader. Reaching for the rifle, the Vietnamese dropped the boots as Steel opened up with the M-16, killing him with a short burst across his chest.

In the next instant the jungle around us was being splintered with enemy small-arms fire. Morris, a veteran team leader, had managed to fit us into the contour of the jungle, using a small rise to our left as protection, while a huge decaying log provided us with the protection we'd need to our front. Smaller trees standing to our right offered immediate protection there, leaving only one exposed area, one that was thick with vines and branches and that the North Vietnamese soldiers could not easily assault.

"Talon Relay. Contact! Over. I say again, Contact!" Zap yelled into the radio handset while firing his rifle. In the background I could hear the Ranger relay station kicking things in motion. The

Pink Team would return immediately to help while a QRF, a quick
reaction force, a recon platoon from a nearby fire support base
would be standing by ready to be ferried in should we need them.

Shoulder-fired rockets slammed into the nearby trees, while
their machine-gun and other small-arms fire tore at the vegetation
around us. The lone soldier who'd stumbled upon us was dead, his
body lying twisted on the bend in the trail, so the others could only
guess who and where we were. They'd fire, trying to draw us out,
and then probe to make certain of our position.

Defended fighting positions and bunker complexes, the base
camps of the Viet Cong and North Vietnamese Army forces, were
interlocked strategic positions that made an attacking force vulnerable. With firing holes and occasional tunnels leading to one
another, they were difficult to penetrate. But once attackers were
inside the circle of fighting positions, the defenders were themselves vulnerable to attack. Somehow, we had managed to move
within their perimeter, and though we were hardly in the exact
center of the complex, we were in far enough to cause considerable confusion.

Time and again, small numbers of enemy soldiers probed at our
position, some even boldly charging down the open trail, only to
hurriedly scramble back with their wounded. After a half hour of
exchanging fire and holding out while the gunships provided impressive support fire, the small battle came to a standoff. The
quick reaction force had touched down in a landing zone five
hundred meters away and would link up with us as soon as they
could.

Morris had saved the claymores for any serious assault, should
one come. "Keep your eyes open!" he said. "They're still not
sure where we are, so they'll push."

Snapping twigs alerted us to a few who had tried to sneak
around to our flank. Removing a grenade, Morris waited, head
tucked behind the small mound of dirt that concealed us, let the
spoon break away from the grenade, counted to three, and then
rolled the grenade over the other side of the hill. The grenade
caught two NVA facing the wrong way; they noticed it too late to
react. Then, it was awkwardly quiet.

"Talon 4-3, Quebec Romeo Foxtrot 6, over," the call came
over the radio.

"Talon 4-3. Go," Zap said into the handset.

"We're five minutes from your location. Pop smoke for veri-
fication."

"The QRF wants us to pop smoke," Zaporozec said to Morris

who turned to Steel. The decision was weighing on both of their minds and evident on their faces.

"If the gooks don't know where we are by now, they will when we pop the smoke." Then, after a moment, he added, "Go ahead" to the RTO, who'd pulled a smoke grenade from his web gear.

Zaporozec pulled the pin and then tossed it out toward the other end of the trail, away from the team but still in sight. The slow hissing noise over the cloud of rising red smoke was drowned out by the enemy machine-gun fire raking across the trail.

Minutes later the radio responded. "Roger, Talon 4-3, we have candy-apple smoke. We're coming in."

We could hear the grunts moving through the jungle to our left until their point man appeared in the trail near the now dead smoke grenade. Shute caught his attention with a slow wave, and the pointman responded with a nod while his head turned up the trail, covering it when he noticed the dead NVA soldier and bullet-riddled foliage. The sun was now high overhead, and the twilight became a comfortable shade as smoke, cordite from the expended ammunition, and the smell of cut vegetation wafted across the jungle.

"Talon 4-3, come back to my location. Over," came the request from the QRF leader.

"Their Six wants you back for a talk," Zap said, passing the message along. Morris nodded, told Steel to take over and, slipping by Shute and me, carefully made his way to the point man and disappeared around a bend in the trail.

Though the jungle and the battle were quiet, my heart was pounding. I hadn't slept well the night before, but I was no longer tired. I now knew what Fabian had felt the night he was in contact—the excitement, the awe, and the mild confusion induced by what had happened. Before the sudden firefight, I assumed that when it finally happened it would almost seem to take place in slow motion. I'd see the enemy, carefully take aim, fire, and then ready to fire again. The assumption was a fabrication, a lie to make the process seem glamorous to me. Had I known otherwise, my enthusiasm might've diminished, and then I'd have to question my other assumptions about the war.

"How many you think we got?" It was Zap.

"I don't know—one for sure," I replied.

"Two more over here," Steel said. "And I think we wounded a few more who came down the trail."

"So is this it? Will we be extracted now?"

Steel turned to Shute and shrugged. "I dunno. We're compromised, but maybe the grunts will want to keep us around to take the point for them when they check this thing out.''

"You think so?'' Zap asked.

"More than likely, because division will want some hard intelligence they can work with.''

Steel was right. When Morris came back he was wearing a solemn expression. Facing the round-faced assistant team leader he frowned. "Their LT [lieutenant] wants us to check out the bunker complex. First though, he wants to come up here and take a look for himself. He doesn't think we found anything major since they didn't encounter any heavy fire coming in.''

"It has got to be at least a platoon out there, maybe even a company,'' Steel said.

"I know but that's his game plan.''

A few minutes later a lieutenant emerged from the trail, followed by his radioman and a squad leader. Map in hand, the officer was trying to get a handle on the extent of the bunker complex. It was a cautious move, but the trio remained standing over the objections of Morris, who pointed out that we had taken heavy fire less than twenty yards away. Things were quiet by then, so the lieutenant decided to take the advice under consideration. As he turned back to his squad leader, the top of the man's head flew off into his jungle fatigue shirt; a machine-gun burst caught the radioman and the squad leader. Pulling the officer down, Morris scrambled to return fire as Zap tried to help the dying squad leader. His brain was shattered, but the body was jerking in heaving spasms. The radioman was crying in pain while the officer yelled for his men to get down. He'd made a costly mistake, one that he wouldn't repeat. The lieutenant grabbed the handset of the wounded man's radio and, looking at his map, directed the gunships on a firing mission.

Blood from the dying squad leader spread across the ground around us, seeping into our fatigues. An M-60 gunner came racing up the trail and sprawled flat. Aiming beyond the dead Vietnamese, he peppered the area where the enemy's machine gun had fired from. Exposed, the man kept up the one-man assault until the NVA forces could be heard running through the woods trying to outflank us. Judging from the din of the Vietnamese yelling, there was at least a platoon.

"We're going to pull back to here!'' the QRF leader said, showing Morris his map and plan. A white pool on the map indicated a small break in the rain forest, not big enough for a landing zone but maybe big enough to defend with a hastily established perimeter.

Enemy fire was coming from three directions as we moved. We heard the distinctive thump of enemy mortars seconds before the inevitable explosions thundered through the treetops and rained over our last position. We were in a serious fight, and we knew it. The Vietnamese had maneuvered into position around us. They knew the full extent of their bunker complex, while we could only guess. From the initial attacks and probes, they had planned their strategy, and the young officer in charge of the infantry quick reaction force knew it. He was damn certain he was going to keep them guessing.

"Keep your heads down!" he yelled as the word had been passed on across our perimeter. An air strike had been called in, and in seconds the deafening roar of the air force jet and rumbling boom of the falling bombs it had released momentarily silenced the battle around us. Radio traffic was loud and manic. Gunship pilots had engaged definite targets, taking out enemy mortar crews and enemy soldiers. Others screamed that they were all over the place, and the platoon-size estimate had been revised to a reinforced-company status.

I had wanted to be part of the war so much that I couldn't wait to get into action. Now, after my first few hours in combat, I wanted to call "Time," pick up my things and go home, just as I had done when I played war as a child. But this wasn't a game. It was a deadly struggle that would play its course.

Across the small clearing someone yelled for a medic, and I caught a glimpse of another soldier running toward the voice with a bag in his hand. It was their platoon medic, who was getting a workout the hard way.

More air strikes didn't end the battle, and though we'd only suffered one dead and three wounded, the Vietnamese had suffered considerably more loss. All around us, dead NVA bodies could be seen. Some had broken through the vegetation only to find themselves in the middle of the American position. Instantly they knew their death was inevitable, but still they came, running, yelling, firing.

Then, once again it was quiet, and we could hear the order going out over the radio for us to withdraw, that an Arc Light, a B-52 bombing mission, would take over where the jets left off. The thousands of five-hundred-pound bombs would destroy the complex, uprooting and splintering ancient, massive trees and leaving deep, pondlike craters where bunkers and jungle had been.

As the lieutenant called for us to move out, he asked for volunteers to help carry the body of the dead squad leader. I said I'd help, while other voices answered as well. Loading the lifeless body into a makeshift litter, we carried him out. The going was rough, uncertain. Knowing the NVA wouldn't use that route, the point man led us through a waist-deep swamp toward the designated pickup zone. The radio was weighing me down, and another man took it, leaving me to pull my share of the litter.

We'd taken shifts carrying the body of the squad leader, who somebody called "C." Giving the body an identity personalized the corpse, making the burden easier to carry. He'd come in to help us and died in the process, and though I'd occasionally slip in the mud, falling into the warm, thick water, I got to my feet, pulling the sagging end of the litter out of the water and continued on, arms aching but refusing to pass along my share of the burden to someone else.

During a short rest break on the other side of the swamp and well into dark, the lieutenant came by, stopping to view the body. Without a word he chewed on his lower lip, shook his head, and asked us how we were doing. When we said we were okay, he nodded and left.

"He's taking it hard," a grunt said to another. "The squad leader helped break him in."

They looked at the dead soldier, whose head lay open before them. The bleeding had stopped long ago. The heart was no longer pumping and the body had taken on a ashen blue color. A terrible smell was coming from the body. Mud from the swamp clung to it and mixed with the dried blood and pieces of severed flesh. Gases were building up inside the stomach.

"The fucking war don't even let you die in peace," the one grunt said.

By the time we reached the pickup zone, my muscles were screaming, cramped from holding the litter for such a long time. Though we'd been given time to rest, it hadn't been enough for tired muscles. We'd have to wait to first light before the helicopters would pick us up. Once we were far enough away, the air force bombers would unload their bomb racks from ten thousand feet then begin their long turns back to Thailand, where the flights originated.

When the sun finally rose over the jungle and the helicopters could be heard in the distance, Morris roused us from our sleep, saying we'd be the last to go out.

"The grunts will go first, and we'll follow. They seem a little pissed at us, so be cool. They lost one and got two wounded coming in to help us.''

"Maybe it would've been better if they took our advice and got down when we told them to,'' Steel said, spitting.

"Yeah, I know, but you can't tell them something they don't want to hear. Anyway, keep watch on the tree line. I don't want any more nasty surprises before we get out of here.''

"How you doing, Jorgy?'' Steel asked when he noticed me bleeding from my chest. A leech had been knocked off leaving a small trickle of blood spilling down my sternum.

"Tired, that's all.'' And I was! Beat, sore, worn, wet, physically and mentally exhausted. I had volunteered for Vietnam, savoring some foolish romantic notion of battle and found a real war instead. '

Steel, noticing the look on my face, said something, drawing me out of my weariness.

"What?''

"I said thanks for volunteering to help carry the body.''

I nodded, staring over at the lifeless body in the poncho.

"It seemed like the thing to do,'' I said, knowing he didn't realize that maybe I was trying to make up for being too gung ho to get to combat. I knew that it could've been me in the poncho. If the situation had been reversed, I hoped he would've helped carry my body out. Who knows? Maybe I helped because I wanted to do something honorable? Wasn't that one of my reasons for being in Vietnam anyway?

There was honor in the action, and that had to count for something.

CHAPTER EIGHT

Transferred to Gary Massitelli's team, I became a a veteran rear scout.

The first two weeks of November held more picnic missions, more walks through the countryside, or so it seemed. Gary was due to go on R&R in a few days, and the ATL came down with malaria and had to be medevaced to Saigon for recovery. As for the rest of us on the team, we were farmed out to fill in the rosters on other teams, which for one reason or another were short personnel. Zap and I went to Jim McIntyre's, where we joined David Torres, who'd be Mack's ATL. I only knew of McIntyre but had worked with Torres on previous missions. He was helpful and friendly, and we had become friends. When we heard we'd be going to Mack's team, the heavy-set Mexican with the flat, broad features of his Indian ancestors and the hot blood and generous demeanor of the Spanish side of his heritage, slapped me on the back. "McIntyre's good people. He's one of the best the company has."

"How does he compare to Massitelli?" a team leader I felt was pretty damn good.

"My friend, if I didn't know any better, I'd swear they were both my home boys. But to put it in Anglo-gringo terms, kiddo, everything's peachy!"

Trying to fill us in, Torres explained how McIntyre had come to the company less than a year earlier as a private first class, the lowly PFC. In the few months that followed, he showed what lay behind the quiet country-boy exterior. When the team he was on got into contact and a grenade fell near their tight circle perimeter, McIntyre, without any hesitation, lifted his heavy rucksack, and threw it on the grenade, lying on the pack for support. The explosion sent him flying back in a sprawling, tumbling roll, and miraculously neither Mack nor any of the others was seriously injured. The team leader and the other members of the team were momentarily stunned by the quick action as well as the explosion. Seconds—and perhaps a lifetime—later they were still impressed with the new PFC, so when they came in they nominated him for a Silver Star. The company commander, George Paccerelli, was just as impressed, as was the division commander who pinned the medal on his chest and immediately promoted him to the rank of Sergeant. Torres went on to say that McIntyre proved himself as a team leader with little fanfare or noise, just good, careful work.

When we reported to McIntyre, he seemed pleased to have Torres working with him again and welcomed me with a nod and a handshake. Unlike the other team leaders, McIntyre was quiet, and though I initially wondered whether I'd been snubbed or not, I soon found out it was McIntyre's way of approaching people and things, saving his judgment for a later, more informed view.

Besides Mack and Torres I was the third "vet" on the team, though I was only a handful of missions ahead of the two remaining team members. Zap was close on my heels, and it would be the first or second mission for the fifth team member. Zap and I were buddies. Besides the patrol we'd been on together, we'd pulled guard on the engineers' tower and on the back gate, and through the long nights of watching over our section of camp perimeter had come to know something about each other. We became "buddies," the army term that goes beyond friendship. In war a buddy might very well save your life, get you drunk when your girlfriend or wife dumped you, or share news from home with you during mail call. Zap and I were friends but, more important, we were buddies, so when I heard he was on the team, I felt good about the mission. The final member of 4-2 was Paul Rogers, whom I knew little about, other than this would be his first mission, and he would serve as the team's medic. After flipping with Zap to see who'd carry the extra weight, I still had the honor of being the radioman. Zap gallantly offered to go two out of three if I'd like.

"Hell no! I'd probably end up having to carry your pack, too!"

The New Jersey native grinned. "You don't suppose the new guy would go for it, do you?"

I shook my head. "He wouldn't touch it with a ten-foot pole."

"Ah, an ethnic slur rears its ugly head. By the way, did your girlfriend ever get those pictures of us you sent, the ones of us on guard?"

I said she had.

A look of consternation crossed his face. "Hmm, I haven't heard from her yet, I mean besides the naked pictures she sent."

I threw a dog-eared paperback at him and he ducked away laughing. "Seriously though, Jorgy, I'll carry the radio, if you want."

"Naw, I'm getting used to it by now. Besides, if we get in contact and I have to scream for help, I want everybody to hear me."

"You think we'll get in contact?"

I knew what was bothering him, the same thing that had bothered me before I found out what it was like to have someone shooting at you—the wondering, that damn insecure feeling of not really knowing how you'll react under fire. Bravado only carries you so far, your action ultimately takes you the rest of the distance.

"I don't know, but at least we're in good company. Dave Torres is good in the jungle, and he seems to look up to Mack as some sort of legend, and now, through a strange twist of fate, you have me on the radio—so partner, I'd say things are looking good for our side. Now, if I can only remember how to work the damn thing."

"Comforting, Jorgy, very comforting."

The operational order took well over an hour. McIntyre was a stickler for details, more so than others had been. He wanted to be certain that everyone on 4-2 knew their roles as well as the roles of the others. When he and Torres were satisfied with our answers in the mission briefing, they grunted their okay and left us to take care of any personal business. As usual there'd be letters to write, personal effects to lock up and store, and maybe the quiet time needed to relax mentally before the five tense days of patrol. In the morning we'd go through a weapons and equipment check, where McIntyre and Torres would tape down anything on our rucksacks or web gear they felt made too much noise or might reflect light. And then, when they were satisfied, we'd line up for the team picture, the customary ritual for our outbound LRRP teams, board the small flatbed mules, and ride to the flight line to the awaiting helicopter.

The mission would be out of Fire Support Base Buttons in Song Be Province. Buttons had been hit with a ground attack two weeks earlier, when hundreds of North Vietnamese sappers and soldiers assaulted the small strategic base and, in a bloody battle, failed. G-2, division intelligence, said the remaining NVA units could very well still be in the area, and so the purpose of our patrol was to determine if that was the case or if they'd withdrawn. I finally fell asleep on my cot, arms and legs crossed, and staring at the corrugated-tin ceiling, listening to the constant hammering of outgoing artillery rounds from the nearby battery and wondering if the NVA had left or if they were still in the region waiting for us.

The helicopter hovered near the landing site the next morning, refusing to touch down because of the stumps and scrub brush in the small opening in the jungle. The LZ was the legacy of an artillery barrage, maybe the one from the night before, and splintered trees and gaping orange holes in the earth looked back at us as we steadied ourselves on the skids of the helicopter, wondering what to do next.

McIntyre yelled at the doorgunner to tell the pilot to take it lower, and when the pilot refused, Mack tapped him on the shoulder and, showing his middle finger, flipped him off.

"Asshole!" he said as he jumped the five feet to the ground. The rest of us followed. I landed hard on all fours, the radio pushing over my neck into the back of my head. Each of the others had been driven to their knees, as well, with the nearly hundred pounds of equipment and weapons weighing them down. There was more than enough pain to go around.

In an instant, Mack motioned for us to move into the tree line. Torres took off first, followed by Zaporozec, McIntyre, and me. Rogers covered the rear.

Concealed by thick vegetation, I established commo while Mack took the radio handset, whispering into the handpiece. Then, after ten minutes of tense waiting, he motioned for Torres to move out to the north. Less than twenty minutes into the mission, we came across a well-used trail, maybe a few days or a week old, from the look of it. The wind and rain had dulled the sharp edges of the enemy's bootprints, leaving them rounded and muddied.

We pushed north and then east, paralleling the trail until dark, when we set up a claymore perimeter and a revolving guard schedule. Other than the swarms of mosquitoes that we battled throughout the long night, everything was reasonably quiet—with the exception being the natural noises of the jungle with the screeching of unseen birds, the groans and croaks of lizards, and occasional grunts from scurrying animals in nocturnal search for food. Though the insect repellent could keep the mosquitoes from biting, their numbers made it impossible to breathe without having several go up your nose with each inhalation.

The following day was a repeat of the previous, more trails

discovered, noted, and paralleled, leading to abandoned bunker complexes. On the third day, while moving through a hilly section of jungle, we lost radio contact.

"Nothing," I whispered to McIntyre.

"When did you change the battery?"

"This morning," I replied.

"Check the connections again." He turned to Torres. "I think it's the terrain. We've got to get to higher ground."

When his suspicions proved correct, and radio communications were established once again after we moved over the crest of the hill, Mack called for a lunch rest. The weather was hot, and the jungle stifled even the slightest breeze. The hump up the hillside left us breathing hard and sweating.

After the break, we moved out again, this time with Mack taking the lead. Fifteen minutes into the walk, his hand shot up in a clenched fist. He'd found something.

To his front a three-foot-wide trail carried the signs of heavy and frequent use. Experience told him that whoever had been using it had been traveling fast and light, the front part of the bootprints deeper than the heel. Sharp edges were evident, and the lack of water seepage in the wet soil told him that whoever had used it was also close by. Very close.

"Quick!" he said scanning the surrounding vegetation. "Across the trail. *Don't step on it!*" his whisper was frenzied. "Set up the long whip antenna," he added, looking at me. On the other side of the trail I pulled out the longer whip antenna and made the connection, storing the smaller one in my pack. Listening, waiting, we heard nothing, which didn't satisfy Torres or Mack. The NVA were here and more than likely they'd be back. The surrounding vegetation was scrub brush, and after ten minutes of waiting, Mack decided to shift back across the trail to a side better suited for an ambush. While Rogers covered one end of the trail and Zap another, Mack led us to a more defendable position. Experience and instinct were his guides, and they had not failed him yet. The new position with its two-foot-high, abandoned ant mound and fallen tree gave us the protection that the other position lacked. Barely moments after we sat down, we heard the Vietnamese moving up the trail. Initially, we counted ten, and judging from their uniforms and equipment, they were NVA regulars. Torres was the closest to the trail and counted their number, while Zap made his count from the other end. In the meantime, the rest of us went through the eye-straining task of quietly counting the number of enemy soldiers less than fifteen feet away.

When they were past us, McIntyre told us to call in the sighting. I'd only finished the transmission, when we heard others coming down the trail. I gave up counting at thirty and prayed they'd keep on going, only God wasn't listening.

Coming to a halt, they milled along the trail, perhaps waiting for an order to move again, when one curious NVA soldier, seeing something striking, walked toward a red ring just off the trail, the red ring of a smoke grenade attached to Torres's pack. A few feet from the assistant team leader, the enemy soldier recognized it for what it was. He screamed and turned his AK-47 on it, but before he could pull the trigger, Torres opened up with his M-14, killing the man instantly.

"*Contact!*" McIntyre yelled as we opened fire on the surprised NVA, who returned fire in every direction, running pell-mell through the surrounding jungle to get out of the ambush site. Only, it wasn't an ambush site because we hadn't had time to set up our claymores. Torres's M-14 must have sounded like the M-60 machine gun that a U.S. platoon-size force might use, but that wouldn't be enough to slow the barrage of bullets that flew through the vegetation around us.

"Oh, Jesus, Jesus," Torres yelled holding his chest, firing into the ground as he sat up in burning pain. A stream of blood rushed out of his chest. Still, he managed to return fire. Next to me Zap was up on one knee firing as well. "Dave!" Mack screamed, pulling him back and down as he kept up his own small-arms fire, but before he could yank his friend down the big Southern Californian took a second burst to his chest.

I felt Zap's arm grabbing mine and tried to shove it off.

"Damn it, Zap, Leave me alone, they—"

There was a strange gurgling sound, and as I threw away his hand, I turned and saw his reason for grabbing me. A bullet had hit him above the upper lip, the hydrostatic pressure of the bullet distorting his face into a grotesque, discolored mask of blood and bone. I pulled him in close, scrambling for a bandage.

Rogers was screaming, too, and rolling over and over on the ground, holding onto his left leg, unable to see the splintered bone and gouged flesh where the bullet had hit him.

"*Keep firing!*" McIntyre yelled when I stopped, stunned by what I was witnessing.

"*Keep firing!*" he yelled again, pulling me back to the tactical situation. The main body of the NVA force had retreated, which was what Mack was hoping for—that they would think they were ambushed and would react accordingly, hurrying to put distance between the Americans and themselves. Had our firing diminished and they'd guessed otherwise, they would've slowly moved in to kill us. As it was, the wounded enemy soldiers or those stuck in the immediate area were still giving us a bitter fight.

Picking up the grenade launcher, McIntyre fired it through the forest, the quick explosions changed the momentum of the fight.

Torres was crying now, a small sob of resignation while Rogers's piercing cries mixed with the assistant team leader's in a frightening chorus. I'd called in the contact and told them the situation.

"Talon Relay, we have three line-twos [wounded], bounce a medevac. I say again, bounce a medevac."

"*Get a gunship out here!*" McIntyre yelled at me.

"Talon Relay, bounce a Pink Team!"

Suddenly realizing that we were taking fire from 360 degrees, I turned and covered 180 of them while McIntyre took the other half. I fired in short bursts, holding my rifle with one hand and trying to wrap a bandage around Zap's face, trying to stop the bleeding.

"Hang in there, buddy. You'll make it. Hang in there!" I was yelling, trying to convince myself he wasn't dying. There was no exit wound from the bullet, and I knew it must be lodged in the base of his skull. But I knew he could make it. Christ! He had to!

Torres held his hands over his chest while pink bubbles pushed out of his nose and mouth. I threw the radio handset to Rogers. "Take it!" I yelled while he turned back to me, bleary-eyed, dirt-stained cheeks from crying on the jungle floor.

"I said *take it*, damn it! Keep in commo with the relay!" I said, trying to work on Dave, while Mack scurried through the under-brush routing the NVA and giving us the time we needed to deal with our injuries. Zap's face had turned that sickening ashen gray, and his face and lip were caked with thick, dark blood. When I tried to secure the bandage, part of his face fell in my hands. Rogers was somehow holding on, but Torres wouldn't be that far behind Zap if he didn't get immediate medical attention. Rogers was on the radio but unable to do much. Taking the radio from his hands I yelled into the handset for help. "Where's the medevac?"

It had been a frustrated call. I knew they were doing everything they could on the other end to get us help, but I had to yell at something, at someone, and the radio was the only place I felt where it would do any good.

"We—we have one line-one and two line-two's, for Christ's sake, get us some help out here!"

An explosion sent small pieces of shrapnel into my left hand, causing me to drop the handset. Meanwhile McIntyre was alternating between the grenade launcher and the rifle, concentrating on the heaviest points of resistance. A gunship arrived on station, and after seeing the smoke that Mack had popped for it, the helicopter gunship rolled in around us, providing our perimeter support and giving the team leader time to assess the situation. Taking the big Mexican-American in his arms, Mack inspected the wounds. Torres was unconscious, and there was no response. I shook my head.

"There's another wound to his head, Mack." My voice was hollow, cracking. We couldn't get a pulse.

The medic was crying, and the noise bothered McIntyre, who couldn't see the extent of his wounds from where he was.

"Keep it down! God damn it!"

Rogers, sucking in his cry, did what he was told, and as the team leader moved in to see what had caused the loud crying he was startled by the large hole in the man's leg.

"Get him some morphine," he said. Going through the medic's shattered pack, I finally found the small needle dispenser. I removed the plastic cover and shoved the needle in his thigh. Seconds later severe blood loss or the pain reliever began to take effect, and his moans were growing weaker.

"Talon 4-2. Talon Relay. Over," the radio handset crackled. Picking up the handset, McIntyre told me to keep an eye open while he replied to the radio request.

"Talon 4-2. Go."

"Roger. Can you Echo-Echo?"

The relay station was asking if we could escape and evade.

"Negative. We have two line-ones and one line-two."

"Oscar 6 requests you leave the line-ones in place and Echo-Echo to the following location—"

"I said *negative!*" McIntyre's face was red with anger. He wouldn't leave the dead team members behind as the quick reaction force's commander had suggested.

"Oscar 6 cannot get a Quebec Romeo Foxtrot to your location at this time and requests—"

"*Negative!* We all go or no one does!"

The sun was going down and a quick reaction force would be waiting for us at a landing zone eight hundred meters to our west. They wouldn't risk trying to link up with us in the dark. It would be easier for us to move to them, they decided, only Mack wouldn't buy it. Finally, Oscar 6 sent in a helicopter to recover the wounded as well as the dead. Talon 6, Captain Griffiths, had readied a reaction force of his own and was standing by to rappel in if there were any problems with the extraction.

As the helicopter hovered hundreds of feet above the trees, the doorgunner kicked out a rescue basket into which we put the wounded medic. Then we attached it to a cable that was lowered.

"Thank you, thank you," Rogers was saying to Mack and me, but I wasn't sure what he was thanking me for. As Mack covered the trail, I guided the basket through the trees until I could no longer reach it. Moments later the basket returned, and I put Torres's body in it, struggling with the weight. When that was done I followed suit with Zap. Then a small seat was dropped, and McIntyre looked at it saying, "Your turn, go ahead." I was pulled up through the limbs and vegetation to find the sky filled with circling gunships and helicopters. From the jungle floor it had seemed we were alone, but once through the trees we could see the support. Torres and Zap lay on the belly of the Huey helicopter's bay, lifeless cargo that the second doorgunner had climbed over to get a better look at the cable. Off to another side, Rogers lay staring out the open door, crying. The back of his leg was splintered and open.

Within moments McIntyre was aboard, and the helicopter dipped its nose and pulled up and away from the kill zone as gunships rolled in on the area behind us.

The crew chief scrambled over Zaporozec's body, sitting on it as he said something to the pilot.

"Get off him!" I said, slamming my hand against his helmet.

"What?" he said, pulling the helmet's radio microphone away from his mouth.

I pointed to my dead friend, to Julius Zaporozec, my buddy. "I said *get the fuck off him*!"

I was holding my rifle at the ready. Seeing that, his expression changed as he nodded for my benefit. He had already accepted them as lifeless cargo, while I still viewed them as friends. I patted Torres on the back for the reassurance I knew he couldn't feel, and as the sky opened up with a sudden monsoon shower, I looked out the door and cried with Rogers, who just kept saying, "Thank you," over and over, while the frustration, anger, and fear kept spilling from my eyes. Looking over the cargo bay, I couldn't find the voice or words to say "you're welcome."

When the helicopter reached Fire Support Base Buttons, the Ranger Commander, Captain Griffiths, and other LRRPs helped us from the aircraft, each catching a glimpse of the grisly scene on the helicopter's floor. My legs were like rubber, and I had to sit down, leaning against a helicopter revetment. I locked my knees to my chest and lowered my head while others mobbed McIntyre, trying to get a better picture of what had happened. How many were there? Who were they? What kind of small arms? Too many questions flew at the team leader, who answered them as he pushed away, walking over to where I was sitting. "You okay?" he asked. On the helicopter, several people were working on Torres.

I nodded. As McIntyre turned back to the others and was led to a nearby bunker for an intelligence debriefing, I heard an officer, a potbellied man in crisp, starched jungle fatigues say, "There couldn't possibly have been that many. Our intell says the gooks are moving out of the area—"

"You dumb fuck, we are your intell!" Mack yelled, while another officer maneuvered himself between the team leader and the officer doing the questioning.

Back at Phuoc Vinh we had separate debriefings in order to determine an accurate picture. Brennan, one of the platoon's lieutenants, carefully probed and asked for comments about McIntyre's actions. I probably looked the way I felt. Worn and frayed at the visceral edges. "If it wasn't for Mack, we all would've been killed. We found the trail, and before we barely got off of it, the gooks showed up. There was no time to put up the claymores, God how I wish there was, but there wasn't. Dave was shot first, Zap or maybe Rogers next. I dunno, it happened too fast."

"What did McIntyre do?"

"Kept us together. I didn't know what to do. It wasn't supposed to happen like that, you know, sir?"

He nodded.

"Mack directed everything and then tried to drive away the NVA by himself."

"What did you do?"

"Survived. I was too scared to do anything else!"

"That's not what he says," Brennan said.

"Sir, I don't know what I did or didn't do. There was just too much going on. It happened too fast, and I was scared shitless." The officer nodded.

Several days later, during the morning formation, the assistant division commander presented McIntyre and me with Silver Stars and Purple Hearts. When the general pinned the medals to our uniforms, saying we performed a difficult job with difficult risks and consequences, I wondered if that was how it really was, with medals that is, making a big deal out of the survival instinct? Did heroes shake at night whenever they thought about how it all happened? Did they, too, feel as though someone or something had plucked away a significant piece of their souls? I wish to God I could have done more, playing the scene over and over again, trying to make some sense of it. My role in life had been dramatically changed by the medal; I'd forever feel the weight and responsibility of it. So as friends closed in around to congratulate me, I felt something more ominous closing in as well.

"Hey, Jorgy, you want to go get a beer?" Ed Beal asked. I wasn't up for celebrating, so I declined.

"Naw."

"Come on, a drink will do you some good."

"No, thanks anyway," I said, bowing out. "I just want to take it easy for a while. Go on. Maybe I'll meet you later."

Beal nodded and then turned toward the door.

I felt guilty about the medal and didn't want to celebrate anything. I questioned why I didn't do something more, something that could've saved Zap's or Torres's life. Maybe I could've cut a hole in Zap's throat, helped him breathe through a plastic tube until the medics on the helicopter could've taken over. Maybe I should have let him carry the radio anyway, maybe then he might've been the one to drop behind the ant mound, protecting it as I had, and in the process saving my own life?

I didn't sleep easily that night, nor would I for a while to come. There was still too much I didn't understand, and there was no way of ever changing what had happened.

Staring at the red, white, and blue ribbon with the gold star medal that held a small silver star in its center, I tossed it on my foot locker and rolled over, facing the barracks wall, swearing and knowing that it wasn't worth their lives.

The comic books never told me about the cost of it all.

On Thanksgiving Day I lay in my bunk, too tired to go to the afternoon dinner the mess hall had prepared. I wasn't hungry—I had lost my appetite entirely. Listless, sore for no apparent reason, when I finally got out of the bunk my head was splitting. By that evening I was sweating more than usual in the too warm Vietnamese night. I knew I'd be all right by morning, and all I really needed was some sleep. The flu maybe.

The chills began that evening and alternated with a high fever. I was nauseous as well, and my stomach was churning over and tumbling violently. Diarrhea had taken over the fight.

"Hey, you don't look so good, Jorgy," Beal said in the morning, when I'd only managed to sit up in the bunk while the rest of the platoon was going about the daily routine.

"I feel like I look. Give me a hand?" I asked as he reached over helping me up. The back of my T-shirt was drenched in sweat.

"The flu," I said, while Beal only watched and nodded.

By late afternoon I had trouble walking. The cramps in my stomach had doubled me over, and every muscle in my body felt ready to tear. It was Beal who finally brought my condition to the attention of the first sergeant. Soon they loomed over my bunk, where I'd taken refuge, curling up in the fetal position.

"Sergeant Jorgenson, I'm going to have Sergeant Beal here take you over to the aid station," the veteran Ranger said, staring down at the pathetic figure in the cot.

"It's just the flu," I said to Beal who helped me up. "I'll be fine tomorrow."

"Take him down there, and I'll have someone pack his things back here," the first sergeant said, while Beal nodded, leading me out the door toward the battalion aid station.

The first sergeant and Beal had seen it before; the pattern was clear and unmistakable. They recognized my "flu" as malaria, and the initial exam at the aid station confirmed it.

"One hundred and three," the med said, reading the thermometer and telling the doctor of the results. "You didn't take your horse pill, did you?" the medic said in a scolding tone. He was referring to the large orange chloroquine-primaquine tablet issued to the soldiers in the division each Monday morning by their unit medics.

I shook my head. "Gives me diarrhea," I said.

"So does malaria, but the pill won't kill you!"

"No, but the gooks might when they catch me with my pants down in the jungle!" I wanted to tell him about the ways I saw myself dying in glorious combat, and that getting shot with my pants down around my ankles wasn't very high on my list. I let it ride. I didn't feel like arguing, and he knew it. All I really wanted to do was crawl into a corner somewhere to lie down and die.

A few hours later I was medevacced to Bien Hoa and finally Saigon, where blood tests confirmed the malaria. On the outskirts of the infamous city, the hospital had a French colonial flair, with broad tiled hallways and large double-hung windows, reflecting the comfortable lifestyle of those who designed it. A guarded check point, hidden behind sandbagged fighting positions and barbed wire, a fence, and a brick wall reminded everyone that for all the hospital's comfort and seemingly safe location, it was still susceptible to attack.

For the first time in a long time, I slept on a bed with sheets, but

I wore the standard hospital-issue blue pajamas. The ward contained others who had suffered a similar fate, and I would have two weeks there before I would be able to return to my unit. I received medicine and lectures three times a day from the doctors, nurses, and medics who, after reading my chart, couldn't believe that anyone would be dumb enough to throw away his malaria pills. Yeah, yeah, yeah, dumb, I know, silly me. It wasn't worth arguing the point. They wouldn't understand. They lived in a clean, antiseptic environment and didn't understand the situation in the field. On my second morning, I outraged a doctor even further after he innocently inquired as to how we LRRPs lived in the field.

"How do you carry all of your equipment, let alone rations? I mean, you're out there in the jungle, you say, for five days at a time?"

"Dehydrated rations. The rucksack contains all of the excess equipment and stuff you can live without if you have to abandon it. We carry forty to forty-five fully loaded magazines, grenades, knife, and McGuire rig on our web gear."

"If you carry so much ammunition on your web gear, then where do you carry your canteens?"

"On the pack."

"How many?"

"One, sometimes two."

"Then, where do you get the rest of the water you drink?"

"Rivers, streams, bomb craters—"

"What?" he yelled, while the nurse at his side looked on horrified

"Well, sir, clean water is a luxury we sometimes can't afford. We make do."

He was outraged, and I was the target of his fury. "*Don't ever drink bomb-crater water!* You hear me?"

"Sometimes it's the only water we can find, Doc."

"I don't care! The purifying tablets don't help much, even with the river water, and they can't do a damn thing with the chemicals and bacteria found in the pools left after a bomb's explosion. Carry more water, go without, but don't ever, *ever*, drink the water from a bomb crater. You understand me, Sergeant?" He'd reverted to his military rank, and any informalities that had once existed were now gone.

After making a few quick notations in my chart, he hurriedly went to the next patient while the nurse remained at the foot of the bed, shaking her head. A first lieutenant in her early twenties. "That water could kill you."

"That and a thousand other things, pilgrim," I said, doing my best John Wayne. "So, when do I get my sponge bath?"

"How old are you?" she asked, her bright green eyes sparkling as she tried to suppress a smile.

"Nineteen. Geeze, you're not gonna pull rank and age on me, are you? You can't be that much older than me anyway."

"No to the sponge bath and pulling rank, or whatever. And thanks for the compliment. However, I am older."

"Twenty-three maybe, twenty-four tops—and, may I add, you've held up well," I said as she just smiled before turning and following the doctor on the morning rounds. She was the smiling, slightly plump, cheerleader type with bright green eyes and a smile that made you want to cheer. Dressed in formal whites that failed to conceal the stocky but athletic build beneath them, the nurse lieutenant was the prettiest woman I'd seen in a while. I suppose I daydreamed about her and me embraced in a passionate affair, but that was little more than an illusion—I was the enlisted patient, and she was the officer nurse, and no matter how things sparked between us, if they did, it was temporary and finite. She knew it and I did, too, so over the weeks we built up a fine attraction for each other, but just the brother-and-sister variety, which didn't do much for my ego.

She made me miss my girlfriend in Seattle and also made me realize that that relationship, too, was finite. She was still in high school, going about the daily high-school routine. Though we'd seemed to have so much in common before the war, I knew we wouldn't have anything in common afterward. It was funny because a quote I recalled from a high school literature class was right—you can't go home again. I was too many light years away from Seattle to return the same person. My sociology course would last one year and would be combined with a construction course that would build walls around my emotions. I could see them being constructed daily in Vietnam; I knew that when I eventually returned home, they'd be too high and thick to scale or break through. Nothing mattered but the war.

"Sergeant Jorgenson, you have a few visitors," the nurse-lieutenant said as two smiling faces came sauntering down the hall. It was Johnny Rodriguez and a veteran team leader I only knew slightly.

"Get the hell outta the rack, shithead. You're coming with us!"

Rod said, tossing me my jungle fatigues that the nurse had given him. "None of the lazy-ass REMF crap for you, son. We're here to take you back to the company."

"Come on, there's an 11:45 flight to Phuoc Vinh so we don't have much time," Rodriguez said. Then to the nurse he added, "If the boy gave you a difficult time, miss, we can have him shot. It's really no trouble." The veteran team leader winked at the nurse. Shaking her head, she walked back to the duty desk.

"So, have you slept with her yet?" the team leader asked, while admiring the nurse as she walked away. I said I hadn't, and they both frowned.

"And he calls himself a Ranger?" Rodriguez added, and then just as quickly said, "Come on, Jorgy. We'll miss the flight."

After I put on the jungle fatigues and laced my boots, the team leader tossed me my black Ranger beret while Rod scooped up my personal effects.

At the desk, the doctor was discussing something with my nurse and another ward nurse, a dark-haired captain who wore a smirk.

"Where do we sign the boy out?" Rod asked as the doctor turned, revealing his gold, oak-leaf major insignia.

"Eh, down at the main desk on the first floor."

"Anything else we need, Major?" Rod asked, while my nurse watched on with concern.

"Maybe a better story, Sergeant," the major replied. "Try not to catch the clap."

"Excuse me, sir," Rod said with mock surprise.

"Never mind, forget it," he said. "Sergeant Jorgenson, remember what I said about the bomb-crater water."

I told him I would, while the two LRRPs headed quickly toward the stairwell.

"Sergeant Jorgenson, can I talk to you for a minute?" the nurse-lieutenant said catching us at the doorway. I told the others to go on, I'd join them in a minute. Rod smiled wickedly and winked at me in appreciation.

"Yes, ma'am?"

"Cut it out," she said, frowning at me as she shifted uncomfortably. "I don't know. Look, just take care of yourself, and don't drink any more bomb-crater water. I'm going to miss you, kiddo. Take care, okay?" she said. Then, with an afterthought, she reached out and gave me a hug.

"And I'll miss your walk. You have a nice butt, ma'am," I said as she broke into a smile.

"Come on, Jorgy!" Rod called from the stairwell. I turned,

thinking that maybe the war had some valuable lessons as well. Even if I was having trouble deciphering their meanings. The nurse, I'm certain, had a better understanding of the war. The hospital had given her that much.

After clearing the hospital, signing me out, and picking up my rifle, we were out on the busy Saigon street.

"Let's catch a cab," the team leader said while Rodriguez agreed.

"What do you mean, cab? Tan Son Nhut is just down the street!" I said, pointing to the direction of the airport.

"Damned if he still doesn't have a touch of the fever," Rodriguez said, his accent turning remarkably English.

"His sense of direction is completely off." The team leader grinned, hailing a cab. "We'd better run him into town here, find a bar and hotel, a few smiling hookers, and see if we can cure him!"

"That's affirmative!" Rod replied.

On the ride through the crowded streets, I learned that the two had actually been on their way to Bien Hoa to pick up some new ropes for rappelling when they cooked up their plan.

"The first sergeant wanted us to take a look and see how you were doing. It seemed to us you were doing fair to middling, so a day or so in Saigon proper just might make you feel a whole hell of a lot better," Rodriguez said.

"And if the MPs stop us, well, we can just say we're poor little sheep who've lost our way. Baa-fucking-baa," piped in the team leader.

"So where are we going?" I asked. After all, it seemed like a reasonable question.

"Tu Do Street," beamed the team leader. "Sin City's finest road to hell in a handbasket. First though, we have to find a place to stay. Hey! cab driver, where's a good hotel?"

"I take you! I take you!" the cab driver said as he veered off on another main street and then delivered us to the U.S. Armed Forces Exchange. Turning in his seat the cab driver produced one-hundred dollars in MPC.

"You buy me cigarettes and whiskey, and I buy your hotel, for all three."

Rod recognized a good thing when he saw it.

"Keep your money down, papa san. Cigarettes and whiskey no problem, but you get us number-one hotel, okay. No fleabag, back-alley, number-ten hotel. Number-one hotel, you bic?"

The cab driver was smiling, showing gold-capped teeth while he nodded in understanding.

Ten minutes or so later, we returned to find our cab driver holding our door before he quickly whisked us away through the streets. He came to a stop in front of a seven-story building in the city's center. A large sign outside read: HOTEL CARAVELLE.

"Numbah-one hotel, you see. Numbah one." And then he raced in the door and came out moments later with our keys, along with a receipt for the room.

As we entered with our rucksacks, rifles, and jungle fatigues, we looked out of place and, seeing this, the clerk behind the desk had someone quickly show us our room. There was a restaurant on the roof of the hotel, but we decided not to use it; too many chances of running into people with questions we couldn't answer. So locking our rifles and equipment in the room, we spruced up as best we could and then left, searching for a decent bar. Half an hour later, we turned into one that had loud rock music coming from its doors. As we entered, three hostesses greeted us. When we took a seat at a booth, they slipped in next to us, and asked us to buy them drinks.

Their "drinks" were called champagne but more than likely were ginger ale or a substitute. But while our drinks went for one dollar a shot, theirs went for two dollars each. After an hour we were down fifty dollars. A short time after that, a hostess led·the team leader through a curtain in back where she was going to give him a rubdown.

"I'm certain it's only therapeutic," Rodriguez said to the Vietnamese woman at his side. The hostess next to me, who said her name was Mary, placed a hand on the inside of my lap.

"You want a rubdown, too?" she cooed.

I said I did, and while we waited, I noticed an MP jeep pull up outside the bar. Two sharply dressed MPs in spit-shined boots, shining helmets, and wearing aviator glasses and sour expressions came through the door.

Sauntering up to our booth, their expressions turned to smiles.

"You guys have any orders on you?" a big spec-four Goliath asked. The second MP, a PFC stood off to the side.

"Sure," Rodriguez replied and, reaching into his pocket, produced the folded forms for the MPs.

"It says here you're on your way to Bien Hoa."

Rod nodded. "That's right and it's good for two days so we thought we'd kill some time in your lovely city. We're tourists."

"What about you?" he said, turning to me when he didn't see my name on the travel orders.

"I just got out of the hospital. Malaria. I'm going to catch a plane later to Phuoc Vinh."

"Neither of you have passes for the city, so we'll have to escort you back to the air base," the big MP said as the team leader came back through the curtain smiling and hugging his hostess.

"He's with us," I said.

"I kinda figured he was, so when you're ready, let's go," he said pointing toward the door.

We paid our tab, said our farewells, and hopped in the back of the jeep. I started to say something about our rifles and equipment, and Rodriguez hushed me up. I wasn't sure what he was up to, but I knew he had a plan—makeshift plans seemed to be what he did best. So as we rode once again through the busy streets, heading for the air force base, I sat back and enjoyed the scenery.

There were thousands of mopeds on the street and an odd assortment of buses, cars, and military vehicles. If there were street lights or traffic signals, they weren't working; driving was based on survival instinct rather than plan.

Pulling up to the gate of the air base, the two army MPs delivered us to the air police.

"They don't have passes," the MPs said to the air police, who nodded solemnly and pointed us toward the air terminal.

Once into the compound, Rodriguez and the team leader smiled as a line of vehicles headed toward the gate.

"Come on," the team leader said, heading for the nearest truck.

"What's up?"

Rod offered an explanation. "We're going to hitch a ride back into the city. See, the air police aren't really concerned with what or who goes out of the base as much as they are with who or what comes in."

"Do you think it'll work?" I asked.

"Jorgy, how do you think we got to the hospital?"

An hour later we returned to the bar, eventually finding our way back to the hotel, escorted by our hostesses. The sins of the city were still intact, and my absolution would only be temporary.

On my return to the company, the platoon leader offered me a job as a radio relay in Tay Ninh province. It would be a safe job, no more missions, just filtering radio traffic while the teams went about their patrols. It was the kind of job a veteran team member or team leader might receive after nine months or more in-country, only I didn't have that much time punched in. I declined the offer, and after a few days of soul-searching, I decided to transfer out of the company. My minor wounds and brief service didn't merit the cushy job.

I didn't have a reasonable explanation or answer for my action, and when Lieutenant Brennan tried to talk me into staying, I told him I couldn't. What I didn't tell him is that I felt I had let the company down. After all, I was one of their honor graduates and a shake 'n' bake. I'd thought I could work miracles. Losing my friends taught me otherwise.

"Where would you like to go?"

"The Blues," I said, knowing that the infantry platoons of the 1st of the 9th Cav spent the majority of their time rescuing downed helicopter crews or serving as quick reaction forces for Ranger teams that had suddenly found themselves in contact and in desperate need of help.

"There are three Blue units in the 1st of the 9th. Which one do you want?"

"A Troop," I said, seeing that the platoon leader was satisfied with my selection. A Troop, the Apache Blues as they were better known in the division, was considered by many of the Rangers to be the best of the twenty-one man reconnaissance units.

"You don't have to go, you know." Lieutenant Brennan said. "You can stay with the company."

"Yes sir, I do . . ." I said, starting to explain my reasoning and deciding against it. Survivor's guilt does strange things. It would sound silly to him; I knew it was deadly serious.

"You're a good Ranger," he said extending his hand. "Take care."

I shook it and then left the platoon hootch, wondering if I'd made the right decision. Several days later my orders came down from division. After clearing the company, I picked up my duffel bag and rifle, said my good-byes and, taking one last look around, started toward the 1st of the 9th's battalion headquarters, a few hundred yards away.

"You need some help?" I turned and saw Beal standing a few feet from the gate.

"Yeah, you know a better travel agent? Mine's got me booked on some silly ass vacations spots. You sure this ain't Rio?"

"Reasonably sure. Take it easy, Jorgy. Keep in touch, huh?"

I told him I would but I knew otherwise. I was already out of touch.

The walk over to battalion headquarters took only ten minutes. It was a slow walk, burdened with the realization that war wasn't like it was in the movies, that good guys don't always win in the end, that good people die for no good reasons. As I walked, I felt the weight of the realization and of the Silver Star pushing down at my shoulders. Like a curse beginning to take effect, I felt the unheard rumbling as of a far-off storm building in the distance and heading towards me. I'd have to prove to myself that I deserved the medal and any respect that went with it. Then I might be able to wear it with some pride or satisfaction. Some, because there would never be a complete sense of worth. A higher price would have to be paid. Heading toward the Blues, I wasn't certain if I could afford it.

I came to Vietnam not really knowing a damn thing about war; with only four months in-country, I now had a working knowledge of what it entailed. I was also painfully aware that soldiers don't write their lines in any war and that, for all of the importance we put into our roles, we could easily be replaced or omitted, written out of the script with a quick stroke. In Paris the peace talks were bogged down over the size of the table the delegates would use, so they wouldn't complete the script for some time to come. The muse was fickle, and the squabbles over joint authorship would keep them from finding excuses not to finish the final chapter.

While they fumbled with their writer's block, toying with various scenarios, those of us confined by their pens would come and go in the story line with cold and indifferent frequency, agonizing and dying over the pages, our blood serving as their ink. We didn't fucking matter.

Two weeks before Christmas of 1969, if there was "a light at the end of the tunnel" as they said, then from our point of view it was the light of an oncoming train. The temperature was in the mid nineties, and Christmas was a world away. Nothing was as it seemed.

CHAPTER NINE

A bored spec-four sat behind a metal-framed desk just inside the door at battalion headquarters. As I walked through the door, he started to rise at attention and then eased back in the seat when he finally noticed the rank insignia on my collar.

"Can I help you, Sarge?"

"I'm reporting in," I said, handing him a copy of my orders. His eyes ran from the name on the orders to my uniform nametag, the Combat Infantryman Badge, and then back to the assignment orders.

"Alpha Troop, huh?"

I nodded. "Yeah, so where do I report?"

"Right here. The battalion sergeant major will want to talk to you first. This your second tour?"

"No, I just transferred from the Ranger company."

"Crazy fuckers, ain't they? I mean, going out with only five guys on a team. I heard one of their teams just got wiped out. You know any of them?"

I nodded.

"It's crazy. Have a seat over there, Sarge." He pointed to a nearby folding chair as he walked the orders through the doorway. A few minutes later the battalion sergeant major walked back through with him, carrying my orders.

"Sergeant Jorgenson?" he said, looking me over, mentally kicking the tires on the new man. "I'm the squadron's sergeant major. Welcome to the 1st of the 9th. I see you were a LRRP." he said, staring at the red, white, and black Ranger scroll over my division patch.

"Yes, Sergeant Major."

"Why did you leave?"

"They offered me a rear-area job, and I wasn't ready for one yet," I said. "I hadn't earned it."

"Is that right?" he said, looking over the orders along with my 201 file. "I see you have a Silver Star."

I nodded again, thinking what a paradox it was: proud and ashamed at the same time.

"I don't suppose you'd like to be the old man's jeep driver, would you? The sergeant here's going home in less than a month, and we need someone we can rely on to do the job."

I shook my head, declining the offer. It'd be too difficult to explain, so I gave him another answer instead, one just as honest. "I eh—I've never driven a jeep before. I can't drive a stick!"

"That's the trouble with the Rangers, they teach you how to blow up the damn things but not how to operate one." The old sergeant laughed while the jeep driver joined in. "Well, I guess that rules you out. Glad to have you in the battalion anyway," he said, deciding that maybe the battalion could use me. The sergeants major of battalions were usually screeners, old-time foremen who liked to see who was transferring into their battalions and why. If they were reasonably satisfied by their appraisal, they'd welcome you into their command; if they felt you might be a potential problem, they could pass you on to someone else. "There's a mail chopper coming down from Alpha Troop at 1600," he said, checking his watch. "You can catch a ride with it. That'll give an hour or so to take it easy. The sergeant here'll give you hand with your things when you're ready to go."

He turned back to his office, while the sergeant sat back down behind the metal desk.

"You should've taken the job. I could've taught you how to drive the jeep in fifteen minutes. With all the potholes and mudpits around here, they wouldn't have even noticed an occasional missed gear, let alone a clutch!"

"Thanks anyway. Look, I'm gonna head over to the flight line and wait for the helicopter. I don't have that much to carry, so you can take it easy."

I grabbed my duffel bag and rifle and walked the few hundred yards to the battalion flight line. I took a seat in the shade against a sandbagged revetment. Somewhere in the distance artillery rounds were thumping, accenting a nearby transistor radio that someone had tuned in to AFVN—the radio station in Saigon. The war was going on, business as usual.

The 1st of the 9th Cavalry had been the original Buffalo Soldiers, the black, horse soldiers and white officers who earned a hard-fought reputation in the American Southwest against the Indians. Over the decades that followed the horses disappeared, replaced first by wheeled vehicles and finally by helicopters in Vietnam. Along with the changes, the segregated unit opened its ranks to all and—if military information officers were to be believed—in its latest struggles, the battalion was still adding to its list of accomplishments.

One thing the unit did retain from its horse cavalry days was its troop designations. Unlike many of the other units in the division that had company units, the 1st of the 9th had troops. In total there were four—A Troop in Tay Ninh, B Troop in Quan Loi, Charlie Troop in Phuoc Vinh, and D or Delta Troop, who were also known as the Rat Patrol, after the World War II unit in North Africa that operated in heavily armed jeeps.

Each of the first three troops was further broken down into platoons—an infantry platoon, known as "Blues" for their infantry color designation, a scout platoon with three-man observation helicopters (called Loaches), and the gunship and lift platoons with the sleek and deadly Cobra helicopters and the awkward Huey transport helicopters that ferried the Blues into combat. Along with these platoons were the support personnel needed to fill in the gaps in the troop personnel roster such as the cooks, clerks, and maintenance.

Together, they added a new dimension to the strategy of the war, whereas infantry or "grunt" units would spend weeks moving in and out of suspected enemy regions, the troops used observations helicopters to locate the enemy by flying at treetop level to spot them. They would then hurriedly veer away to let the gunships attack and the lift ships (Hueys) ferry in the Blues to engage the enemy on the ground. It was a practical working arrangement that met with success. While the grunts would go out for weeks on end, the troops fought a banker's war, a nine-to-five operation every day of the year. The Blues also carried the responsibility of rescuing shot-down helicopter crews, as well as reconnaissance and quick reaction forces (QRF) roles for units within the division.

Operating with twenty-one men, the Blues and platoons within the troops spent more time in actual combat than did most grunt companies, and their casualty lists reflected that fact.

The scout platoon, with its small number of assigned helicopters, saw the number dwindle due to staggering losses over a six-month period. One helicopter, nicknamed "Queer John," in A Troop had been downed eleven times. The Blues suffered similar losses and everyone within the troops was familiar with the Chu Phong incident—the Blues had been inserted into an enemy-held area and took a number of prisoners, only to learn that there was a battalion-size North Vietnamese Army unit in the immediate vicinity. Then, when the Blues were trapped by the larger force and their lift ships desperately tried to pull them out to safety, two of the three lift ships were shot down in the attempt, killing fifteen of the twenty-one soldiers. Two-thirds of the unit was wiped out in the heavy fighting.

I knew this was going in, so I was aware of the situation and the probabilities. For me it would be a chance to start over again, to earn the Silver Star and make up for mistakes and misgivings with the Rangers. I hadn't let them down as much as I let myself down, and I knew I wouldn't get a chance to correct that if I didn't *make* the chance. I didn't have a real plan, and I wasn't certain how I'd do it. All I knew is that I had to try.

Maybe the jeep driver was right—maybe we were all a bunch of "crazy fuckers," trying hard to live up to the image of ourselves we created in our minds. Of course, while it must have seemed crazy to some, it was the only way we knew. As Rangers we were taught to be independent, but there was a price for that independence. At nineteen years of age the price hadn't seemed all that expensive; even though I was aware of the possibilities, deep down inside I knew I was invincible, that I couldn't die, that it wasn't in the cards. I also knew I couldn't win but that it was enough to simply be in the game. The stakes seemed trivial, but it was the principle that was everything; until I came to terms with the war and myself, I couldn't go home, and I couldn't take a comfortable rear-area job, either. Honor had to count for something.

I didn't know what hand fate held, and I knew that, at best, I was bluffing. I was in over my head and too proud to fold.

The mail chopper from Tay Ninh touched down a little after 1600, and a doorgunner emerged from the back of the small Loach (LOH) scout ship, carrying a bright orange mailbag of outgoing mail. The pilot, a slender, quiet warrant officer, wearing a Nomex flight suit and dark aviator glasses, waited with the bird. A .38 pistol in a shoulder holster was strapped in place for business. His flight helmet was custom painted with his call sign.

Grabbing my things, I walked toward the aircraft.

"Mind if I catch a ride?"

"Where you going?"

"Apache Troop, 1st of the 9th, the Blues," I said. He nodded, thumbing over his shoulder towards the open bay of the small observation helicopter.

"Throw your things in there. My 60 gunner went to drop off the mail and pick up a few things on the other side of the base camp. It might be a while, so you might as well stow your things and make yourself comfortable."

When I started to climb in the back, he protested. "Naw, that's for the gunner and the mail. You'll ride up here as the observer."

Though I had flown in the cargo bays of a number of aircraft since arriving in Nam, I had yet to fly up front.

"You a LRRP?" he said, looking at the Ranger scroll.

"Used to be," I said and left it at that.

"Apache Troop's not so bad," he said casually, ignoring the barrier of rank. But then, warrant officers were the only officer rank to do so. In the scheme of things they were the bridge between the two rank structures. They weren't "sirs," nor were they "soldiers," instead they were "misters." Neither fish nor fowl, but able to move about comfortably in both environments.

"The old man, Captain Funk's got his shit together. He's a good guy and a good pilot, but he's getting short—maybe one hundred days—so who knows what they'll send us next. Probably some dildo with no flying time."

"You a scout?" I said, asking the obvious. Taking things for granted wasn't the best policy and the question provided me with an opportunity to learn something more about the unit I was transferring into.

The pilot nodded, producing a wry smile. "To quote everybody, if you ain't a scout, you ain't shit! so I guess that makes me shit." He held out his hand. "Tad Yanika," he said. "Scouts."

"Jorgenson," I said, shaking it.

"You know, if you're transferring in, you can always give scouts a try?"

It was an interesting idea, and for a moment I pictured myself as a character out of Errol Flynn's *Dawn Patrol*, white scarf around my neck, cocky walk—more of a strut really—and then added a few of the war's personal touches, dark sunglasses and a custom-painted helmet, but then I quickly realized that it was little more than a daydream.

For all the glamorous notions, the small helicopters were little more than fiberglass and paper-thin metal. Their mission was to fly at treetop level and draw enemy fire for the gunships circling above. The system worked well when things went according to plan, but the Loaches frequently took hits and fell in flames to the jungle below. I'd heard their casualty rate was high, and sitting in the front of the helicopter, it was easy to see why. There was no protection, even the helicopter rides at county fairs seemed to have more substance to them than did the real things. And though flak jackets could protect a soldier's chest and back from direct small-arms fire, they couldn't stop a shoulder-fired rocket, one of the chief weapons used against the treetop fliers.

I told the pilot I'd consider it and actually did so. A few minutes later Chris Gray, the doorgunner, came running back, carrying another mail bag and a small cardboard box. With little preparation, we were ready to go. Plugging the commo cord into his helmet headset, Gray said something to the pilot and they laughed. He motioned for me to put on the extra flight helmet. After I did, he plugged me into the conversation.

"—so I told him the NVA pit helmet was worth at least a fifth or two of Jack Daniels, which didn't exactly go over well . . ." Yanika said. "Chris, this is Jorgenson. He's just coming into the troop, so he'll be heading back with us."

Gray nodded with a thumbs-up as Yanika cranked the Loach. "The booze is a bonus," Yanika explained. "We alternate mail runs, and depending on who's got it, we try to pick up the things we want or need or can't get in Tay Ninh by bartering with whatever we have." It was an old system, one that everyone used to get the basics or luxuries that for one reason or another weren't available. It was rumored that at one Special Forces camp you could get anything from Thompson machine guns to NVA flame throwers for a pound of fresh coffee or whatever they were short of at the time. Free enterprise extended beyond the business world.

"Hey, Chris, Jorgenson here may be interested in coming over to the scouts."

"Is that right?" Chris asked when I told him I was considering it.

"I don't really have any flight time," I said.

"No sweat, GI," he said laughing. "After a few months with us you'll be an ace aviator, courtesy of Apache Troop." Then, running through the flight check, Yanika brought the machine to life, first to a hip-high hover and then, dipping the skids, took off in a rushing run down the small flight line. Clearing the camp's barbed-wire perimeter, he took the Loach a few thousand feet in the air, leaving my stomach and Phuoc Vinh behind to settle in the dust cloud he'd created. The flight would take roughly forty minutes, and he'd fly by rote, taking the same visual route he'd taken so many times before.

Ten minutes out of Phuoc Vinh, he told me to take the stick.

"First lesson, it's about the same as riding a motorcycle, gas, brakes, speedometer, and everything but a decent radio station."

"I dunno . . ." I said, trying to leave the flying to him.

"Come on, give it a try. Most observers got more air time than most Stateside pilots, and if you become an observer, you'll have to know the basics anyway," Yanika said. He went on to explain that the observers had to know how to fly the aircraft since there was a very good likelihood of a pilot's getting wounded on a mission. It happened all the time, he said, and then told me about an observer in the troop who'd just earned a Distinguished Flying Cross for doing exactly that. When the pilot was shot in the neck, the observer, a big Hawaiian named David Ham, managed to bring the ship to safety.

"It ain't authorized but it's smart policy," Yanika said. "Our policy. Okay, slowly, carefully, take the stick."

In a brief lesson Yanika had me holding on to the controls while keeping a careful vigil over my actions, his hands poised and ready to retake control in an instant if need be. After a few minutes of what seemed like five hours of tense, restricted movement, I told him to take it, which he did, grinning. Afterward, I learned he had never relinquished control.

"Not bad, Gray. What you think?"

"I think he'll do fine, but he won't be able to jerk off for a week. Flying's better than sex!"

The jungle below was a carpet of browns and greens, and an occasional brown, winding river cut the pattern into living jigsaw puzzle pieces. Small bare patches of ponds or dried depressions were holes in the jungle floor, natural clearings that often became landing or pickup zones.

"We have guests," Gray's voice boomed over the intercom.

"What?" Mr. Yanika asked, becoming all business.

"Gooks, with boats on the river at three o'clock," he said, turning his machine gun down toward the river a thousand feet or so below. Though it was difficult to make out at first, the unmistakable outline of the long open sampans could be seen paralleling the bank of the muddied river. There were no villages in the vicinity, and the river they were trying to cross was in enemy territory.

Yanika circled around, too high to worry about taking fire. He wanted to get a better look.

"Looks like three boats. There's another one hugging the bank. We'll call it in, but other than that we can't do a whole hell of a lot.'' While the pilot called the sighting in, Gray and I could do little more than watch the action below.

The Vietnamese had been fighting the same kind of war for one thousand years, a hide-and-seek, guerrilla-action war, usually against better armed and equipped opponents. With their determination and cunning, they had usually outlasted their enemies. Well into the sixth year of direct involvement, we were getting a dose of what they gave the French before us, the Japanese before them, and the countless other armies over the centuries who thought they, too, could beat these little people.

Twenty minutes later the Nui Ba Den, the towering Black Virgin Mountain, loomed in the distance like a moody giant, sulking over the province. I'd seen it several times before but not from the air inside a Loach.

''We've got to make a pickup at the top of it,'' Yanika said, then added, ''Keep your 60 ready,'' to his doorgunner.

The ''60'' was the M-60 machine gun, the only real weapon the small observation helicopters had. Gray had removed the tight, metal stand that restricted its movement and connected the machine gun to a flexible strap bolted to the ceiling of the aircraft that enabled him to move the weapon in any direction and to lean out on the skids, as many scout doorgunners did, to get a better shot at the enemy below.

As we neared the mountain, I saw that great pock marks and shell holes dotted the approach to the small camp at its peak. It was said that, with the small fortified position at the top of the mountain and the basecamp in its shadow, we controlled the far reaches, while the Viet Cong and North Vietnamese Army held the middle and the miles of tunnels, caves, and cathedrallike caverns that they'd carved out over the ages. Three sides of the mountain were rubble and craters, while the fourth side, where the Buddhist monastery lay perched overlooking the countryside, was undisturbed. It was rumored that the key to the secret of the mountain lay in the monastery but that it was off-limits as a military target.

''Close up it looks like gravel,'' I said looking down the long, erratic slope. Rubble had replaced any natural growth.

''Yeah, it does,'' Yanika replied, ''and it still doesn't stop them from digging out and taking pot shots at us. Last week we lost a lift ship that flew too close to the mountain and was downed with antiaircraft fire. I don't know what they've got in there, but it's probably more than any of us will ever guess.''

A grunt guided us into the helipad, half visible from the purple smoke grenade he used to show the wind's direction. On landing, Gray unloaded a small packet of letters from the orange sack, while picking up the outgoing mail and then, just as fast as we landed, we were off again.

"The 25th Infantry Division owns the camp at the top. We just have a few radio-relay people stationed on it. Get ready, we're going down," Yanika said, pulling the helicopter suddenly down and then racing over the flat rice paddies that led to the Tay Ninh base camp, my new home.

Tay Ninh Province bordered on Cambodia, and because of its location it had earned the nickname of Rocket City for the nightly rocket and mortar attacks the North Vietnamese would set before scurrying back into the sanctuary of nearby Cambodia. Because of the constant incoming—meaning incoming rocket and mortar rounds—many of the hootches and command posts took on the appearance of fortified fighting bunkers, with sandbagged walls skirting the structures. Of those who lived there, many would remain underground until the monsoons, when the torrential downpours turned their underground homes into mud-filled swimming holes.

Yanika had contact with the troop's tower, whose air traffic controllers gave us landing clearance. Hovering into place between two sandbagged revetment walls—the garage for the scout helicopters—we touched down on Alpha Troop, Apache Troop as a portal-way sign claimed. A Russian .51 machine gun was welded to one of the two steel columns that supported the archway sign.

"The orderly room's over there," Yanika said, pointing across the compound area to a series of huts. "Think about the scouts. We can always use good people."

"Thanks a lot, sir," I said with a salute. He just waved it off.

"Don't do that, Sarge. You'll hurt his feelings," Gray said, grinning.

Apache Troop was just a collection of hootches and bunkers that lay within the L-shaped flight line and small helicopter parking area that housed the unit's many helicopters. It was easy to see that the troop catered to the helicopters and relied on them for its success, so if I chose not to go with the scouts, then I'd surely get my air time in the Huey lift ships as the Blues were ferried into battle.

After reporting in, I was assigned to an NCO hootch near the perimeter road that circled the large base camp. The Tay Ninh base camp belonged to the 25th Infantry Division, though other units such as the 1st Cav shared its facilities and responsibilities.

Apache Troop was only one of several helicopter assault units, though the only Cav troop in the area of operations. Cav Division grunts worked the regions of the province, living out of such unlikely named fire support bases as Ike, Jamie, Carolyn, Grant, and Becky. Fire support bases were named innocently enough by staff officers who couldn't begin to guess the ominous actions that would plague the small defensive outposts along the enemy infiltration routes.

The Blues and the scouts were both short on personnel, and I could take a few days to make up my mind between them. Anyway, the minor wounds I'd received in the last Ranger mission still had not healed; they were still infected and foul smelling beneath the bandages. Besides the small cuts I received in my hand, a razorlike piece of exploding metal had cut across the Achilles tendon of my left foot, not a major wound by any standards. I didn't even know I'd been wounded in the foot until back at the company, when I found a pool of blood in the boot. The small piece of metal that had cut the tendon was still lodged in the jungle boot. I removed it, wondering what it might've done had it hit me in the head. I couldn't help but recall a single bullet to the front of the face, another small piece of flying metal.

I'd seen Mister Yanika and Gray heading out over the barbed wire toward the jungle and a mission the following morning. The Blues were on a two-day stand-down, but their four hootches near the flight line were busy. Several soldiers sat in front of the general-store-like facades of the hootches, cleaning weapons and equipment. Loud rock music came from a hootch-size hut that served as a club for the troop's enlisted men. A dirt road cut through the compound. Across the flight line, maintenance personnel were working on helicopters. A Troop seemed to be self-supporting.

Closer to the orderly room were the officers facilities that served the many warrant officers within the unit. Unlike most infantry companies, which had only a handful of officers out of the one hundred or so men within their command, a third of A Troop was officers. The other two-thirds were divided between the combat and support personnel. Directly across the compound road from the enlisted men's club, sat the troop's mess tent. Across from it was the TOC or tactical operations center, the radio-filled, fortified briefing and command center for the troop. Farther along behind it lay the perimeter road where the bunkers and fighting positions and layers of barbed wire defined the troop's base-camp responsibilities. In the camp's overall defense, the troop was required to mount a night guide to man the bunkers and fighting position in its sector and to supply a day guard as well.

The senior NCO hootch was the closest living quarters to the perimeter, which was known as the Greenline. The hootch was divided into small rooms for most of the senior noncommissioned officers in the troop. Others, like the unit's first sergeant, had living quarters directly off the orderly room. Temporarily, I'd set up house in the NCO hootch until I determined which platoon to go to. My choice would begin on the second day, when I'd go out on my first mission as an observer, a get-acquainted ride to try to sell me on the scouts. So far that seemed like a reasonable idea, but a mail flight and an actual mission were two different things, and I'd have to learn the difference. After that I'd get a shot at the Blues to see how I'd fit with them. Being a scout appealed to my sense of imagination, but deep down I knew I was better suited for the Blues, on the ground, utilizing the skills I'd received in State-side training as well as the real world ones I'd picked up from the LRRPs.

My flight training would be with another round pilot, WO Bill McIntosh, who looked all of fourteen years of age. Even his thin mustache couldn't hide his youthful look. What I didn't know was that "Minimac" was perhaps one of the finest pilots in the troop. For him the check-out mission would be a hayride. We were to reconnoiter a region northwest of the base camp for signs of enemy activity. Minimac gave Nui ba Den a wide berth then settled on an altitude that would carry us safely to the region. Once there we'd begin the dangerous descent to the jungle below to attract enemy fire, while the Cobra gunship that remained perched high above us waited for the action to begin.

"Jorgy, let's see what's down there," McIntosh said as he brought the helicopter lower. We were worms on the hook going down to attract the fish in the water. Of course, just as crafty as some fish that'll strip the bait off the hook, the North Vietnamese soldiers lay hidden in shadows, waiting for the fishermen.

From treetop level, the jungle takes on a different perspective. Brightly colored birds, suddenly interrupted, screeched and flew away as alarmed monkeys leaped from their branches, yelling their displeasure, as we slowly toured the forest. Small trails would occasionally be seen through small openings and then disappeared beneath the lush foliage.

"Got a bunker," the door gunner, Terry 'Mugsy' Delorme said, firing a burst from his machine gun. The worm was wiggling on the hook.

I hadn't seen it yet, but the machine-gun rounds slamming into the earth below brought it out—a small earthen mound with log-supported openings was the target below. Then the floor revealed more fighting positions, at first unseen even to the trained or familiar eye. For an eternity, Mugsy raked the bunker complex but with no result. If the North Vietnamese were down there, they were lying low, knowing that sooner or later we'd have to give up and go away. The helicopter only had so much fuel, and if we were to make it back to Tay Ninh, then we'd only have a few more minutes on station to find anything.

"Doesn't look like anybody's home," Delorme said.

"That's a rog. Let's see what the high bird would like to do."

The "high bird" was the gunship, to whom the flight was becoming a bore. We at least had the bunker complex to scout, while the gunship went around time and again in slow, lazy circles.

"Looks like nobody's home, folks—either that or they're being terribly antisocial. What do you suggest? Over."

"Let's head back, 1-1. Out," came the static-charged voice over my headset.

"Hang on folks. We're outta here!" McIntosh said, peeling away in a sharp turn and instantly taking her up in a roller-coaster climb to join the sleek gunship. Once there, he radioed that he wanted to do a little contour flying home to see what else might pop up. The high bird gave him permission, and the small helicopter slid down to the treetops, flying over the multilevel trees, frightening birds and wildlife below. And there was more.

"Jorgy, you don't look so good, partner!" Minimac said, looking over at me as I held on to the seat frame with white knuckles bared. It wasn't the knuckles that caught his attention, it was my green complexion.

I felt a sudden surge in my stomach and knew that, while I liked the idea of the aviator glasses and the painted helmet, I couldn't tolerate the roller-coaster effect.

"I—I think I'm gonna be sick," I said in a voice I didn't recognize. Seconds later I was leaning out the opened door vomiting over the rain forest.

"Hey, no sweat, GI!" he said, taking it all in. "We all go through it. After a week or two you'll get used to it."

"I know that shooting, bombing, or napalming the enemy isn't a war crime, but puking on them from above has to be up there with gassing kids and grandmothers," Minimac said when I turned back. Part of what I'd jettisoned rested on the shoulder of my flight suit.

My stomach was in knots, and even my toes hurt. I couldn't take another flight, let alone a few weeks of them. Like the skeptics who watched the Wright brothers before they made their maiden flight, I, too, was convinced that man wasn't meant to fly.

The Blues were looking better and better.

CHAPTER TEN

"I decided to go with the Blues," I said a little sheepishly. The first sergeant leaned back in his chair and smiled. "Yeah, I heard," he said, smothering a small laugh. "Christ! I can't stand those damn things, either! Too much like being a yo-yo on a two-thousand-foot string in the hands of some silly ass, goofy-looking kid trying out new tricks to make everyone else go 'ooh' and 'aah.'

"They're a special breed though, like the kind of wild-eyed folks you see at state fairs who ride the roller coaster over and over again, hoping that maybe they can get it to tilt just a little more on its tracks when they lean into the corners. They scare the hell outta me sometimes, and riding with them makes me sicker than a three-night drunk, which, I suppose, is why we have other jobs for folks like me to do in the army. And," he said, grinning, "folks like you.

"Schwenke here will take you over and introduce you to Staff Sergeant Burrows, who'll show you around." Then, scowling at the company clerk who was coming around the desk, he added, "He used to be their 60 gunner before he got this job, only he still thinks he's one of them. He can shoot a thousand rounds a minute with the damn 60 accurately enough, but he can't seem to type out more than three words a minute without two corrections and an operating manual."

The round-faced soldier with the scraggly mustache, ignoring the first sergeant's comments, led me out the door. "Back in a minute, Top."

Schwenke's jungle fatigues had faded to a pale green. His restless eyes and fidgets gave him the appearance of someone caught at a social function in the wrong attire and painfully aware of it. I'd seen the look before on other vets, who suddenly found themselves with a safe, comfortable rear-area job and wondering, if perhaps, they should still be out in the jungle. They were feeling a little guilty about leaving their buddies behind.

"Jorgenson, Seattle," I said extending my hand.

"Bob Schwenke, Montana," he replied. "Come on, I'll show you where you can find Burrows."

"Burrows" was SSgt. Roberts Payton Burrows, six two or three and well over two hundred pounds. His quarters were in the senior NCO hootch near the perimeter line, and judging from their Spartan appearance, not to mention the spit-polished jungle boot perched on the regulation-made bunk, he took his position seriously. Schwenke said something about him being in line for the position of platoon sergeant since the outgoing one, a former cook, would soon be leaving the troop.

Professionally friendly, even if I did appear to be too young to be a sergeant in his eyes, Burrows let the brief doubt pass as he took in my 75th Ranger scroll and welcomed me into the platoon.

He was cleaning his rifle, and his bearing became less rigid as he talked about the platoon and something more. "I fought with Patton at the Bulge, you know," he said, inspecting the chamber of the already clean rifle. I thought that that was odd, since the big staff sergeant appeared to be in his early thirties, which would've made him too young for World War II.

"And I was with the Legion," he added.

"French?"

"No. Roman," he said. "Reincarnation. Come on, I'll show you around. So you're a Ranger. Good. Very professional, the LRRPs. That's what the platoon needs, more professionals."

Following Burrows across the troop area was like trailing behind a drill sergeant on a parade field, the gait more of a march than an informal walk.

"We have some highly skilled soldiers in the platoon. Amateurs mostly, you know. Shake 'n' bakes and the like, but still they're not bad for nonprofessionals."

I wanted to tell him I was a shake 'n' bake but let it pass. Instead, just took in the guided tour.

"We have four squads, one medic, a sniper, a number of accomplished machine gunners—Specialists Cortez, Esquibel, Bloor, and Schwenke, whom you've already met. We also have two of the best RTOs in the battalion—Specialists Paul Englebretsen and Jim Braun. Besides firepower, commo's the most important thing in the field. Let's see, who else?" he said, then immediately following up with the answer. "One or two dopes," he said dejectedly.

"Heroin?" I asked, somewhat surprised.

"What?"

"The one's you're talking about, they on drugs?"

Looking at me oddly, Burrows shook his head. "No, dopes as in real fucking stupid. Some real bricks, but even with bricks a skilled craftsman can build a solid foundation. You think I'm crazy, right?"

"Eh . . . I don't know," I said, which seemed like a safe answer.

"More people here do. They have little use or time for professional soldiers these days, and make no mistake about it, I am a professional. The army is more than my career. It's my life and has been for centuries. Jorgenson, that's Danish, isn't it?"

"And Norwegian."

"Good! The Berserkers—the bear-shirt Vikings! Good, capable fighters. No wonder you're a Ranger. Here we are," he said as we headed into the Blue platoon area.

The platoon, he said, was in transition. There was a new platoon leader or "Blue," along with several other new arrivals filling positions that were vacated when the platoon had been ambushed, several of its members wounded, and one was killed.

"The new lieutenant's name is Hugele. A Special Forces type. Seems a little young, but then everyone is these days. We'll also be getting a new platoon sergeant, too," his voice carrying a noticeable edge. "His name is Sergeant First Class Andreu, and he'll be arriving soon.

"We have four squads. Our table of organization chart says we're authorized one 60 machine gun, but we carry three. More firepower, and since we're in a helicopter unit, it's easy to get the ammunition. Not that that's a real problem anyway, since one of our primary jobs is picking up shot-down helicopters, which, by the way, is where we got our extra machine guns.

"You'll more than likely be taking over the 4th Squad—4-4. We rotate the squads on point with each mission. Do you have any problem with that?"

"No. That's fine," I said.

"Some people don't like to walk point."

"I don't mind."

Burrows studied me for a moment and then said, "We'll see."

The Blues' area was made up of three hootches and a CP or command post. The hootches were little more than boomtown shacks—tin-roofed, wooden structures that housed up to ten or so soldiers in sectioned-off rooms. Adjacent to the scout hootches, the latrine, and a small enlisted men's club, the Blues area was just off of the troop's helicopter flight line.

Burrows explained that the mission of the platoon was three-fold. First, it was platoon-size recon, that is, "sticking our noses into Viet Cong or North Vietnamese Army areas in order to draw them out for further contact.

"Secondly, it's to serve as a quick reaction force for division units who suddenly find themselves in need of an additional platoon. And finally," Burrows said, "the Blues are responsible for crew rescue of downed helicopters, which in this area alone could be a full-time occupation."

It was no secret that in the AO (area of operations), over half of the scout helicopters in the troop had been downed at one time or another, *Queer John*, of course, was setting new records in that area.

A "downed helicopter" could be for anything from simple mechanical problems to a fatally destructive crash caused by enemy gunfire. A single bullet or a shoulder-fired rocket could bring them down in a tumbling, fiery ball.

"Ninety-nine percent of them are caused by gunfire, and our mission is to get to the crash sites as soon as we can, to get to any survivors before the NVA do."

"We lose any prisoners to the NVA?"

"No," Burrows said succinctly. "They usually don't take them prisoners. They kill whoever's on board. You'll see."

And I did. The first mission with the Blues was a cross between a LRRP operation and a Sunday stroll—a by-the-numbers recon of an abandoned enemy base camp just outside of Fire Support Base Jamie. That was a platoon familiarization exercise really, with the new lieutenant getting a chance to see how the platoon operated in the bush. Judging from initial appearances, Hugele seemed to know his business.

Unlike the Rangers or grunts, who carried everything they owned in their packs for extended stays in the field, the Blues went in light. We carried weapons and ammunition only because we were concerned with daylight operations. However, unlike the grunts, who might only come in contact with the enemy once a month, or the LRRPs whose primary mission was to watch for but avoid contact with the enemy, our job was to find the enemy, engage him in combat, and then call in the necessary support or forces to beat him.

Apache Troop was self-sufficient. We had our own scout helicopters—the small ones that would ferret out the enemy in the jungle, the pilots going in at treetop level to draw them out. We had our Cobra gunships that would fly well above the area, waiting to take their role in the deadly game of hide-and-seek, which was to swoop down on the area where the scouts took gunfire. With miniguns that fired thousands of rounds a minute, automatic grenade launchers, and deadly rockets, the Cobras would keep the enemy at bay until the Blues worked their way in on the ground to confront them.

The Hueys, or lift ships, were the primary means of transportation for the Blues. They performed jungle insertions by quick landings or hovering over the dense, carpet-thick rain forests as we rappelled in.

Besides these groups, the troop also had its own maintenance section, cooks, supply room, orderly room operations, and TOC or the tactical operations center, which controlled the action.

Each platoon was color coded. The scouts were white, the gunships red. Together they could make up a Pink Team. Finally, the infantry, we Blues, were blue.

Breaking into a new unit takes time, and the Blues were no exception. There were initial suspicions to quell, faces and names to remember, fears to relieve, and all that would take time. But of that, we all seemed to have a lot, if the short-timers' calendars, which were on everything from helmets to hootch walls, were accurate indicators.

Although there were twenty-one or so members in the platoon, the ones I came into contact with were the members of my squad, along with a few others who, for one reason or another, gravitated to the hootch area. Duane Bloor was my 60 gunner; Mark Esquibel, an infantryman who sometimes doubled as a machine gunner; Alan Stephenson and Bill Lugenbeal rounded out the small squad as riflemen. Lungenbeal, Stephenson, and Esquibel were all southern Californians. Bloor was from Hillsboro, Wisconsin. All were vets, and each knew his job in the field, which made my job easy. Well, at least on the first mission. Time and combat testing might prove otherwise, but then I was certain they were wondering the same things about me. After all, they'd been working together. To them I had to be the unknown factor. But I wasn't alone.

The new platoon leader, the new Blue (the call sign for the lieutenant), was a tall, lanky twenty-two-year-old Texan named

Jack Hugele, who, on his first mission-briefing, did something that won him over with the platoon. After the operational order, he let down his authoritarian tone and said: "Now I know how you felt about your old platoon leader, and I know it's tough to break in a new lieutenant on such short notice, so I'll do my best to listen to your advice before I make up my mind. Just because I'm an officer doesn't mean I know everything. That's the platoon sergeant's job," he said looking at the platoon sergeant, who seemed satisfied with the appraisal. "My job is to lead, and with your experience and help, I can do that. I'd like to talk with the squad leaders for a few minutes. Gentlemen, that's it."

Hugele didn't give us a pep talk, he just wanted to talk to us close up to get to know something about us and the rest of the platoon. He seemed intent on listening to discussion of problem areas or potential problem areas, and behind that southern drawl was an analytical mind that was taking in everything that was said and storing it for future reference. The subdued spearhead patch of the Special Forces, as well as his jump wings, told us that he had more than the basic officer candidate training. To what extent and degree we'd soon find out.

Initially there were picnic missions in Tay Ninh, seemingly useless walks through the jungle, searching for the enemy. The next few missions led to the discovery of weapons caches and underground food storage areas containing tons of bagged rice, but there was little or no contact with the North Vietnamese or Viet Cong.

The loud, screaming cry of the siren sent us scrambling like firemen toward the flight line, grabbing our weapons and equipment, while the helicopter crews readied the aircraft. In a matter of minutes the first lift was filled, while the remaining two quickly loaded.

Bloor was readying his machine gun, while Stephenson, taking on the job of the squad's radioman, ran a quick check on the PRC-25. A new spec four, Chuck Manning, joined the squad as did a veteran Blue named Tony Cortez. Cortez was talking to Lugenbeal and laughing. Bill Lugenbeal was a biker from southern California with a bandit mustache and a sweatband tied across his brow, not to keep his hair out of his eyes—years of riding his Harley-Davidson without a helmet had seen to that, and the wind-blown hair was permanently brushed back. A draftee, Lugenbeal was "doing his time," he said, and then he would be free to continue his biker life. For all of his posturing and badass biker routines, he was a competent and efficient soldier.

Manning was new, but with a little training came to handle the job well. Bloor was a vet like Cortez. Bloor always answered the bell, swearing he didn't like the job and hated the Army. But he always somehow made it to the first helicopter before it lifted over the wire. Trying to make up for his newness, Manning raced to be on the lead helicopter as well.

A scout ship had been shot down along the border, and the gunship that accompanied it was providing immediate security for the downed bird. The gunship gunner and pilot couldn't tell if any of the crew was still alive. Burning wreckage was showing out of a jungle hub. The gunship was taking ground fire, small arms mostly, and had enough fuel to remain on station for another ten minutes.

There was another hitch—the second and third helicopters were delayed getting off the ground so we'd be going in alone for a while.

"Roger, Blue," I said over the radio. "We'll set up a perimeter when we get there and wait for your arrival. Four-four, out."

There wasn't much more we could do. When it came to shot-down aircraft, I'd come to learn that seconds were critical and the sooner we arrived on station to help the better the crew's chances for survival.

Minutes out from the crash site, we could see the column of dense, black smoke coming from the rain forest. A grassland field, small enough for one helicopter, stood nearby. It looked as though the pilot had tried to make the small clearing but failed.

"Blue 4-4, be advised that Blue wants us to prep for LZ," the gunship pilot said over the radio.

"Roger, we'll follow you in," I said, feeling a little better that the new lieutenant was looking after us. Blue wanted to provide us with a running start. If anyone was waiting for us in the open landing zone, then they'd have a hell of a surprise when the Cobra gunship rolled in on them with a wall of fire. The downed helicopter was one hundred or so meters off, and if the crew was alive, they would keep their heads down and wait near the aircraft, knowing we'd go directly to the crash site for them. So as the gunship roared into the landing zone, firing up the surrounding jungle, the Huey liftship followed her deadly trail, its own door-gunners firing into the tree line. Before the ship had even touched down, we were standing on the Huey's skids, then leaping off and racing into the tree line. It quickly lifted off. Directly above us, a scout helicopter hovered at the ready.

With a compass direction from the gunship for guidance, we

hurriedly moved through the jungle. There were no man-made
trails in the immediate vicinity, and that would be a plus for the
crew. If we'd have trouble moving toward them, then so would
the North Vietnamese Army soldiers. Brushing aside branches
and limbs, I took the point, struggling to find a way into the site.
I could smell the burning wreckage and hear the crackling of the
vegetation that burned with it. At least I though it was the vegetation. I wasn't prepared for what I found, and judging by the
expressions on the faces of the rest of the rescue team, neither
were they.

"Set up a perimeter!" I yelled to Bloor, who nodded and took
over, while I scrambled around the wreckage looking for survivors.

I could smell the heavy, sweet smell of burning flesh before I
caught sight of the first crew member—not that it was easy to
recognize him as a person. Leaning back and locked in death, the
body was literally melting into the wreckage.

What could burn and disintegrate already had; ears, eyes, nose,
lips, and hair were gone along with the flight helmet.

What would not burn slowly charred.

A lazy cloud of slow, billowing, caustic smoke from the burning helicopter, its lifeless cargo, the surrounding vegetation, and
excess JP-4 jet fuel in the exploded tanks hung over the crash site.

Severed pieces of fiberglass and metal were strewn over the
area. The smell of burning flesh had filled my nostrils and lungs.
Choking back the thick, black smoke, I caught sight of a second
burning crew member, although it hardly looked like a human
being. Tangled in the splintered wreckage, a lump of meat sizzled
and burned before us. The only evidence that it was a man was the
outstretched hand reaching out for something that wasn't there to
help—a final desperate lunge at eternity.

"Oh, Christ!" I heard a voice say off to my left, pulling my
attention from the grisly sight to a lifeless body, half in and half
out of the burning helicopter. "It's our people," the voice said,
breaking. "Oh, fuck, it's one of our birds."

We watched in horror and despair. The only recognizable body
was that of the pilot, Tan Yanika. I turned back to the other two
burning bodies, knowing that one had to be Chris Gray. My head
was spinning, and I had to drop to one knee to slow it down. Jack
Daniels and party favors. I studied the forest, trying without success to blow the smell of the burning bodies out of my nose.

In the distance a helicopter touched down and Minimac—Mr.
McIntosh—came running over, desperately trying to see if there

was anything he could do to help and knowing instantly the futility of the attempt. The frustration and anger were evident on his drawn face.

Trying to pull Yanika free, Minimac and the rest of us were overpowered by the heat and the nature of the task. There was nothing to do but secure the perimeter and recover the bodies after the fire was extinguished.

McIntosh was swearing under his breath, clenching and un-clenching his fists. He ran back to his helicopter still determined to do something, anything to help. His eyes were glazed and fixed on a miracle in the distance. I learned later that he and Yanika had been best friends.

"Keep your eyes open," Burrows said to no one in particular.

He meant that we should stay alert toward the surrounding jungle, but the focus of our attention was on the crash site. Later, we sullenly loaded the remains into the olive drab, rubber body-bags, placing them in a small, neat row. Rubber envelopes with dead letters to be forwarded home. Postage due.

The mounted bayonet held the M-16 rifle in place in the hard-packed, orange soil. The helmet rested on the upturned butt of the rifle's stock, while a pair of polished jungle boots stood beside the rifle, forming a quiet monument, an outdoor altar.

The battalion chaplain was reciting a final prayer before the memorial service was officially over. When he'd finished, he looked up at the faces of the soldiers who stood in formation before the memorial; somber faces, cynical faces, some still with adolescent acne. But their eyes made them different, they had the cold, hard stares of people who'd seen too much in too short a time.

The actual funeral service would take place thousands of miles away, "Back in the world," as the saying went—the phrase for anyplace other than the war. This memorial was more for us than it was for the fallen soldiers.

"Take solace in that Thaddeus Yanika, Chris Gray and Barry Kletta—"

"Kaletta. His name was Kaletta," someone yelled from the rear of the formation as heads turned. An officer scowled at the soldier who'd interrupted the service.

"And Barry Kaletta," the chaplain said, carefully pronouncing the name. "To those of you who knew them, they were special people, performing a special mission. Though I didn't know them,

I don't intend to let their memory die without pausing to think of the personal sacrifice they endured—''

"—In a bullshit cause!'' someone else said.

The ceremonies were never easy, and usually very emotional. Though the senior NCOs and officers would yell, "At ease!'' they knew they could do little to quell the feelings that arose.

"The war is more than politics, more than duty. It is a commitment to friendship between you and those who have died. Yours is a personal war with personal tragedies and extraordinary sacrifices for that friendship. I urge you not to let those friendships or memories die in this war. Remember Tad Yanika, Chris Gray, and Barry Kaletta and remember their names and their sacrifice for you, rather than to a cause or political purpose. Speak their names and share your stories about their friendships.

"I—I wish you safety and peace in your lives as well as in the war, and I pray to God to this end.''

The chaplain walked off toward the command post. His was an awkward, uncomfortable gait.

CHAPTER ELEVEN

Ed Beal, with whom I had gone through Ranger training, arrived in Tay Ninh just after the New Year, transferring into the troop after he decided to leave the Rangers. "It was time," he said, explaining how he felt he was pushing it with each new mission. Taking more chances than he needed to.

"The trouble with five-man recon teams eventually comes down to a matter of firepower. I don't know. I guess I just want to see what we can do when we go after these suckers head-on. What can I say? I'm here."

There was more, I was certain, and Beal would get around to it in his own way and time. Not that it mattered anyway because it was good seeing a familiar face and having one I knew I could rely on.

As I led him over to the NCO hootch and briefly filled him in on what I knew of Apache Troop and how they operated, Beal grinned.

"A heavily armed platoon with their own gunship support and scouts," he said in admiration.

"Yep, and these guys are good. Of the three troops, Apache has the highest rating. The pilots are good. Crazy maybe, but good. The Blues go out with more fire support than God. So, you'll enjoy the Blues," I said.

He shook his head, depositing his duffel bag and gear in the hootch. "I don't know. The first sergeant wants to know if I want to give the scouts a try."

"How's your stomach?"

"What do you mean?"

"Never mind. You'll find out," I said with a smirk. "Have they assigned you to a hootch yet?"

"No."

"Then make yourself at home here until they do."

"Thanks," Beal said. "So how do you like the Blues?"

I shrugged. "They're okay. The role's different, and I like the firepower. These guys got more machine guns than Al Capone."

"I hear you're walking point?" His grin turned solemn.

"Not much choice, really. I have five people in my squad counting me. One's a 60 gunner, another the radioman, another carries the M-79, plus one who's too new to let waltz us into an ambush. So, through the process of elimination, that leaves me. Besides, it's a piece of cake after being a LRRP. We go out light, no rucksacks. Nothing but web gear and ammo. It's pretty much a banker's war, nine to five, and thank you but we're closed, you'll have to come back tomorrow."

"What do you mean?"

"I mean, they don't stay out overnight. At least they try to avoid it. The only drawback I can see is that they go out damn near every day looking for trouble."

"Nine to five, huh?"

"Yep. They're a helicopter rifle platoon, and the birds come in to roost by dark," I said.

Beal was weighing the possibilities. It was evident from his concerned expression. "Lots of 60s, huh?"

I nodded. "When they do find Charlie they like to give him the greeting he deserves."

"Well," he said, dismissing it all with a smile, "it doesn't apply to me anyway. I'm going to be a scout. I don't intend to ever walk through the jungle again."

I wanted to tell him I had felt the same way a month earlier, before my stomach convinced me otherwise. He knew about the inherent dangers involved with being a scout and considered it part of the job. It was the danger and the glory that everyone associated with the job that gave it its appeal and attraction, the lure that drew them in, but it was the everyday aspects, including airsickness, that changed the face of the picture. I wondered if his face would be as green as mine.

Three days later I had my answer when a more subdued and muttering Beal joined the rifle platoon. Manning went to another squad, leaving room in 4-4 for the North Carolinian. He could handle the wild rides and sudden slips in altitude, but what he couldn't take was knowing that after they drew the enemy's frantic attention and sudden gunfire, there was little he could do but watch as the doorgunner returned fire.

"I felt like a sitting duck staring down at the hunters! There was nothing for me to do but spot the little bastards and hope the 60 gunner could hit them. There's nothing to hide behind but occasional low clouds, and they don't block bullets. No thank you, at least on the ground I have a rifle, and if need be, I can find a tree to hide behind,'' he said, summing up the experience. Like Cortez, who'd been Ranger trained before coming to the Blues, the platoon was taking on a distinct Ranger flavor, not that it really needed it. The Blues were good without us; we just added to their overall game plan, taking up the slack and slowly becoming Blues ourselves, proud of each role we secured and willing to argue with either side the merits of each.

From the process of elimination in response to a growing challenge, I became the platoon's point man, the first man in the long line of soldiers as we moved carefully through the jungle. Time and experience became my best allies in the position, that and the help of Sgt. Nguyen Hue, our Vietnamese interpreter, who, after a crash course, helped me refine my skills.

At five feet, five inches, and maybe 120 pounds, Nguyen Hue looked comical—the too-thin, always-smiling, South Vietnamese soldier with the uncombed hair, complete with cowlick, dressed in loose-fitting jungle fatigues. He looked like someone's little brother playing soldier. Appearances do deceive; Hue came from that same stubborn race of people which had steadfastly and successfully fought off larger and better equipped armies for well over one thousand years. Hue was already in his fourth year of fighting the war as an infantryman, the last with our platoon, during which he'd earned the respect of most of the Blues, that is, those who worked directly with him. There were others, inexperienced soldiers, who grouped all Vietnamese soldiers into the "gook" category, viewing them all as lazy and cowardly. But then, they were in the minority in the platoon as to the way they felt about the small interpreter. What's more, the critics were usually in the *middle* of the walking formation, never on point where Hue spent a great deal of his time.

Initially, I didn't feel there was much he could teach me since I was a Ranger. Besides, he was Vietnamese, and we'd come over to his country to help his people fight their war. They needed our help, so what could he possibly teach me? After several missions, I found what a patient teacher he could be for those who cared to listen and learn. Whenever we came across a trail in the jungle, his eyes and analytical mind went to work. Doing a quick study, he'd take in everything—the size and shape of the trail, the sounds of the jungle, and the detailed condition of any boot or sandal prints we might find.

"VC and NVA like anyone else, they no ghosts—they leave tracks and signs like everyone else," he'd say taking me into his pathfinding confidence. "You just have to look for signs."

On my third mission on point, Hue kept me from walking by a well-concealed fighting position several feet off of the side of the trail. In another instance, he abruptly pushed me back and down moments before a Viet Cong soldier sprayed the area we'd been standing in with a burst from his AK-47.

For his efforts Hue was paid roughly forty-five dollars a month by his government. Soldiers in the platoon supplemented his meager pay with gifts and minor extravagances such as room fans, Levi's jeans, and an acoustic guitar, on which he played—or tried to—his interpretations of country and western music.

In his late twenties, Hue wanted to be a Vietnamese cowboy, a real-life range rider, tending water buffalo from the back of a John Wayne horse, complete with western saddle and bedroll. His favorite movies were westerns, and whenever the unit received a cowboy movie to show, Hue would be sitting cross-legged up front and as close to the outdoor screen as he could get, squealing with delight whenever the movie's hero and his trusty steed rode off.

After a while Hue gave up his uniform at night for the faded Levi's that someone had brought back for him while on R&R. He was also confused about why we didn't bring any horses with us to Vietnam.

"Too much equipment breakdown all the time—jeeps, helicopters, everything. But horse no breakdown, and cavalry without horse can't catch VC Indians."

I wanted to tell him about General Custer, but decided to let it pass. Hue was our Indian scout and as such couldn't change the direction of the travel but could advise us on the situation. Unlike Custer, who never listened to his Indian scouts, we paid close attention to Hue's suggestions. After his initial mission, Lieutenant Hugele always added Hue's evaluation into his own overall plan. Even though the new Blue had less than a month in the field, he was quickly becoming field smart, an attitude and characteristic that soon quelled any misgivings about the new lieutenant.

January saw more shot-down helicopters and crew rescues. The AO (area of operations) was getting busy. Tet, the Vietnamese New Year, was the traditional time for significant increase in enemy actions, and it was the division's idea to keep a close eye on known infiltration areas. That's where we came in, as it became our assignment to patrol those areas looking for signs of increased activity. Blue was getting weaned on his platoon and jungle responsibilities, while the rest of us seemed to be getting a good feel for one another. Since Sergeant Andreu, the new platoon sergeant, hadn't arrived yet, Burrows, for all practical purposes, took the job. Although another senior NCO officially had the title, it was Burrows who got us to function as a unit. No easy task.

Manning was still having a little trouble reading a map, but he seemed to handle his other responsibilities well enough. The outgoing medic developed a short-timer's attitude since he'd soon be replaced. Medics were only required to do six months in the field, so he was looking forward to leaving the platoon. Burrows, swearing and shaking his head along with the rest of us, promised we'd get rid of him as soon as possible. At times he even suggested that we could make do without one until an adequate replacement could be found. Another NCO proved to be as useless, always yelling at the men in his squad for some trivial reason. He was just practicing the old trick: if you don't know what you're doing, yell at somebody else and make him look bad. The NCO wouldn't listen, at least not to us, since we were "hippies" and "punk-ass sergeants who got their ranks the easy way." Once, on a helicopter recovery mission, when the platoon had to rappel into a crash site, the NCO wouldn't listen as we tried to tell him he was rappelling the wrong way.

"Shut up!" he barked, as he slipped out the door of the hovering helicopter and stood on the skids. "I know what I'm doing."

"Sure you do," Beal said, winking, as the other sergeant leaned back and then pushed off, holding the rappelling ropes in front of him. The sudden realization that what he was doing was wrong instantly showed on his face as he went down the one hundred feet of nylon rope too fast, his leather gloves smoldering as the friction wore holes through them and then burned his hands before he landed hard on his butt on the jungle floor.

"The guy doesn't listen," I said to Beal, as he hooked up correctly.

"A pity," he said smiling, "a real pity. Look at the bright side, He makes the rest of us look good!"

Alan Stephenson, my radioman, was working out well. He had an affinity for the shoulder-carried radio, and he'd found his place in the war and knew it. Bloor, a veteran 60 gunner in the platoon, took on the nickname ''Porky'' for the way he liked to eat his C rations. The affable machine gunner strapped the linked ammunition across his chest, Mexican-bandit style, and in a swinging motion when firing, could cover a wide swath of jungle in a firefight, and the rest of us knew that no one would be coming at us from his direction. He could also troubleshoot the M-60 better than anyone in the platoon, doing a quick fix on jammed rounds or misfires and getting it back on line in instant working order.

One by one we began to know how the others would react, and we also knew that sooner or later we'd get a chance to find out more because we knew we were due. So far things had been relatively quiet, safe, and reasonably comfortable, but how long could that last? How many picnic missions would we get before the party came to a close? After we caught three NVA prisoners on a sweep through a jungle bunker complex and divisions intelligence told us they were part of an enemy division that hadn't been seen in the area before, we knew the tide was changing.

Throughout February more scout observation helicopters were getting shot down in our AO, and though many of the crews were pulled out with only minor injuries, others were less fortunate. The body bags and frustration tally were growing.

By early March, Captain Funk, the troop commander, was getting short. He had a month to do, and his replacement would be in before he left. Rumor had it we'd be getting an officer from another unit. Rumor also had it that someone had tried to frag and kill him.

''I hear the man's a real asshole.'' Lugenbeal said to Burrows, who turned away, frowning.

''I hear a lot of things, too. What can I say? Let's wait and see how he does before we make up our minds.'' Burrows's speech wasn't very convincing and more rumors were going around the troop concerning the new replacement for Captain Paul ''Butch'' Funk. At thirty years of age, the ''old man'' from Montana had earned our respect; his incoming replacement would have a lot to prove if the rumors proved correct.

The new commander was rated as an F-I, a helicopter flight instructor, while Jim Braun, the lieutenant's RTO, said that from what he heard the initials should've meant he was a ''fucking idiot'' instead. But we had nothing substantial to go on other than the rumors, and rumors seldom panned out. So we'd wait and see. We had the present to contend with anyway.

We were overdue for contact and we knew it. The other two

Blue troops in the battalion had their share of action, while we had somehow avoided it. Tensions were fanned by the anticipation as well as the rumors.

The quiet days couldn't last.

Also, by early March, Beal and I had established ourselves as the platoon's point men. We were good and, what's worse, we knew it. That was the edge and, too, that became the lure. These were the reputation days, the "no sweat," action-without-casualties missions where cockiness was right up there with us. We rappelled after downed helicopter crews, uncovered enemy booby traps and punji pits, cleared bunkers and occasional tunnels, and became reasonable trackers under Hue's careful tutoring.

While the job rotated within the platoon, few argued when Ed and I took the lead. After a while it became expected.

"Who's got point today?" Blue would ask during the mission briefing. I'd volunteer to take it, only to have Beal follow my lead.

"They don't know the meaning of the word 'fear,' do they?" Cortez asked after one mission briefing.

"Beal does," Jim Braun replied, "but as for Jorgy, well there's a lot of words he doesn't understand the meaning of—"

"Like common sense," Cortez said, nodding to me.

"Yep, and stupidity—"

"And fuck off," I added.

"Not Anton Fuckoff, the famous Moscow writer?" Cortez asked Braun.

"Wrote *Russian to the Point*, I think," Braun added, "or was that Pissoff?"

"That, too," I said. "Sorry to leave you like this, but I have to get ready for the mission. You bozos done and care to join me?"

"To the point, isn't he?" Cortez said, as the big man fell in, still smiling.

"Usually, but only because he keeps volunteering," Braun said sarcastically. "Of course, if he doesn't then Beal will."

"Funny. I didn't recognize them without their bat capes. Why, they're the Dynamic Duo!"

"Yes, we are," Beal piped in, then listened as our buddies tore into us goodnaturedly.

"Legends, too, for that matter."

"Goes without saying," Cortez agreed, lying; nothing went without saying in the platoon, especially sarcasm.

*   *   *

The explosion and staccato burst of automatic rifle fire sent soldiers scurrying for safety while the camp's warning siren alerted the rest of the base camp of pending danger.

When there were no follow-up explosions or returned gunfire, ducked heads slowly began to raise and wonder if they should perhaps try to make it to better fighting positions before the next assault.

"What in the hell is going on?" Sergeant Burrows asked, his voice quaking from anger and surprise. The explosion had come from one of the troop's bunkers, and as the veteran NCO he was responsible for the day guards who manned it. Winded from the quick sprint, Burrows lay on the sandbagged bunker, waiting for an answer, while his eyes scanned the perimeter and the thick grass field outside of the barbed wire. The Vietnamese morning was quiet. Too quiet.

"We got him!" the new PFC there said as the older soldier's eyes darted over the perimeter searching for the wounded or dead enemy soldier that his quick glance must have missed. The soldier started to rise, but Burrows's thick hand yanked him back down.

"Stay down. There might be more of them out there. Get on the radio and get a helicopter up in the air just in case."

"For a dead rat?" the PFC asked.

"A what?"

"A rat, a damn big one!" he replied, his hands showing the rat's size the way a fisherman might describe his catch. "He was foaming at the mouth and trying to bite us, so I killed him."

"What are you talking about?"

"Me and the new guy here," the soldier said, while the other GI on the bunker nodded vigorously. "We were sitting here watching the perimeter like we were supposed to, when this big rat came outta nowhere and attacked us. Swear to God!"

"Me, too!" echoed the new guy.

Still trying to comprehend what the private, first class, had said, Burrows turned his gaze to the second young soldier who was still nodding.

"He ran right at us, and we tried to beat him with our rifles. I think we stunned him some, and that's when we shot him as he ran over the side," the new guy said.

"So I threw a grenade at him and wasted him!" The PFC beamed.

"We got him!" the second soldier agreed.

Peering over the side of the bunker Burrows could see pieces of what appeared to have been an extremely large rodent. Air bubbles foamed over the rodent's bloodied teeth and jaw.

"Let me get this straight. You threw a grenade at a rat?" the staff sergeant asked quietly.

The PFC nodded.

"After we shot him," the new guy added.

"Gentlemen, let me explain something to you," he said, regaining his composure, voice containing his controlled rage. "If you ever, I say again, if you *ever* do anything like this again, I won't recommend an Article 15 and take away any of your money. I won't even suggest a court-martial for anything as stupid as this either. Instead I'll rip out your weak little spines and rake up the shit for brains that you two have between you. And you know what?—it'll be a small pile! Do you hear me?" he said, looming over the two disillusioned soldiers who stood there meekly. Though they nodded, mumbling their understanding, it wasn't good enough for Burrows.

"I said, *DO YOU HEAR ME?*"

"Yes, sergeant!" they yelled, finally comprehending Burrows's message.

Turning to head back to the TOC, Burrows knew he'd have to try to explain it to the first sergeant and the troop commander, who in turn, would have to explain the incident to the base camp TOC and the base camp's commanding general, who'd want to know who was attacking his camp.

"War is hell," Burrows thought, trying to dream up a better excuse than the one he had, "and sometimes it's a real pain in the ass!"

CHAPTER TWELVE

"At 0900 hours we'll be inserted at the landing zone at these coordinates," Blue said, writing the numbers on the wall map with a black grease pencil. "Division wants us to check this area out and see what we come up with."

"That's the Dog's Head, isn't it? I thought the 25th had that region?" asked Sergeant May.

"It was," Blue replied. "It's ours now. The 25th said there hasn't been any activity there in months and that the mission should be a piece of cake. Gentlemen, cakes can sometimes be half-baked, so we'll take every precaution simply because of its location and proximity to the border."

On the map, the area did resemble the profile of a dog's head. It was adjacent to Cambodia, less than a mile from the border, and surrounded with thick vegetation. If the enemy were there, they might be hard to root out since cover and concealment were on their side. Our air support wouldn't be much help, and if there was fighting, the situation would be touch and go.

"I want everyone to carry extra ammunition for the 60s and take it slow and easy today. We'll be in no hurry, and I don't want you to overlook anything."

"Any ground support?" Burrows asked, studying the map.

The lieutenant nodded. "Grunts from Carolyn will serve as our QRF if we need one," he said.

"Be on the flight line by 0845 for a weapons check. If nobody has any questions, then that's it," Blue added, taking a look at the somber faces in front of him. "Sergeant Andreu," he said, turning to the platoon sergeant, "they're all yours." The Puerto Rican nodded.

After the lieutenant had left, the veteran soldier looked around the platoon's CP, surveying our faces, looking for any questions on our faces that our mouths wouldn't ask.

"It may be a piece of cake, but cakes are funny business, and you'll never know who'll be doing the cutting, so we won't take any unnecessary chances. Beside the extra M-60 rounds, I want the squad leaders to carry extra grenades. Sergeant May, Doc Devalle, the new medic, will be in your squad. Sergeant Jorgenson, you'll take the point."

I nodded, knowing that whatever happened it wouldn't be so bad since Beal and Hue were up there with me. Satisfied, Sergeant Andreu left us to get ready, while the new medic, a nineteen-year-old New Guy from New Jersey, attached himself to May's squad. Having arrived a short time earlier, Doc Devalle was bearing his newness fairly well.

Since he was the latest replacement from the division's replacement station in Bien Hoa, Doc was also the platoon's latest source of entertainment. He hated the term FNG, telling us in a nonthreatening way not to call him that. His thick New Jersey accent made the plea comical, and though we were happy to have him, we still harassed him. Liking him had little to do with the fact he was new. In Vietnam there was no greater sin or more laughable condition.

We'd yet to find out if he was a better medic than the last one, but he even reminded us to take our salt pills on the mission. He also reminded Cortez and a few of us who were sitting on our web gear waiting to go out on a mission one day to change our socks and underwear on a regular basis so we wouldn't develop jungle or crotch rot.

"Doc, you mean well. However, we don't wear any," Cortez said.

"What? You mean you don't wear socks or underwear?"

Cortez and the rest of us shook our heads.

"And you won't either, if you know what's good for you. The jungle will turn them into sandpaper on your ass and feet, and take our word for it, you don't need that kind of aggravation."

"But your old medic wore them . . ."

"We know, we never told him," Cortez replied.

"But he was your medic!"

"Doc, we didn't care for him. We were hoping his balls would fall off and they'd have to transfer him to the WAC."

"So why did you tell me?"

"You're still new, and you have potential. Don't blow it," Cortez said. He leaned back against his helmet and closed his eyes.

So Devalle adopted our ways, and we quit threatening him whenever he caught us throwing away the large, orange antimalaria horse pills and chewed us out. Doc Devalle meant well, and he seemed to know his business. That was good enough.

By 0815 most of the platoon was on the flight line going over their equipment and weapons, making certain that everything was in working order. By 0850, after the weapons check from Sergeant Andreu, under the watchful eye of Blue, we were ready to go. When the Pink Team gunship and observation helicopters flew out ahead of us, we broke into our flight formation groups to meet the lift ships that were lumbering out to greet us.

With a thumbs-up from Blue, we boarded the Hueys. Moments later we were airborne, with the Tay Ninh base camp disappearing behind us. As was the tradition, many of us replaced our steel helmets with the bush cap or a simple sweatband tied around our foreheads to keep the sweat from our eyes.

Division policy required us to wear the helmets and the heavy vestlike flak jackets, but the steel pots were heavy, useless to a direct hit, and, what's more, frequently fell over a soldier's eyes when he moved. It impeded eyesight and hearing. So, even though we were required to have them during the weapons and equipment inspection just before a mission, they would very often be left behind on the helicopters when we landed or fell out of the open helicopter doors and, oh darn, be lost forever, while the smiling GI would pull out the bush hat or sweat rag.

The flak jackets were sometimes abandoned on the helicopters as well. Soldiers used them as seats, finding them preferable to the hard metal flooring of the lift ship helicopters. In this position, the jackets also served as protection against incoming small-arms fire to the underside of the helicopter and, of course, the soldiers' balls.

The platoon's policy toward steel pots and flak jackets left their use to individual choice, since our primary and secondary missions called for speed and ease of movement, which required clear vision and hearing.

Around his head Beal wore a green arm sling twisted into a sweatband. Esquibel wore his helmet, and Cortez did the same. Lugenbeal opted to wear nothing on his head. Bloor rode on the first bird with us and was dressed the "gypsy role," as Burrows called it—cutaway sleeves on his uniform, a helmet with bug spray in the band, crossed, belted ammunition for his machine gun, and a leather glove on his left hand. The glove was for the machine-gun barrel that would glow an odd shade of orange after too much firing—at that point it had to be replaced. Like Beal, I went without a helmet or sweatband. After twenty or so missions walking point, I didn't want to wear anything that would inhibit my senses. Hue had taught me that much.

"You go slow. You listen and watch!" he'd said one day, the veteran soldier lecturing the foreign rookie. "No wear helmet because if you don't see or hear VC, then helmet won't stop ambush."

So I listened on point, walking carefully and cautiously slow, looking for signs out of the ordinary, tracking those who'd sometimes track us.

It was a long flight out. Even so, no one talked. It was the quiet time for reflection, for nervous fidgeting, and for the checking and rechecking of weapons and equipment. A few minutes out, we could hear the gunships opening up on the landing zone. The AO was out of reach of the artillery of the closest fire support base, so the gunships were prepping the tree line. If anyone was there waiting for us, then we'd at least have a few precious moments to leap off of the aircraft and return fire. On the short final approach, the lift ship doorgunners took over firing as we stood on the skids, rifles and weapons poised toward the tree line, waiting to touch down.

Seconds later we were there, with no return fire and nothing to fight but a small fire ignited from one of the gunship's tracer rounds. Just on the edge of the rain forest, Blue motioned to move out.

"Move to your west on a 265-degree bearing," he whispered over the radio while Stephenson relayed the message.

"Roger, Blue. Out," I answered as Beal nodded for confirmation. Pointing the direction, I nodded to Hue. The South Vietnamese soldier moved out. Over the previous month, Beal and I developed a split-point method of patrolling, the first person moving ten yards ahead while the second would leapfrog, moving fifteen, and so on. It became a practical method of moving through enemy territory, enabling us to cover each other while we moved. We'd use the same method today, with Hue and the rest of the platoon moving right behind us.

Ten yards into the tree line, we found a trail, and judging from the spoor, the trail was well used. Flakes of dropped balled rice, still moist and sticky—indicating it had been prepared only minutes before—littered portions of the trail. On closer inspection of the trees that lined the trail, we found placards and notes were tacked in place.

"Gung ho type talk," Hue said, reading the notes. "Victory, brotherhood, same old shit," he added kneeling.

"What do you think?" I asked, already knowing the answer.

"They here a few minutes ago. Hear helicopter, maybe run for the border. Maybe not."

I passed along the information to Jim Braun, Blue's RTO, who relayed the information.

"Blue wants you to parallel the trail and see what you can find," Braun said.

Farther along the trail, we came to the edge of the immense bunker complex and, unlike the others we'd found in the region that had been well concealed, this one was blatant. While the double canopied vegetation provided a growing ceiling overhead, beneath the green and brown roof lay hundreds of fighting positions, small "spider holes"—one-man positions—and underground, fortified living quarters. The jungle was very quiet, too quiet for Hue's liking. As the observation helicopter overhead raced across the treetrops, rotor blades chopping in the wind, our movement was drowned out by the mechanical noise.

For as far as we could see in the rain forest, bunkers and fighting positions were visible. While Hue carefully slipped into the first we came upon, I covered the others in the immediate area. Finding nothing, we moved into the next one, this time with me easing myself into the small dirt opening, peering around earthen corners for the enemy we knew was there. Nothing again! Maybe they had gone back across the border when they heard the gunships. It was a logical assumption; they knew they were safe in Cambodia. Then again, maybe they decided to sit it out, knowing the Americans would eventually fly away.

The bunker complex looked like a training facility. Outlines of fire support bases had been carved into the ground. Small wooden models showing the layout of our bases along with pointers and arrows showing the best method of attack. Hanging from the trees were wooden helicopters—gunships, the Huey lift ships, and the small observation helicopters in miniature, for the North Vietnamese soldiers to study. Farther along, aboveground storage huts were evident, as were kitchens and meeting areas. In less than an hour, we'd managed to work our way into the center of the large jungle base without locating the enemy.

"Hold it up!" Stephenson whispered, listening on the handset of the radio as Blue directed our action. Then, motioning us back, the RTO passed along the plan. "The gunship's breaking station. Has to refuel, so Blue wants us to wait until it returns."

It seemed like a reasonable idea. Without the gunship for support, we'd be in a world of trouble should we come across the inhabitants of the bunker complex.

As the chopping of the gunship and the buzzing of the smaller Loach observation helicopter diminished, Hue decided to give one more fighting position a try.

"Cover me," he said, as I walked over to a small bunker and put one foot up on the small mount to rest. My rifle lay across my thigh while I watched him carefully work his way toward the small opening in the ground. He was always careful even though the last fifteen or so bunkers and fighting positions we'd cleared were empty, and maybe that's how he'd lasted four years in combat. I started to wipe the sweat from my brow, when Hue began firing into the hole, his quick rifle burst shattering the morning silence while a North Vietnamese soldier replied with his AK-47.

Contact! Only it wasn't anything to be happy about. In that forever moment of sudden understanding, the forest floor began to come alive with enemy soldiers scrambling to get out of their bunkers at the urging of an NVA officer. Thinking that ours was just another helicopter reconnaissance, they hadn't heard us move into the bunker complex. Suddenly aware something was drastically wrong, the NVA now struggled to correct his tactical mistake.

All around me, action was unfolding, the entire picture blocked out by my immediate concerns. Hue had shot the soldier in the fighting position, but the man was still firing, and as Hue came racing back to my position, the cone of a B-40 shoulder-fired rocket nosed out of the bunker I was standing on. Blocked from view by the dirt mound, the soldier carrying it couldn't see me. He could, however, see Hue as he hurriedly tried to get the weapon out of the bunker. The enemy soldier couldn't fire it until he cleared the bunker, otherwise the backblast from the rocket would surely kill him. Seeing the rocket, Hue stopped and tried to load another magazine into his rifle. He was too late, and he knew it. As the North Vietnamese soldier cleared the bunker, I kicked him in the head, grabbing the RPG-7 as he fell and flinging it over my shoulder. The soldier came back with a knife, slashing wildly. Falling back I fired a short burst across his chest. I saw Beal go down several feet behind me, holding the left side of his head, letting out a sickening piercing scream as he fell, blood spilling over his face while a hand fought to hold back the flow. Manning screamed as well when a bullet to his right thigh sent him flying back against a tree.

Porky, catching four enemy soldiers assaulting us from the left, dropped them with a spray from his machine gun, catching them chest high. They were flung back and down under the impact of the machine-gun rounds. Behind them the other advancing NVA soldiers quickly withdrew.

Trying to shore up an instant perimeter, I reached over and pulled Beal back, only to have him struggle to free himself. The left side of his head and shoulders were caked with blood and dirt, but Beal was clear-eyed and angry.

"Just—just a graze," he said, firing his rifle at a North Vietnamese soldier who'd tried to assault us from a nearby position. The rifle fire caught the man across the ridge of his eyebrows, throwing his green pith helmet back along with what was left of his head. Cortez joined us, and we set up a three-pronged defense. If they were to overrun us, they'd have to get by our position, and since fighting positions usually were designed against opponents who attacked from the outside, the North Vietnamese would have an uphill battle; we'd penetrated their perimeter. Their firing ports faced *out*, and the entry positions were to our front. To attack us successfully, they'd have to climb out of the bunkers, get their bearings, and then assault. We were in the driver's seat in a race for survival.

We could hear the heavy firing the rest of the platoon was under and hoped Blue could keep the platoon tight and together. The radio was alive with traffic as Blue relayed the platoon's situation back to Six, the company commander in Tay Ninh. Funk, a veteran commander, sent out the gunships he suspected we needed and had the quick-reaction force from the nearest fire support base ready to go, if need be.

Lugenbeal scurried around to help Porky get to better cover, as I scrambled around to find a head bandage. As I started to move, the barrel of an AK-47 stuck itself out of the bunker's second opening and, knowing that I'd already killed the soldier with the rocket, I wondered how many more were down there. Not wanting to stick my head over to see, I reached over, grabbing the front wooden grip of the assault rifle and jerked it out of the soldier's hands. With no real plan other than survival, I popped the pin on a grenade, yelled "Fire in the hole!" for the other Blues, and released the spoon to count to a quick three before rolling it into the opening. Covering my head and ears, I turned away. Seconds later the earthen structure rocked violently as secondary explosions from the extra rockets in the bunker turned it into a volcano, first throwing dirt and debris skyward and then falling into itself.

Suddenly, I found myself in a depression, my ears bleeding, and trying hard to keep from passing out.

I should've thought about the rockets, but I had been too scared to think. There was only time to act and react, and any actions or reactions were, at best, incomplete. There wasn't time to get up and check the body of the person you shot or dig out the bunker to insure that that was all of it. The dam was cracking, and holes had to be plugged where the force and flow was the heaviest.

Beal was back at my side, checking to see how I was doing. He and his words were coming in and out of focus. My head was pounding, and I wanted to throw my rifle down and quit.

"You okay?" he asked.

"Yeah," I lied. Okay or not, I wasn't about to give in to the pain; as long as I ran on its edge, I was still in control. I also knew that when and if I did give in to the pain, I might not wake up. I had a concussion at least.

The firing turned away from our position, and we could see and hear the battle moving to our rear, where the rest of the platoon lay scattered along the complex trail. Porky fired into a second group of North Vietnamese who'd tried to work their way toward the platoon behind us. They couldn't see what he was doing because of the vegetation, but they could hear the fire and the cries from the soldiers as they fell. Bloor was on the money.

Troop gunships screamed on station in strafing runs as Blue directed their fire. After several passes, the North Vietnamese gave up trying to overrun us. Unable to link up, there were small pools of soldiers confined to separate holes in the ground.

The battle was growing quiet, waiting for its second wind. Checking our situation and equipment, we had time now to survey the damage.

Beal, Manning, and I were wounded. Stephenson, Hue, and Cortez were okay but Bloor was taking on a pale, gray color. The heat from the constant firing combined with the humidity and the temperature were taking their toll on him. Around us we had eight, maybe nine dead North Vietnamese soldiers. Others were dead in their fighting positions.

Blue was on the radio calling for a kickout, a resupply of ammunition kicked out of a helicopter's door, hopefully near our location. We were getting low on M-60 rounds for the machine gun, and even the spare one hundred rounds that each of us carried for Porky would quickly be used up in the next assault we knew had to come. We couldn't get out of the bunker complex until the North Vietnamese were routed; if we tried, they'd cut us to pieces from the defensive positions. We'd have to get them to retreat, but so far it seemed as though they were dug in to stay.

A short burst from an AK-47 sent us down. We returned fire, driving the soldier back into his fighting position. Less than ten yards away, the incoming automatic-rifle rounds had a slamming impact against the dirt and wood barriers. We were relatively safe so long as the soldier remained in the hole.

"Cover me, Ed," I said to Beal, pulling a concussion grenade from the canteen pouch where I'd stored four. With one down, I had three left—two after this. I crawled toward the hole while Beal and Cortez provided the gunfire to support me. They'd keep his head down for a while longer, and that's what I was counting on. Pulling the pin on the grenade, I let out my breath, propped myself up and tossed it in a high arc toward the hole. I wanted to be certain it went in, so I used an easy toss. I didn't want to miss with a hard, overhand throw and suddenly find myself without cover and still in the immediate blast area.

I wasn't John Wayne, and I knew I had pushed my luck by releasing the spoon on the last grenade and counting to three before throwing it. I'd been too frightened by the thought of the soldier picking it up and throwing it back at me. I didn't have that kind of guts anymore, and counted on this soldier's being so startled by the grenade tumbling at his feet that he wouldn't have time to think about what he'd do.

The hunch paid off. When it finally blew, the force went sky-ward. Crawling over to the edge of the fighting position, I caught a glimpse of the dead soldier, half-covered with dirt from the collapsing position. A dark pool of red oozed over his ruptured intestines. I started to gag, caught myself, and scrambled back to the others.

"You get him?" Hue asked.

"Yeah," I said, suddenly exhausted. My stomach was dry heaving from the sight of the dead soldier in the fighting position, and I had to take several deep breaths to quell it.

"You saved me," Hue said, wearing a stern face. "I no forget."

I wasn't sure what he was talking about, and it must have showed.

"He almost fire RPG," Hue said, looking at the weapon laying on the ground nearby where I'd tossed it. "No forget," he said, retrieving it and then patting me on the back, as he went to see how the others were doing.

"Think they'll try again?" I said to Beal, who was busy pulling weapons out of a nearby bunker.

He nodded. "They have to. What other choice is there? Come on, Jorgy. Give me a hand with the bodies."

Climbing into the small, two-man position, we pulled out the first dead NVA soldier, searching through his pockets and coming up with a map and documents. The second body produced only personal effects; a thin wallet with North Vietnamese currency, a few stamps, and a picture of a young woman holding a smiling baby. You don't feel proud at moments like that. You feel relieved that it wasn't you. Staring at the faces in the picture, I caught a glimpse of the personal tragedy of war, of the wife who'd lost a husband and the small child who'd never know her father. I tried hard to hate the dead soldiers but couldn't. I wanted to so I could feel better about taking their lives. They were the enemy, my enemy, and I wouldn't cry over their deaths. But I wouldn't celebrate their deaths, either.

I felt good that I'd helped Hue and that he thought I'd done something to save his life. I wanted to feel good about being in Vietnam and about being so anxious to get there. Any sense of enthusiasm for the war, I had lost with my last LRRP mission. By my actions in the Dog's Head, I knew I'd done something to redeem myself for the Silver Star. But any sense of satisfaction disappeared when the North Vietnamese tried their next push, this time from up the trail, where a group had massed and now came running down the small jungle path, firing and yelling.

Kneeling to a steady aiming position, Porky opened up, as did Beal and I. One soldier had managed to reach a few feet from our position before we finally nailed him. We looked at each other in astonishment. Why didn't he fire? He could have fired and maybe caught us both. But why didn't he? It was then I noticed the rag sticking out of the barrel of the assault rifle and the bayonet locked out to strike.

"He wanted to stab us," I said, staring at the dead soldier. "He wanted to bayonet us."

In the distance we could hear the QRF coming in from the landing zone. Cortez crawled up to tell us that the QRF would be linking up with us and that they were maybe ten minutes out. They hadn't taken any fire coming in, and their leader, a first lieutenant, opted to have the infantry platoon move through the jungle toward our location rather than following our original route. That was a wise decision since the North Vietnamese would have it covered.

Minutes later we heard the grunts breaking through the bush, moving toward our position. The jungle was quiet again, with the exception of the noise that the grunts were making. A platoon of twenty to thirty soldiers makes a lot of noise when you're straining to hear the slightest sound of enemy movement; movement that could spell your life or death. To us the grunts sounded as though they were breaking every damn twig and limb they could find in the rain forest.

"Christ! They're noisy!" Beal said, staring in the direction the grunts were coming from.

I nodded, knowing it was one of the flaws in the way our army was fighting the war. Too much equipment and too many men made the grunt companies susceptible to ambush and attacks. Their heavy packs made the going slow and awkward, and too many men meant too much noise.

When they were less than a hundred meters out, we confirmed our position with a smoke grenade signal. Moments later the grunt's point man lumbered through the underbrush, eyes and rifle going to and from the dead bodies of the NVA in front of our positions. His lips mouthed a quiet obscenity.

The linkup would provide our platoon with additional manpower. After a brief meeting between the two junior officers in charge, it was decided that we'd head out to the landing zone in another direction, both officers realizing that the enemy would first monitor our movement and then set up to react to it. The war often became a deadly game of chess, where each move anticipated another move, opening up the opponent for attack.

Still on point, we began to head out. The North Vietnamese struck again. It was their final chance to trap us in the jungle labyrinth. In a flanking attack they moved at us in groups, only to have their attack fall short of their desperate expectations. Our additional twenty to thirty men gave us the firepower we needed to fend them off. A rough count of enemy bodies and captured weapons left the number at thirty-nine. Though probably inaccurate, we knew the count was reasonably close. Blood trails and collapsed bunkers suggested a higher count, but to us that really didn't matter. Body-count figures were for analysts; surviving was our primary concern.

My head was spinning again, pounding as it turned, and I knew I couldn't go on for much longer. When would the damn NVA give up anyway? When would they finally call it quits, knowing that we'd outmaneuvered them this time?

"Jorgy?" Beal said looking at me with a troubled expression.

Kregg Jorgenson,
March, 1970.

A LRRP team practicing immediate action drills.
Fall, 1969.

H Company trainee tent—home for Rangers-in-training. Fall, 1969.

The author at H company. Fall, 1969.

Ranger Julius Zaporozec, killed in action. November 17, 1969.

Rangers Leon McLaughlin and Johnny Rodriguez. Fall, 1969.

The Blues' M-60 gunner Duane Bloor on patrol.
Spring, 1970.

Blues recovering downed helicopter and crew. Ed Beal
in background, Jim Braun with radio. Spring, 1970.

Ed Beal and Lt. Jack Hugele inspecting damage from downed helicopter. Spring, 1970.

Kregg Jorgenson and machine gunner Mark Esquibel at the site of another downed helicopter. Spring, 1970.

Blues on patrol in Tay Ninh Province, the Dog's
Head. Spring, 1970.

Blues Jack Miller and Dennis Henderson emerging
from a Viet Cong tunnel. Spring, 1970.

Kregg Jorgenson
during close contact
with an NVA company
northwest of Tay Ninh.
March, 1970. *UPI*

Blues guiding Hueys in to landing zone during pickup northwest of
Tay Ninh. April, 1970. *Art Dockter*

Blues being exfilled by helicopter after recon along
Cambodian border northwest of Tay Ninh.
April, 1970. *Art Dockter*

Blues with equipment captured from one of the largest known enemy
bunker complexes. Cambodia, June, 1970. *Art Dockter*

I stared at him, not understanding what he was saying. What in the hell was happening?

"Sit down," he said, helping me. Seconds later Doc Devalle was looking at me with the same troubled expression that Beal had.

My shirt was covered with blood and mixed with dirt and sweat. I was holding two AK-47s that I'd pulled from a bunker, and if I didn't look like something the cat dragged in, then I was surely a candidate for something he had abandoned.

"I think you have a concussion," Doc said, studying my eyes and ears.

"I feel like hell," I said.

Porky was sitting next to me, his once florid, chipmunk face now pale and clammy.

". . . think they should both be medevacced," I heard Doc Devalle saying into the radio and then nodding at the response he received from Blue.

"Come on, Sarge," he said, helping me to my feet. "Let's get out of here."

In the landing zone I could see the rest of the grunt company spread out, securing it for the medevac helicopter that could be heard coming in over the rain forest.

The platoon had suffered four wounded—Ed Beal with a head wound, Porky with heat exhaustion, Manning with a leg wound, and me with a concussion. Of the five people in the first squad, four of us had been wounded in the initial attack, but we managed to hold on.

"How you feeling?" Blue asked, looking over the squad.

"A bitch of a headache," I said, "and a ringing that won't go away."

"I want you, Manning, and the others to take the medevac out," he said, while Beal protested.

"Boss, Jorgy and the others need it, but this is just a graze," he said pointing to the ugly purple wound that ran across the left side of his head.

Blue started to protest, when Braun strolled over, saying the helicopter only had room for three, and if there were more wounded, then they'd send out another dustoff. Beal again said he was fine, and Blue let it go at that.

"You guys did a damn fine job," he said quietly. "I don't know what happened up on point. From the looks of it, you ran into it, but that gave the rest of us time to react. Sergeant Beal, get your people on the medevac helicopter and then prepare for extraction.'' The lieutenant headed back to the QRF Platoon leader.

When he was out of earshot, Sergeant Andreu said, ''And if it wasn't for him keeping a level head and coordinating those gunships, then we might've not done so well. The guy's got his shit together, and that's good for us.''

''Think he'll get a medal?'' someone asked.

''At least, and I have a sneaking suspicion you folks in the point squad are going to be up there with him!'' the Puerto Rican platoon sergeant said, as the medevac helicopter touched down, and he helped me to the aircraft.

A medic on the helicopter got busy with Manning after he gave Porky and me a preliminary once-over. The new guy had taken it well. The bullet had ripped across the front right thigh, throwing the blue-white muscle out of the skin and giving it the appearance of a bloodied growth on the leg. When we landed in Tay Ninh at the field hospital, we were greeted with open-mouth stares from the people on or near the helipad. What are they looking at? I wondered, and then turned to the others and saw it. We were the embodiment of war, the walking wounded with blank and bloodied expressions, covered with caked blood and dirt, smelling of sweat and fear and looking quite unlike the heroic victors. We made them feel uneasy, and it was evident from their expressions. We'd brought the war home to them, and perhaps that was closer than they wanted it to be.

''I'll take those,'' a medic said, reaching for the Russian assault rifles I had slung over my shoulder as well as my web gear.

''Go ahead, take one, if you like,'' I said, while the medic's eyes went wide with excitement.

''You mean it?''

I nodded. ''Sure, why not?''

Manning was on one table while Porky occupied another. After a going-over, the doctor gave his diagnosis. ''You have a concussion,'' he said, confirming Devalle's suspicions. ''It's nothing critical, but you're going to have a headache for a while. I want you to take it easy. Come back and see me next week,'' he added, writing out a note for me to give the first sergeant.

''What about them?'' I said looking at the others. ''I'm their squad leader.''

The doctor shrugged. ''One's suffering from heat exhaustion. We'll keep him here for a while. The other one will probably be medevacced to Long Binh. It's not serious, but they can keep an eye on the wound a little better than we can. Sometimes the infection that's inevitable is worse than the wound. Take it easy, Sergeant. Looks like you earned that much."

Still dizzy I walked over to Manning, who managed a smile. His jungle fatigue trousers were ripped at the thigh, and a clean white bandage gleamed over the soiled uniform.

"They'll keep you for a while. Enjoy the time off," I said as the shake 'n' bake nodded. "By the way, did I ever tell you I'm a shake 'n' bake, too?" At that, Manning smiled.

Porky was lying on a gurney, the line from an IV bottle taped behind his hand. The needle fed the salt-and-water solution into his veins.

"How you doing?" I asked the machine gunner, who was beginning to get back some color.

"Tired," he said.

More than likely he'd saved the point squads' lives when he brought down the four NVA. "Good shooting this morning."

"It seemed like the thing to do," Bloor said, dismissing the accomplishment.

"Sergeant Jorgenson?" a voice called from the doorway. It was Schwenke, the company clerk and part-time machine gunner.

"Yes?"

"The first sergeant sent me to see how you're doing," he said surveying the field hospital emergency room. Porky gave him a thumbs-up, Manning grinned. It was a certain bet that Schwenke had been out the orderly room door and heading toward the field hospital even before the first sergeant had made the suggestion.

"I thought you could use a ride back to the company area," he said, picking up some gear and equipment. "Okay, Doc?" he asked as the doctor nodded his approval.

"He can go with you. The others will have to stay for a little longer. He also has a mild concussion. Bed rest for at least two days, and bring him back then for a follow-up."

Schwenke nodded. "Come on, Sarge. The old man's got a barbecue going for the platoon. Steaks and cold beer."

"Is the platoon back yet?"

Schwenke shook his head. "Not yet. They're still a few minutes out, so the old man wanted to have something special for you guys when you came in."

As the jeep pulled into the troop area, the lift ships had just touched down. The troop commander, Captain Funk, was there to greet them, pointing them in the direction of the barbecue that the mess hall had set up in the compound area. Two fifty-five-gallon barrels had been cut in half and formed the kettle part of the barbecue, while steel mesh provided the grille. Blue was shaking hands and smiling, while the cooks were passing out cold drinks and paper plates.

Catching sight of me getting out of the jeep, Blue veered away from the barbecue and walked over. "You okay?" he asked.

I nodded. "Headache."

"Concussion," Schwenke corrected. "Manning, the new guy, and Specialist Bloor are doing fine, too."

"Good." the lieutenant sighed.

Moments later we were joined by Captain Funk. "Lieutenant, I'm happy the way things worked out. We'll have a debriefing later. You and your people did an outstanding job. Now, get your weapons and equipment stored and then get your platoon over there and get them their steaks. That's an order, Lieutenant!"

"You heard the man, Sergeant," Blue said, patting me on the back, as Beal joined us. His head carried a caplike bandage covering the grazing head wound.

"I'm proud of you guys," the lieutenant said to Beal and me.

"You're not so bad yourself, Blue—that is, for an officer," Beal added, smiling. Hugele returned the smile.

After storing my equipment, I decided to skip the party. My head was aching, and my ears and forehead felt like a well-worn tire with too much pressure. Lying on my cot, I began to tremble. The hero hiding away. What would they think of me now?

In my quest for absolution with the false-front, John Wayne penance I'd created for myself, I was now paying for my own human misgivings. Lying in the dark I was trembling because I was afraid, and while I could, maybe, fool the others, I couldn't fool myself. I kept telling myself I was in control, even as the war spiraled down around me.

It had worked better this time. Restless, I couldn't sleep. In control, like a deckhand on the bridge of the *Titanic*.

There was a rap at the door of my hootch area.

"Sergeant Jorgenson, you in there?" It was the platoon sergeant, Andreu.

"Yeah, just a minute," I said, unlatching the door and staring at the weathered face of the platoon sergeant who was standing in the darkened hallway.

"What's up, Sarge?"

"Can I come in?" he said a little sheepishly. His head was bowed, and I could see that whatever it was, he was having trouble with it.

"This probably isn't the time," he said, fidgeting. "I don't know how to put this."

"Try me."

"I just left the first sergeant and the company commander, and they've nominated five of us in the platoon for Silver Stars for what happened today, you included."

"So?"

"So, there are only four allocations. The Old Man has nominated Blue and me, and we put you, Beal, and Bloor in for them. I'm embarrassed to be here like this but . . ."

"But they figure since I already have one, would I bow out?"

Andreu nodded. "They want to know if you'll accept a Bronze Star instead? Now, you don't have to. You just say the word and you can have mine. I don't feel right asking you."

I shook my head. "That's fine. The Bronze Star's more than enough."

I'd heard from Burrows that during the fighting Andreu ran from squad to squad, shoring up any holes in the thin perimeter, helping to keep the NVA from overrunning us. The Old Man, I knew, would make sure that Blue and Andreu received their awards, and rightfully so, while Bloor, Beal, and I would be in a lottery for the two remaining slots. Porky deserved one, and Ed did, too, for that matter. I couldn't take them out of the running either.

"The write-up would still be the same," Andreu added, trying to diminish the sting he apparently thought he'd caused me.

Pleased for the others, I said, "That's great."

"You sure?" His expression was genuine concern.

"It really is. I'm just happy things worked out the way they did. I mean it." Andreu was a professional soldier who overlooked many of our military shortcomings—such as the length of our hair and our casual lack of military courtesy and dress habits—so long as we did our jobs and did what was expected of us. He was also a man who operated by an old-world sense of honor and ethics, and though it must have seemed comical to some, I found his way to my liking. We were all chasing windmills, and our impossible dreams seemed easier to handle with people like the platoon sergeant, Blue, Captain Funk, and the others.

"I'm proud to have you in the platoon," he said, holding out his hand.

"Thanks," I said, shaking it. I was proud to be there.

At the presentation of the awards and decorations several days later, Beal, Porky, and the others viewed my Bronze Star as some sort of consolation prize. They didn't understand that it was enough, that the action meant everything.

I had a friend back in Seattle who was a fireman, and he used to say that he loved and hated his job. That initially he was afraid the alarm would sound, that the bell would go off, and he'd have to respond. Then, after a while, he was afraid that it wouldn't go off. He said there was a great sense of satisfaction and frustration with each call—satisfaction, when they could help those who desperately needed it. Frustration, when all they could do was stand by and watch as someone died.

He used to drink a lot, saying from time to time that it was getting to him and he wasn't sure how much more he could take.

"Maybe you ought to change professions? Get out of it and try something else?" I said. The look he gave me could've frozen water. He couldn't, even though he knew the work would eventually take its toll.

"I have to do it, don't you see?"

I said I did, but didn't then. Now it was beginning to come into focus. There were all kinds of fires the world over. Nam was no exception. Maybe we were all firemen in one way or another. Always waiting, and afraid of the next call, but still there to man the pumps.

It wasn't a time to be proud to be in the service, and yet all around me I saw the pride of good, well-meaning, professional people doing extraordinary things to be proud about.

For all of the rhetoric and protests, as well as the questions on the validity of the war back home, the deeds of our men mattered.

CHAPTER THIRTEEN

I knew even less of personal relationships and love than I knew of the war. Any experience I had came from high-school crushes and youthful emotional romances. My sexual experiences were limited as well, and prior to arriving in Vietnam I had been a virgin in various senses of the word. My first encounter with a prostitute in Saigon, when Rodriguez and the veteran team leader checked me out of the hospital, was clumsy, hurried, and awkward. I fumbled with a condom so long that the woman finally took it out of the package and deftly put it on me. Afterward, the woman swore I was "Numbah one good-time lover," and lying there in the dark, I knew I had lost more than my virginity. I'd lost an opportunity for the first time to mean something special, and it should have been. I wanted to hug her and hold her close. But to her it was just business.

In many ways I was old fashioned, the spitting image of the naive kid down the block, too filled with idealism to believe that love or war would be anything less than romantic and daring. As with the war, I was in love with being in love and didn't know the first damn thing about it.

My relationship with my girlfriend during my senior year of high school was an innocent, maybe naive, relationship. We kissed a great deal, said the right things, and believed it was something special. Then, maybe it was. Now, was another matter.

I was becoming jaded while learning how to cope and survive. I wanted to be closer to my girlfriend, but knew there was an emotional distance building between us. I wasn't writing her or even my family as much as I should have because I was finding that I didn't know how to best say what was happening to me.

Honey,

So how's school? Are you going to homecoming? Oh by the way, I killed seven people earlier this week. Blew their shit away. Slept with a hooker, too, a real pro. I'm becoming somewhat of a pro, too, at loading bent and burnt corpses into body bags. Sometimes you have to bend rigid arms or legs to get them to fit in the bags. But don't worry, I'm still the same guy I was before.

Love
Kregg.

High school dances and senior proms were a lifetime away, too far to matter, and too trivial ever to mean anything again. While I was on leave before going to Vietnam, we'd talked about love and eventual marriage the way starry-eyed young lovers do. All good times and no bad. Maximized emotion, minimized commitment or responsibility. Jesus, I missed it.

So while soldiers around cursed and cried over Dear John letters, they received during their tours, I knew we were the ones who'd deserted our loved ones. It was our emotions that had packed up and walked out the door, not theirs. We were worn and lonely and looking for comfort anywhere we could find it. The people back in the World found others to cling to for support; we had no one but ourselves. The platoon mattered. The squad mattered. Your buddies mattered. Everything else did not. And, too, because each of our tours was an individual tour, we each had our own schedules to keep; we pulled our emotions in further, confined for our own emotional survival.

I knew I'd survive, and like the Cowardly Lion in the Land of Oz I, too, had a medal to show how brave I was. And, maybe, like the Lion, I also knew there were flying monkeys and dangerous things lurking in the darkness. Dorothy was back in Kansas, and you couldn't hide behind medals anyway.

There's no place like home, but I'd be damned if I could find the ruby slippers!

"Congratulations, you got the clap!" Doc Devalle said to Manning, who took the news as well as could be expected.

"Oh, God, no!" he said with a wail. "Are you sure?"

The medic nodded, showing Manning the results of the lab report. "Yep. Looks like you been sticking your lizard in some funny resting holes. Steam bath?"

Now it was Manning's turn to nod. The steam bath was adjacent to the base camp's post exchange and officially sanctioned—at least overlooked—by the 25th Infantry Division, which operated the base camp.

"You gotta use a rubber next time. I mean it, otherwise you'll end up with something worse than the clap, something like the Black Syph, and you'll end up on the island they have just off the coast."

Beal and I were cleaning our rifles nearby, and we smiled at each other. Doc was at it again.

"The island?"

"Yeah, you've heard about it, haven't you?"

Still new, Manning didn't want to admit that he hadn't learned everything he should have yet. "Yeah," he replied.

"Sure you have, because that's where they send GIs who get the Black Syph. Their dicks turn green and then black and eventually rot off. The army can't send GIs home with Black Syph because they can't cure it yet. So they send them to the island to die with dignity. Here," he said, flipping Manning a bottle of pills.

"What are they?"

"Tetracycline. Take one of them three times a day until they're all gone. Drink plenty of water and remember what I said about using rubbers next time."

"I will! I swear! Thanks, Doc. Thanks a lot!" Manning said, clutching the bottle in his hands and hurrying off to take the first pill.

"The 'island off the coast'?" Beal said, cocking his head to the side while Devalle beamed.

"It's a good story anyway. Besides, next time he'll remember to use a rubber."

"Doc, you amaze me!"

"Sarge," the medic said, looking pleased with himself, "sometimes I amaze myself!"

At a little over 220 pounds and maybe six two, Braun was the largest man in the platoon, not large as in tall but large as in heavy. He wasn't fat, just muscle heavy, and when he came to the Blues the former high school athlete was the obvious choice for the platoon's main radio telephone operator, the platoon's RTO. His bearlike size and square features belied the quick mind behind the facade. An obvious choice isn't necessarily the only choice, but Braun adapted to the position quite easily and knew instinctively what to do and when to do it, sometimes even before the lieutenant he trailed. Prior to Lieutenant Hugele's arriving, the former Blue had tried once or twice to get the St. Louis resident to sign up for OCS.

"You have the education, the ability, and the uncanny knack of knowing what to do in damn near any situation!" The lieutenant said, trying to get Braun to become an officer.

"Naw, I don't think so, Blue. First of all, I'm a draftee. I didn't volunteer for the army, they came and got me. Secondly, OCS would mean another tour of duty over here as an officer. No, thank you. One tour is enough. And, finally, my father was an officer, and my brother is an officer, and somebody has to keep the family name honest, so thanks for the offer, but like the man says, 'no sale!' "

Then, the last was a lie but made its point when the platoon leader and the others were hit, it was Braun who called in the dustoff medevac helicopter, while Burrows coordinated the ground action. Even Burrows knew that Braun could take care of radio support operations better than he could, and he left the big man to do it.

Braun was also bushwise and had a keen grasp of the world, let alone of army matters, so when he lumbered across the compound area heading towards the CP in an agitated gait, the rest of us wondered what was up.

"Que Pasa?" I asked while the bear frowned.

"The Fucking Idiot's taking over," he replied.

"What?"

"The Flight Instructor, Funks's replacement," he explained. "The pilots are all pissed off, and from what I hear, the only people happy to see him coming here are the people in his old unit."

"Where did you hear that?" the veteran NCO had asked, causing Braun to scowl.

"Radio Free Rumor Mill on your Apache Troop dial. He's coming in soon."

"When's the change of command?"

"A few weeks or so," the RTO said.

"Maybe he ain't so bad," the veteran NCO said, giving the new troop commander the benefit of the doubt. Braun, considering the source, dismissed it.

"And maybe there's the slight possibility you might know what you're talking about, which isn't likely."

"At ease!" the veteran NCO yelled at Braun, who just smiled instead.

"Read my lips, Sarge. Fuck you. You're dead weight that we've carried this far, and you know what, you're getting heavy.

The new CO, from what the pilots say, is a yahoo. You, you're just stupid, so save that regular army stuff for some new guy who'll shiver and shake like a basic trainee.'' The veteran NCO was furious and his fat hands clenched and released as though he was threatening to strike. But even he knew better than to try.

"I ought to—"

"Yeah, you ought to do a lot of things, but you won't. That's the difference between you and me," Braun said, staring him down until the older sergeant walked off in a huff.

"A little hard on him, weren't you?" Beal asked.

"Not really. The guy's incompetent and has no business being here. The old platoon sergeant, the one before Andreu, was his buddy. He let him take over a squad so he could get a Combat Infantryman Badge, only that wasn't enough. When the old Blue got hit, our hero there didn't do squat. After we came back, though, it was a different story, and he wrote himself up for a medal, saying he deserved it. Funk denied it, and since then, everytime something happens, he's there doing some creative writing. Burrows was telling me that he even had his own version how things went last week in the Dog's Head. Straight out of a movie script, folks.''

"You're kidding?" I said.

Braun shook his big, square head. "Nope. It seems like he fought the battle without anyone's assistance. Top is still laughing, I guess, but I don't think Blue and Andreu are.''

"So is this new CO bad?" This time it was Cortez with a question.

"None of them are all bad. From what I hear, the guy's a good pilot, but he likes to take chances with other people's lives. The pilots say he's arrogant, and it's hard to find anyone who'll sing his praises.'' If Braun sounded bitter, it was because when the old lieutenant was wounded, a good friend of his was killed, and he didn't like the idea of anyone's profiting from the loss.

When Braun left for his hootch in a sulking mood, Manning was the first to speak. "The man's got his opinions," he said.

"They're usually on the mark," Cortez said, defending the RTO. Manning wasn't a fan of the NCO whom Braun had confronted, but he was just expressing his concern. Manning felt he had to defend him out of loyalty because the NCO was a fellow member of the platoon, but he wasn't really sure if he wanted to. Still he had to say something. "Yeah, well . . .''

"Yeah, well what?" Beal said, taking the challenge.

"He's persistent?" Manning said finally.

"So are the Viet Cong, but that doesn't mean we like them, either. Nice try, kid."

"You could've tried something better," Cortez said, "like maybe he doesn't sweat much for a fat man."

"Or maybe he's big enough for the whole squad to hide behind in a firefight," said Beal, smiling.

"Or that he's fun to watch rappel," I piped in, causing Beal to smile.

"Okay, okay, okay. But I still have to work with him," he said, giving in to the barrage of insults.

"With who?" Cortez asked.

"With that dumbshit!" Manning finally said. We applauded.

"You know, I think that qualifies you for a Purple Heart, at least. Hey, Jorgy, give him one of yours. You have a million of them anyway!"

"Two!" I said, holding up two fingers to Beal. "And they actually gave me the medal."

"What?"

"They pin them on you in the presentation ceremony and give you a copy of the orders. Afterward, they take back the medal, put it back in the box, and then present it over and over again whenever they need it. So I have the paperwork, which I'll be more than happy to give him," I said while everyone laughed.

"When I was in Airborne training," Beal said, "our TAC sergeant told us that we had two good parachutes to use when we jumped, and if by some chance the main chute didn't open, then the reserve chute would. Then, he said there'd be a truck to pick us up after we landed and take us back to camp. Well, I jumped, and then this one old boy jumped behind me, and you know what? His main chute didn't open, so he released it and then scrambled to pull the rip cord of his reserve parachute. Know what?" It was a rhetorical question, and Beal didn't really want an answer.

"The reserve chute didn't open, either. As he passed me on the way down, falling at 120 miles an hour, he said, 'You know, I bet the truck won't be there either'!"

While Beal was telling his story, Cortez was cutting out a paper medal with his bayonet. When he had finished he pinned it to Manning's chest. The new guy was one of us now.

"Congratulations, new guy," Cortez said. "You've just joined the rest of us walking wounded!"

CHAPTER FOURTEEN

═══════════

The first mission after the run-in with the NVA force in the Dog's Head was a picnic mission just east of Fire Support Base Ike. Division intelligence wanted us to check out the results of an Arc Light, the code name for a B-52 bombing mission.

When we were just a few minutes out of the target area, we could see the effects of the blanket-bombing strategy. In the midst of the lime greens and fading browns of the rain forest, blue water pockets lay ringed with orange-brown rims where five-hundred-pound bombs had ripped large chucks of earth out of the jungle and scattered them the way a farmer might scatter seed over a field. From our height of a few thousand feet, the pockets and pools seemed to go on for miles. As we descended we saw the going would be difficult. It always was after an Arc Light because nothing was where it should have been. Trees were uprooted and splintered, sometimes hanging in other trees. Fire ants once housed in three-foot-high mounds were blown into the vegetation where they clung to leaves, stinging anyone or thing that brushed past them. Small animals and birds lay on the ground dazed, too stunned to move. If there had been any North Vietnamese Army units in the immediate area when the bombs fell, then they would be in much the same condition.

We would have to move through the bombed-out area, going around the deep craters, getting stung by the angered ants while trying to find survivors or bodies.

When our Huey liftships touched down, Blue had us take the tree line and then gave us a direction of movement. Beal and I took the point. Minutes later we were standing next to the first of the many bomb craters. Water from a monsoon storm the night before filled the crater, and the chemical residue from the bomb had turned the water a swimming-pool blue.

I covered Ed as he skirted the crater. Once on the other side, he provided me with protection to move. At the third crater, we came across a section of jungle trail and what looked to be a collapsed bunker. If there had been anyone in the underground facility, then they were buried alive beneath tons of dirt and debris. Not that it mattered. If anyone happened to be in the bunker when the bombs fell, the concussion and pressure from the massive explosions would have killed them anyway, their skin ripping open under the incredible pressure. For forty-five minutes we moved through a dead land that even birds refused to return to. It was strangely quiet, but most cemeteries all seem to have the same sound and feel—that awkward quiet and the smell of upturned earth.

"Blue says to hold up!" Stephenson said, as we searched the area. We had found no signs of recent enemy activity.

As we stood grouped in a perimeter, the unlikeable sergeant brought a discovery to our attention "Over here!" he yelled. "I found something!" he added, kicking at the unseen object. Manning was next to him, looking pale and drawn.

"He probably found a body," Beal said, getting to his feet and heading over to see what the staff sergeant had found, while I radioed the news to Braun who, in turn, relayed it to Blue and the TOC. Less than twenty yards away I saw Beal's back go rigid with surprise, and he yelled something in anger to the staff sergeant, who mumbled a reply as they stepped back from what they'd found.

Ed Beal's face was flushed with anger. "It's a dud, a five-hundred-pounder that didn't go off, and the dumb fucker was kicking it! Can you believe that?" Beal was visibly shaken, while Manning walked over to join us. "I swear to God if I ever say anything good about him again, I want you to shoot me, you *bic* GI?" he said, using the Vietnamese term for "do you understand?"

When we relayed the information to Blue, he told us to slowly, carefully ease away from the dud and to keep reasonable distance from it. "We'll place a charge on it and blow it in place," he said over the radio to Apache 6, who was flying in a gunship a few thousand feet above us.

"Roger," came the static response from the gunship. "Blow it in place."

"Six says blow it," Braun said, relaying the information to us.

"Maybe we can request permission to have the sergeant who discovered it kick it one more time instead. God, what a dumb fuck," Manning said.

Beal and I were tasked with setting the charge to blow the undetonated bomb. It's amazing how cautious you can be when you know that one wrong move might set off five hundred pounds of explosive, especially after one of your fellow soldiers had spent a few minutes kicking it.

"Now would be the perfect time for our hero to earn the medal he wants so badly," Beal said, placing the white, claylike block of C-4 explosive on the exposed section of the bomb.

"How's that?" I asked, rigging a blasting cap to fit in the C-4.

"He could sit on this with a grenade and then pull the pin."

"Uh-uh," I said shaking my head. "It'd be the waste of a perfectly good grenade."

I set a ten-minute fuse, and we scurried back to the platoon. Blue had us quickly move out of the area, and although ten minutes doesn't sound like a lot of time, when you know that a bomb will be going off behind you, you'd be surprised how fast and far you can move in that short time. With less than two minutes to go, the lieutenant had us take cover.

"Keep your heads down," someone said, passing along the comment that had filtered down the line.

After two minutes, I began to wonder if I had timed the fuse correctly, then the explosion shattered the jungle. Hot fragments of metal spattered down on the ruined rain forest, burning through our uniforms when they landed. We suffered minor burns and major fright from the pain until we realized it was only topical.

"Proceed to the Papa Zulu," Apache Six's voice said over the radio net, while Blue's voice rogered the command. We'd head to the designated pickup zone.

Something was up; the mission had been too short. We wondered what was going on while we pushed through the underbrush, heading for the grassland opening where the troop's liftships would, after we secured the PZ, fly in to pick us up.

"Short day?" Cortez asked. I shrugged.

Once at the pickup zone, we received more information. Apache Six had spotted another bunker complex from the air that he wanted us to check out. Murmurs and scowls filled the pickup zone. By the time we were flying into the new landing zone, the new Apache Six must have heard the cloud of insults wafting up toward his direction. Even Burrows was mumbling; after the two-plus hours of getting into the first area and then getting back out we were tired, exhausted, from the tense searching and sweat-drenched movement. We weren't at our peak. Combat assaults take something out of you, and our job and sole business with the

1st of the 9th seemed to be combat assaults. The adrenaline could only pump so long.

"Going in hot!" The doorgunner yelled over the din of the loud hacking of helicopter blades as the line of the helicopters lowered into the landing zone.

"Going in hot" meant that the doorgunners would fire into the tree line to keep down the heads of whomever might be waiting for us. Rifles locked and loaded, we stood on the skids of the helicopter, holding on with one hand while aiming out with the other. Usually on a combat assault, half of the platoon would remain in the center of the helicopters, thinking that they were safer than those who were standing on the skids. After all, the enemy fire would hit those outside first. Those of us standing on the skids reasoned that we did not want to get shot down with the helicopter and have it explode in a burning ball around us. We could at least jump for it.

When the three helicopters touched down again, we raced into the tree line, adrenaline pumping wildly. I was no longer tired, the adrenaline had kicked in again—the excitement of the action, coupled with the constant firing of the helicopters' machine guns had seen to that.

Beal and I took the lead again, while the platoon filed in behind us. Unlike the previous mission, where the bombs had drastically changed the rain forest, this expanse of jungle hid more bunkers and fighting positions, and I guessed that after one thousand years of fighting that there couldn't have been a stretch of jungle in the entire country that didn't contain some kind of fighting positions. Here, I spotted the first one, Beal found a second. The thin Vietnamese interpreter watched the area around us as I descended headfirst into the opening. It took my eyes a second to adjust to the cool, blue light of the underground position. Five feet by six with an L-shaped entrance, the bunker was empty except for a small cooking pot on an earthen shelf. I felt the pot. It was cold, which made me breathe a little easier. If anyone had been using the bunker, it had probably been a while since he'd been there. When I exited the bunker, Hue's eyes confirmed it.

"Old bunker complex," he said, visibly relaxed. Still he studied the tree line with a watchful eye. After four years of actual combat, he wasn't about to take any unnecessary chances.

I told Braun what we'd found, and he relayed the message to Blue, while Apache Six interrupted to say he wanted us to move farther into it. Easy for him, all he had to do was fly in lazy circles above us. We had to push up and around the countryside. Typical grunt thinking, but then when you're worn and tired, it's easy.

Blue rogered the command and had us move deeper into the bunker complex. An hour slipped by with little result. The bunker complex was empty, and when we finally reached its perimeter, where a lone trail led off into the thick rain forest, Blue had us turn around, going back at it from another direction. Then, when that too failed to produce any results, he told Apache Six that the complex was a bust.

"It's an old facility," Lieutenant Hugele said over the radio. "There's no recent activity from what we can tell. Looks abandoned."

After a while, Apache Six replied.

"Roger. Secure the Papa-Zulu and prepare to get lifted out."

We'd reenter the landing zone and use it as our pickup zone, only like the second trip through the bunker complex, we'd come at it from another direction, avoiding unnecessary risks. As we came out of the jungle into the large field, Beal noticed something odd. A small pond, covered from the air by the shade of a large tree, lay tucked away in one corner of the field.

"What's wrong with this picture?" he said, going down on one knee while drawing our attention to the pond.

"What is it?" I asked.

"I don't know," he said, and then he asked Hue: "What do you make of it?"

The Vietnamese sergeant looked it over for a moment before venturing his guess. "For food," he said with a slight hesitation in his voice, and then more firmly, "Yes, for food. It's a fishpond."

"You're kidding?" Beal said, surprised.

"They use it to grow their fish, for food. Come, I show you," he said, moving back within the tree line as he skirted the landing zone toward the pond. Braun had called it in, and Apache Six's interest was sparked again.

"Blue leader, move to the enemy area and check it out. Over," the Troop Commander ordered in hurried excitement.

Hue's assessment was correct. In the small knee-deep pool, hundreds of carplike fish moved through dirty brown water that was fed by a small stream through a bamboo pipe.

"What a fishing hole!" May said when his squad moved in with the others to get a better look at what we'd found.

"So what do we do with it?" Cortez asked. Blue wasn't quite sure. There wasn't a whole hell of a lot we really could do to destroy it, and he knew it.

"Apache Six. Blue leader. Over," the platoon leader called over the radio.

"Six. Go."

"Roger, Six. We have a fish farm at this location. Any suggestions, over?"

Braun knew Six's answer even before it came over the radio. "He'll want us to blow it. What do you bet, Boss?" he said to the lieutenant. Blue only grinned at his RTO, who instinctively and accurately always summed up any situation the platoon seemed to come across. Blue couldn't explain it, but knowing Braun was around made him feel comfortable.

"Blue leader. Blow it in place," came the reply over the radio.

"Ah, but how?" Beal said with a smile.

"How much explosive do we have?" the lieutenant asked Andreu, who did a quick count.

"Maybe two pounds of C-4, plus some det cord," the platoon sergeant replied.

"What do you think?" he asked me.

I said it was more than enough to do the trick. "I can set it in the pond, but I don't think it'll do much good. There's not much to blow up but the fish!"

"Six says blow it, so let's give me an explosion," Blue said, pulling the platoon back and telling the squad leaders to keep their people down.

"This I gotta see." Beal gave me a hand with the explosive.

We decided to detonate it with a concussion grenade, wrapped with a roll of det cord and set in the C-4. It seemed like a reasonable assumption that the quarter-block of dynamite that made up the concussion grenade would set off the rest of the C-4. We knew the delayed fuse of the grenade would give us the few critical seconds needed to get down. We wouldn't have to go too far since the explosion would radiate through the pond and then push skyward. All in all, it seemed like a reasonable assumption.

"Now!" I said, pulling the pin to the grenade, while Beal helped lower it in place. In less than a second, we were out of the pond and lying flat against the grass field. My concussion had taught me a great deal about the effects of an explosion, so I covered my ears and opened my mouth as the charge went off. The ground thundered in protest beneath us as a giant *whoosh* sent water and mud in a growing mushroom. And the fish, too.

It was Braun's voice that I first heard in protest.

"Son of a bitch!" he said as fish fragments and mud rained down on the platoon.

When I looked up, I saw Beal laced with fish pieces, and the tree that shaded the small pond had sprouted with fish in its limbs. The pond, slightly lower, was a coffee-sludge brown, while dead fish and fish fragments littered the surface.

"Too much C-4," I said to Beal, who was laughing.

"Nice bomb, Jorgy!" Cortez yelled, scraping away the debris from his uniform. "Too nice." Then, turning to the lieutenant, Sergeant Andreu added, "The battalion of NVA fish, Kilo India Alphaed all to hell and gone! Madre 'Dios.'"

Blue couldn't keep from laughing as he called in the report to Apache Six. By the time we returned to the Tay Ninh base camp, the doorgunners were eyeing us with disdain. It was bad enough we had to stink up their helicopters, but now they'd have to clean the fish guts and fragments from the helicopters as well.

When we exited the aircraft, there was a mad dash to put our weapons and equipment away before racing to the shower area. We had no way of knowing the showers were broken.

The next morning found us just outside Fire Support Base Ike, set up in a loose perimeter in the cleared deadman's land, just on the other side of the barbed wire that protected the small jungle outpost. We were standing by to serve as a QRF for a LRRP team, if needed. The night before, NVA soldiers moved past its position, using flashlights to find their way through the wet, dark jungle. It had been tense for a while, but with the sunlight, the NVA movement ceased, leaving the five-man Ranger team wondering where the enemy soldiers had stopped. It was waiting to see if perhaps the NVA would move again, this time in front of the LRRPs' claymore mines and ambush. When and if they did, we'd be standing by to help the Ranger team.

When Beal and I heard we'd be helping a LRRP team, we spent a good deal of our time that morning trying to find out which team. After all, we had friends in the Rangers, and though we were no longer in the company, we still considered ourselves Rangers. Periodically Rangers from the company would stop in to see us on their way out or to share a beer while waiting for a helicopter back to Phuoc Vinh.

On his way up to the top of Black Virgin Mountain, Jim McIntyre had stopped in to see me shortly after the Dog's Head incident. He had some business with the relay people on the tall mountain, and when he had some time to kill, he stopped in to see how I was doing with the Blues. It was an awkward reunion with evasive social talk, the kind that makes you feel uncomfortable and leaves you with the feeling that nothing much had actually been said. We hadn't really known each other well before the ill-fated mission, and the only experience we shared was surviving it.

"How are you doing?" he asked.

"Fine. You?"

"Okay." Then, after a long pause he added, "I heard you got wounded again."

"Nothing big. A concussion."

McIntyre laughed slightly. "The little ones add up," he said.

There was little more to say, and after an awkward silence, we wished each other well, shook hands, and said our good-byes. Watching him leave, I felt as though I should call him back and say something more, something that would get past the mission, beyond the memory of how the others had died. But I didn't because I realized that's the only way we'd ever view each other, that there would always be a distance between us·if for no other reason than our emotional survival.

Why couldn't we express our true emotions and sentiments to others without feeling weak or ineffectual? Was it because we viewed ourselves as Rangers, warriors with brass balls and fire for breath? Christ, I should have told him I was glad that he'd helped to save my life and that there wasn't a damn thing he or I could've done to change the outcome of the battle. And that I hurt whenever I thought about the others and how they died and how helpless I felt because I couldn't stop it. I hoped I'd get another chance to tell him I was proud to have been on his team, and that Torres had felt the same way, glad to be working with someone like him. None of us counted on war's manipulative hand reaching in and prying away our expectations and shaping its own. I had played the "if-only" game too many times. There was no way to make any sense of what had happened, and all of the wishing, crying, frustration, and rage would never change the outcome.

The game of the LRRP was not getting caught; the reality was that we sometimes did. Unfortunately, knowing that didn't lessen the pain.

Resting outside of Fire Support Base Ike, we waited for the call which never came; the Ranger long range recon patrol team was extracted and lifted to Ike. When the helicopter touched down, it was Rodriguez who smiled out of the open bay of the aircraft. "Hey, Jorgy," he said walking toward me, "how in the hell are you doing?"

"Fine. So it was your team we've been waiting for?"

The Ranger team leader nodded. "The NVA were pretty busy last night. We couldn't be certain if they were just traveling at night or if they were out looking for us. Either way, they came close enough as it was. So what's this I hear about you and Beal John Wayning in some big-ass firefight?"

"That's Audie Murphy, asshole," Beal said, coming up behind him and catching a few sneers from two of the new guys on Johnny's team. "John Wayne is celluloid fiction. Murphy, like us, is pure flesh, muscle, and nerve."

"Not to mention fourteen-inch peckers," I added.

"Goes without saying," Beal said. "And speaking of peckers, how've you been, Rod?"

"Relax boys," Rodriguez said to his newbies. "These bozos here are two LRRPs I carried through training with the company. The skinny one's Ed Beal, and the one with the silly-ass grin is Jorgenson," he said. The LRRPs' expressions changed from tough-guy challenge to new-guy guffawing. Three of the five team members were cherries. The assistant team leader was a LRRP named Cochran.

We shook hands, asked about some mutual friends and then talked about their mission.

"So what happened last night that brought us out here today?"

"Nothing much. Just the whole North Viet-fucking-namese Army deciding that it was time for a moonlight stroll. Five hundred of them to the right of us. Five hundred of them to the left. Five hundred to the front and five hundred to the rear and you know what? We—"

"Took no prisoners," I said, stealing his thunder.

"Actually, we snuck into a North Vietnamese Army bunker complex and things got tense for a while. But all just a normal part of our workday," Rodriguez said, making light of it, which seemed to be a standard method for explaining away actions. Fear masked with light bravado. Hell, even Clint Eastwood wore makeup in his acting roles!

"What's this I heard about Old Sarge?" Beal asked.

Rod and the others broke into a collective laugh. Old Sarge was a veteran noncommissioned officer and Ranger, who during his downtime brought our spirits up with his antics and humor.

Through the rumor mill we'd heard that some acting first sergeant for the Rangers had angered the new commanding general at an officer's club function at Phuoc Vinh, a dog-and-pony-show, ice-breaking get-together for various division unit officers and

their top NCOs. "Some wild-assed enlisted man," the story teller
had said. "A Ranger."

"Gotta be Old Sarge," Beal said. I nodded. "So what did he
do?"

"I dunno," the warrant officer pilot replied, smiling, "but he
really pissed off the new general." And that was the extent of
what we'd heard until Rod provided the rest.

"The first sergeant was on emergency leave, so they made Old
Sarge the acting first sergeant, and he wasn't too thrilled; he liked
the field and couldn't stand rear-area candy-ass tea parties. The
only consolation he had was that the party had an open bar. So Old
Sarge and the old man were at this get-together, drinking, while
everyone else was standing around smiling and kissing ass. Then
the new general told everyone to relax and take it easy.

"Never one to disobey orders, especially if they're favorable
orders, Old Sarge had a few drinks and was enjoying himself and
winking at the nurses and Donut Dollies who'd also been invited
to the get-together," Rodriguez said.

Among the enlisted men and maybe even a few of the officers,
it was rumored that some of the Donut Dollies peddled more than
donuts and coffee to the troops, and that among the civilian cheerleader types there were also some hookers.

Never one to believe half the crap that circulated through the
rumor mills, Old Sarge probably tried flirting with them, as did
everyone else who came in contact with the "round eyes."

"So he's eyeing this one tall blond who was standing across the
room talking to some pilots, and she catches him staring at her.
She gives the lowly enlisted swine a hard-ass glare and turns
away, like, how could such a commoner put the make on her. I
heard she wasn't anything special, but in Nam she was a round
eye, which made her unique; in Savannah or Chicago she'd have
been considered ordinary.

"Anyhow, she turned again. This time Old Sarge smiled at her.
In a huff she went to join a few full birds [colonels] she knew
across the room, and away from Old Sarge. Taking matters into
his own hands, Old Sarge downs a shot of whiskey, chases it with
a beer, then does recon of his target area. With her back to him,
the dolly couldn't see that he was slowly working his way toward
her. Stopping short of his objective, he surveyed the enemy's
strength like a good LRRP and hastily planned his attack. One of
the full-bird colonels saw him behind her but couldn't figure out
what Old Sarge was up to until the Ranger bent over and bit her
on the ass—a small bite, to be sure, but enough to produce a

piercing scream. Old Sarge just stood smiling then bowed to the collection of colonels and turned to walk away.

"The woman, crying and stammering mad, ran behind the safety of the nearby commanding general's gleaming stars, as the Ranger began his escape and evasion route. A quick order from the outraged general turned him around, heels locked at attention, while the old man was ready to shit. Old Sarge, as we know, has been read the riot act more than a few times in his career, so when the general had finished his speech, our friend spoke his lines in this one-act play.

"Get this, he said, 'Is that all?' knowing damn well it wasn't, so the general screams back at him, 'No that isn't all, soldier. You'll apologize to the young lady for your actions. Second, you'll apologize to me and everyone else here, and finally, you'll be relieved of your duties as your company's first sergeant.' At that, Old Sarge says 'Yes, sir,' and when he had finished with his apologies, the old man escorted him back to the company. The next day he was back as a team leader doing what he likes best!"

We all laughed at the story, which we'd embellish even more in future retellings. Old Sarge had gone from the status of mere mortal to that of demigod.

A sudden shout took us away from the laughter. "Lookie what I found!" a grunt said. He was holding up a small ball-like object. Walking closer, we recognized that the "ball" was a decaying human head with an ant colony making its home in the bridge of the eaten-away nose.

"It's a gook head," he said while we studied the macabre object curiously. Part of the skull had been ripped away, leaving a silver-dollarlike jagged hole.

"Put it down," Rodriguez said, suddenly, angry.

"What?" The grunt was pissed. He didn't like having others tell him what to do, especially a hotdog, fucking Ranger. The army's rank structure made him obey those above him, but those equal to or below him were fair game.

"I said put it down. How would you like someone digging away at your skull after you died?"

"No big thing," the grunt replied, still digging at the skull.

"Hell, they wouldn't find anything in there anyway," his squad leader said, breaking the tension. "Nothing but a record skip in his memory that keeps him sharpening his knife."

"A sharp knife never lets you down!" the soldier said.

"Sure. Whatever," the squad leader said, patronizing the soldier. Then he said, "You know, a while back one of our guys cut off the ears of the dead gook and made the mistake of bragging about it in the enlisted club. The news got back to the MPs and finally the general, and our entire company, along with a company or two of grunts who secured the area where it happened, joined us while we searched for the remains of the body. I mean, he's an enemy soldier, and one of a few that were blown away in an ambush, and the dumb fuck decides he wants a souvenirs, so he cuts off the ears of one of the dead gooks.''

"So?'' the grunt said.

"So the fucking army is bent on crucifying anyone who they think's committing war crimes, and digging away at a partially decomposed skull might just qualify.''

"Bullshit!'' the grunt said. "This is war.''

The squad leader shook his head. "No, man, it's a conflict, like the one we're having now. Put it back. Funny business we're in,'' he said, while the rest of us just looked at the grunt who nervously backed away, taking the severed head back to where he'd found it, grumbling as he did.

"A stupid fucking way to run a war,'' the grunt said grumbling.

"And he's on our side,'' Rodriguez said after he'd left.

"Cross section of America, man,'' the squad leader said.

"What?''

"The draft takes in a cross section of America so you get all kinds, like our man there. The armed forces takes them in, teaches them how to do all kinds of dangerous shit, and then sends them off somewhere to do it. Frightening concept, huh?''

We all nodded.

"Say, you guys don't need another good soldier in your unit, do you?'' he asked. It was easy to see where he was going with the question.

"Sorry, my friend,'' Rodriguez said, "but he's all yours.''

"What if we toss in a case of beer or two? Besides, I thought there's supposed to be a bounty on your Rangers?''

Rumor had it that the North Vietnamese placed a bounty on the Rangers they referred to as "the men with the painted faces'' because of the impact LRRP units were making on their operations.

"We could say he was a LRRP and then leave him out in the jungle. I wonder who we'd have to talk to about it?''

"Any hootch maid might do.'' Cortez laughed. "But tell her you'll settle for a whole lot less.''

"Yeah, like fifty piastas for a blue light special," laughed the squad leader. "Hey, you guys take care."

Saying good-bye to the grunts who were heading back to the fire support base, I thought about what he'd said about a cross section of America being in uniform, only it wasn't very comforting. I'd been lucky so far. The units I was with, Hotel Company and Apache Troop, were made up of good people. But then, they were special units. We couldn't tolerate fuck-ups. In fact, the more I thought about it the better our own yahoos looked, by comparison.

"I see you carry a lot of fire power," Rodriguez said, taking inventory of the Blues.

"Yeah. It gives us an edge until the gunships arrive," Beal said. "In fact, it probably kept that NVA unit we crossed paths with from overrunning us. I hear some LRRP units up north take out a machine gun."

"Might prove useful. I tell you, last night I would've felt better knowing we had one. We had a lot of gooks go by. A few even tripped over our claymore wires in the dark," Rodriguez shuddered thinking about it.

"All this and free C rations, too," Beal said, drawing him out of the sudden bad mood. Rodriguez laughed.

"Except lima beans. I hate ham and lima beans!"

"Ham 'n motherfuckers," Cortez corrected.

"That's right." Rodriguez grinned. "You guys take care, huh?"

In the deadman's land west of the small outpost, their return helicopter began cranking in the clearing. A helmeted doorgunner waved them on. It was Art Dockter, one of ours.

"Time to go, folks. Take it easy, you guys," Rod said, leading his team back to the awaiting helicopter. Stopping and turning back around, Rod said to me, "You should've taken the radio-relay job. You really should have."

I nodded. Maybe I should have, but it wasn't in the cards. I was part of the Blues by then, and in the short time I'd been with them, I'd learned something about myself that the Rangers had kept from me. I was a nineteen-year-old kid when I arrived. I was all of twenty years old now, but my brass balls didn't clink anymore, and I was no longer afraid to walk in thunder storms the way the Rangers told me I should be. But then, how could you keep those nineteen- and twenty-year-old kids doing the tough job they were doing if they didn't believe they were superhuman? How could you keep them motivated? There was a time when I wondered why some of the Rangers in the company, especially the older ones, got blind drunk on their stand-down time. Not anymore. I'd already fallen from Olympus; now I wondered why anyone in the damned country wanted to stay sober!

The helicopter returned a short time later after dropping the LRRPs off in Tay Ninh. Just in time for something else the higher-ups had planned.

"How would you and Beal like to go on a snatch mission?" the platoon sergeant asked, while Beal looked from where he was, stretched out and grinned.

"Did somebody say snatch?"

"Not as in pussy, as in, 'swoop down in a screaming helicopter, land, race out in a clearing, capture a Viet Cong suspect, and bring him back'? One of the scouts discovered a woodcutter out of his territory in a free fire-zone and bordering a bunker complex. It's an NVA bunker complex and recently used, too, and this old woodcutter shouldn't be anywhere near it, if in fact, he is a woodcutter."

"Sure, why not?" I said.

Beal slowly got to his feet. "Why did I know he was going to say that? I knew it! I swear I did." And then to Andreu he said: "So what's the plan?"

"Exactly as I said, only don't take any unnecessary chances. A Pink Team will cover you, but that don't mean shit when you're the only ones on the ground. If it looks bad, do what you have to and get out, you hear me?" The old Puerto Rican was concerned for our welfare as was the platoon leader, who had coordinated the action with Apache Six.

"Six wants the guy snatched, and he wants the Blues to do it. I suggested you two. What do you think?" the lieutenant asked.

"I think if the helicopter stays cranked, we can be in and out of there with the guy in a few minutes," I said.

Beal added his own. "I agree. No sweat on snatching the guy, Boss. But I'd like the scouts to give the guy's surroundings the once-over just to be on the safe side."

The lieutenant listened, nodded, and said he'd do it. While Beal and I put on our web gear, one of the lift ships from the squadron was coming in to get us. We traveled light: M-16s and web gear only. From our time with the Rangers, we were used to carrying forty magazines, with eighteen rounds in each clip, in canteen pouches around the pistol belt of the web gear. Since the firefight in the Dog's Head, when many of the Blues had run out of ammunition, they'd carried the extra ammunition that they'd once laughed at us for hauling.

It was a short, hectic ride to the jungle area where the wood-cutter was spotted, with a water buffalo that was pulling a short, high cart. From the air it was easy to see why they wanted to pick him up. The closest village was miles away, and the woodcutter was definitely in the area designated a free-fire zone, which meant that anyone or anything in the area that wasn't obviously on our side was fair game. He was lucky the scouts hadn't blown him away. Technically, the woodcutter was a legitimate target—legally, too, for that matter. The villagers had been warned time and again and, though it was common knowledge that many harbored and supported the Viet Cong and NVA units in the region, they could not be considered fair game—unless they were in a free-fire zone. Like the kid standing on a chair in the kitchen, arm reaching for the forbidden cookie jar, the woodcutter would be hard-pressed to explain away his presence in the area, especially when there were wild forests and trees so much closer to the village.

"Keep an eye on the tree line," Beal yelled to Dockter, who trained his machine gun on the wood line and nodded as we veered down in a thunderous charge. The high tech troopers were swooping in on a Stone Age woodcutter.

As we landed, the small scout observation helicopter flew tree-top level over the jungle that surrounded the small dirt road that ran the length of the region. As we ran out to intercept the Vietnamese woodcutter, I was surprised at first how he just sat there in the cart and waited patiently. But then, what could I really expect from a race of people whose land had been invaded so many times and even the little children grew up knowing that open resentment or sudden movement might result in death? He could've been or he could've not been exactly what he appeared to be, a woodcutter waiting and watching while yet another military force made demands on him. But we were the Good Guys, the Cavalry, for crying out loud! Didn't he know that? Maybe he did, and maybe he thought that we thought he was an Indian as Beal yelled and motioned for him to get down, while I searched the immediate tree line for any sign of an ambush. Nothing! No movement or suspicious signs. I turned back to Ed and the old man and saw that the woodcutter didn't really understand what we had wanted him to do—or maybe he did, thinking that we intended to kill him. Stranger things had happened.

Resigned to his fate, the old man finally climbed down from the cart and stood waiting for the bullets that never came. Ed was swearing now. We'd already been on the ground longer than we needed to be. I tied the old man's hands behind him, then Beal put a sandbag over his head and led him off to the helicopter. Searching the cart, I found nothing but the wood and the old man's tools. The water buffalo would eventually pull the cart to the village without the old man, leaving others to wonder about his fate. This wasn't anything new. The NVA used similar infiltration tactics before.

After sprinting back to the aircraft while an anxious crew nervously prepared to take off, I noticed that the old man was shaking. Did he think we were going to throw him out of the aircraft? What kind of people did he take us for anyway? Screaming madmen with rifles, yelling in a language he didn't understand to get down and be gagged, hooded, and then abducted on one of their strange flying machines?

"We did it!" I said to Ed, who smiled in relief and satisfaction.

"Yeah, we sure did."

"We're the good guys," I said to myself, glancing at the old man who still sat trembling.

He'd be flown back to the Tay Ninh base camp where he'd be interrogated by intelligence people; people who used the good guy, bad guy routine to extract information.

"You think they'll ring him up?" Beal asked. To ring someone up meant taping the bare wires of a field telephone to the prisoner's testicles and then cranking the telephone's generator, sending a jolt of electricity surging through his body. We'd never seen it done, but we'd heard about it through the rumor mill.

"No, they'll just question him, that's all. We're the good guys."

After laagering at Ike for the day, the platoon had been lifted back to Tay Ninh, and after Beal and I were finally dropped off near our troop area, we watched as the helicopter flew off into the sunset.

"Weren't *we* supposed to do that?" I asked.

Beal shook his head. "That's only in the movies."

"You think he was a gook officer or something?"

Ed turned back to me with a tired face. "I hope so,' he said. "Christ! I hope so."

Braun was standing at the door of the troop's small enlisted club, drinking a cold beer when we entered the troop area. "My God, two gen-u-wine war hee-rows. You boys gonna join us for a drink, or maybe go back out for a night ambush?"

"Anything besides Black Label beer?" Beal asked.

Braun nodded. "A kindly old helicopter pilot was good enough to donate a bottle of Johnny Walker to the cause."

Beal pushed past him into the club, where a few of the troop scouts had already finished off a quarter of the fifth. "I need a drink," he said to Porky, who was acting as the evening's bartender. "And a sodie pop for my underage friend," he added as I came through the door.

"Beer," I said while Porky pushed a cold can from the ice chest beneath the bar.

"Aren't you gonna check my ID?"

Porky shook his head and left Braun to sum it up.

"There ain't no young men left over here anymore. Not even you new nineteen-year-old John Waynes who still think you're invincible. Cheers, kid, and stop taking any more unnecessary chances."

I passed out on my cot, still wearing my web gear, and when the incoming mortar rounds exploded inside the camp, I was still too drunk to get up.

"Incoming!" someone yelled as the *whoompf* of mortar rounds exploded in the night. The camp's siren screamed over the explosions. *Whoompf!* and the mortars were hitting closer, probably the flight line this time. Screw it! By the time I managed to prop myself up into a questionable seated position, my head was pounding worse than the concussion I'd received in combat. My stomach was tied in a tumbling knot, and I was going to be sick. *Whoompf!* Inside the compound area this time, maybe near the TOC. *Whoompf!* and I was trying to get to my feet with little success. I sat back down on the cot, deciding against trying to make it to a bunker. If I died, I died. But I wouldn't die stooped in a hootch hallway vomiting over myself! *Whoompf! Whoompf!* and the mortar explosions were moving away from the compound area. Charlie was walking them over the camp. The distant *thump* from the dump area told us that the Viet Cong were using the refuse area again to mortar us. Standard Operating Procedure: Sneak out to the dump near the camp's back gate, hide behind the piles of garbage and in the craters that the engineers had dug with their large machines, then fire off a handful of rounds. Charlie had the routine down, and because of his modest success with the tactic, Tay Ninh was dubbed Rocket City. For the most part it was a misnomer. The majority of incoming rounds seemed to be mortar rounds, accented from time to time by 122mm rockets fired from farther off in the jungle.

Our artillery immediately answered the incoming rounds with a barrage of 155mm rounds in the area where the attack originated. Too late. Charlie was already halfway home, wondering how much damage he had inflicted and perhaps hoping he hadn't accidentally hit the mess hall, barbershop, or laundry where he worked. Nothing personal, GI.

Listening to the outgoing artillery rounds, I rolled off the bed and stopped my spinning stomach with the floor. I awoke a dark century later, listening to the scratching of a rat searching for something in the corner of my sleeping area. My rifle was leaning against the door frame, and feeling around my web gear, I found something in a pouch to keep my new enemy away. One eye open, mouth drooling on the dusty floor, and staring at the rodent—I was ready! The concussion grenade would do the trick.

"You dirty rat!" I mouthed dryly, while the rat gave me his best Bogart look and then ignored me.

Just then Burrows was walking through the squad hootch, pounding on doors. When he came to mine, the partially open door gave way under his knocking. "Sergeant Jorgenson?" he said, looking down at the fully dressed soldier huddled in a fetal position and holding a grenade. "You okay?"

"What? . . ." I turned over, seeing the veteran's half-scowl and confused look.

"First call. You—uh, okay?"

"Rats," I said, while he just looked around the room and nodded.

"Uh-huh," he added, turning to leave. "I usually set up a trap. I never gave any serious thought about ambushing them." He was still chuckling as he walked out the hootch heading for the 2d Squad's building.

"I tell you Bangkok's the place to go!" Cortez was arguing with Braun while they played a game of blackjack.

"Taipei," Braun replied, dealing Cortez a king while he peeled a look at a five of hearts he had dealt himself.

"Hit me!" Cortez said. "Uh-uh, Manning spent seven days in Bangkok with a dark-eyed beauty who introduced him to the basket trick, and the boy's never been the same since. Hell, he even took a seven-day leave just to go back!"

"What's a basket trick?" I asked. Braun gave me a look usually reserved for new guys. Manning was sitting in the corner of the platoon's CP, cleaning his rifle. He smiled. Finally someone else would catch it for a while. Besides, the story damn near made him a new-guy legend.

"The basket trick involves a pretty little woman who lays you out on a bed with your pecker pointing skyward while she loads herself in an open basket that's connected to the ceiling over the bed, and then she twists it in a circle, round and round until there's torque on the basket rope," explained Cortez, while Braun dealt him another card. It was a seven of diamonds. "Hit me again!" he said as Braun peeled another card from the deck. "Anyhow, the lady then lowers herself on your pecker and lets spin."

The third card was a two of clubs, and the grinning Cortez patted the cards and then told Braun to hit him again.

"Wouldn't that hurt?" I said, while Cortez stared at me along with Braun. Even Manning was staring at me with amused awe.

"It hurts good," Manning said as Cortez swore, "Shit!" The card showing was another face card. He was over.

"A pilot I know went to Taipei," Braun said, collecting the cards and reshuffling. "Came back with bootlegged records, a buck an album, three or four tailored suits for next to nothing, and a suitcase filled with contracts."

"Contracts?" I said. It seemed like a reasonable question, while the card players stopped what they were doing again, this time so Braun could explain it to me. First though, there were a few questions to ask.

"Haven't you been on R&R yet?"

I shook my head.

"How long have you been in-country?" the big RTO asked.

"Seven months," I replied.

"And you haven't taken a leave or an R&R?"

"Well, I put in for one when I was with the Rangers, but I came down with malaria. Then, I put in for one to Taipei the same time Lugenbeal did and got a concussion. But I put in for Bangkok yesterday!"

"Boy, you've had a run of bad luck when it comes to R&R," Braun finally said. He continued his explanation. "The prostitutes in Taipei are contracted services. When you go to a bar and see one you like, you work out a deal with the bartender, sign a contract, and off you go with your purchase."

"You buy a prostitute?" This time it was Manning with a question, and I faked it, giving him a frown along with the others.

"Hell no! You don't *buy* a hooker, you *rent* her. You see, prostitution is an honorable profession in the Far East and the ladies are licensed, card-carrying business professionals who'll bring up your Dow-Jones faster than a technological break-through!"

"No kidding!" I said, while Manning nodded in agreement. I was certain that a few of the others didn't know what a real Dow-Jones was, either, but understood that it was another way of saying pecker, and that was enough to get the point across to the rest of us.

"A case filled with contracts, huh?" I said.

"Yep," Braun replied, dealing the cards again.

"I wonder if it's too late to take my name off of the Bangkok list and put in for Taipei?"

Cortez said it wasn't. "Top won't take the requests off of the board until the end of the week. But talk to Manning before you do. After all, if you're gonna get fucked by the army and the war, then your pecker might as well have something to feel good about afterward!"

I wrestled with visions of the basket trick and of a suitcase filled with contracts the entire day, and when I finally made my way over to the orderly room with my decision, the allocations for the seven-day rest and recuperation leaves to Taipei were filled. I'd have to settle on Bangkok. It took another hour before the smile on my face finally faded.

CHAPTER FIFTEEN

The next mission took us near the former site of Fire Support Base Becky, just a few miles north of Carolyn, where the grunts of the 2d of the 8th Cav and the artillery of the 1st of the 30th fought one of the bloodiest battles of the war. That battle had been one of the reasons Frank Duggan came to the Rangers when he did. Duggan was on Becky when it was hit, and as we flew over the now abandoned outpost I remembered the story he told me about the attack.

It was their second night running on Red Alert. Their nerves were frayed, he said, and everyone was visibly on edge. But then they had good reason to be. The morning before, a little after three A.M., the North Vietnamese had begun their first assault.

Fifty mortar and 122mm rocket rounds slammed into a little outpost that from the air looked no bigger than a small city park, the kind that might hold two baseball fields back to back. Anyway, Duggan said that while the gooks were throwing in the rockets and mortars, an eleven-man NVA sapper team was busy working its way through the perimeter defenses, crawling past the three rows of barbed wire and around the antipersonnel mines. While that was going on, the officers and NCOs for two North Vietnamese infantry companies yelled for the soldiers to get on line for the ground attack. Then, with a piercing bugle call, they attacked. Duggan said the defenders fought like hell for two hours, pushing them back. Finally, by dawn, the North Vietnamese had withdrawn to the jungle. The grunts on Becky lost four killed and ten wounded. The count of dead NVA soldiers in the wire was seventeen. Blood trails snaked into the jungle, and while the artillery on Becky and the Cobra gunships from Tay Ninh hit the jungle around the camp, Becky still received return fire throughout the day.

Later that night, radar on the fire support base picked up North Vietnamese Army trucks as they sped in from nearby Cambodia and dropped off their cargo for yet another attack. This time, though, they were determined to take the outpost. Three hundred fifty mortars and rockets slammed into Becky, taking out one of the base's three tubes and destroying the ammo dump. A sapper team managed to blow up two bunkers and the wire in front of them, creating a hole for the main force to push in on. The battle that Duggan told us about in hushed tones back at Phuoc Vinh was tense. His hands shook and trembled when he retold the story, and his eyes darted to and from the platoon hootch door as though the NVA force he was telling us about would come through the opening any second.

The outpost was less fortunate than it had been the previous night. NVA soldiers raced through the fire support base, firing into and blowing up bunker and fighting positions as they ran. But the grunts held. In close, confused fighting, they somehow forced the North Vietnamese Army forces out again. This time, though, the cost was higher: seventeen dead and forty-nine wounded; half of the attacking force had been killed.

"We lost the base. They overran us," Duggan said.

But a lieutenant who'd been listening disagreed with him. "No, that's not right. We closed down the base."

"Yes, sir, that very night at 1800 hours."

"You kicked their asses!" the lieutenant said, his macho and enthusiasm helping him make his point.

Duggan just looked at him, stopping him with a cold, hard stare. "If you say so, Lieutenant, but that doesn't change what happened."

The look said everything. The same look that McIntyre and I shared after our team was hit so hard in Song Be. There were those who'd say we won, those who hadn't been there and wanted to believe that we were always kicking ass, but the survivors would know better.

I thought of Frank and the battle as we flew over the remains of Becky.

"Which one's that?" Manning asked, staring down at the dust-blown outpost.

"Becky," I said.

He nodded. "Hey!" he said excitedly, "It's empty."

To him it was. But I saw a small fragment of Duggan's war and an omen of the outcome of the war in the deserted outpost. Like the deserted French outposts strung throughout the countryside, ours, too, would fight and struggle to keep from reverting to jungle. And there was also the argument I had with Braun the week before because he casually said that it didn't really matter what battles we won over here since we'd lose in the end anyway.

"What are you saying? You saying we'll lose?" I asked, the too young, gung ho enthusiast arguing with the better educated and informed radioman.

"It's inevitable, kid," he said. "Sooner or later we'll give up and go home, and that's what they're counting on. Take a look at their history. They did it to the Chinese, the Cambodians, the French, Japanese, and everyone else who tried to colonize this country."

"But we're not here to colonize their country, we're here to help them."

"How? By building golden arches and supplying every family with a Big Mac? We can't stop the Vietnamese from becoming Vietnamese."

"But we're winning the battles! We're winning the war!"

Braun looked at me, started to say something, decided against it and instead said, "This isn't the kind of war you win, it's the kind you survive. We'll survive, but we'll also pull out eventually because the hearts of the South Vietnamese ain't in it, and if they're not, then we're only kidding ourselves thinking that we can save them. Come on, Jorgy, you can see that, can't you?"

I didn't reply. I was too angry with him; I knew he was right. Everything he said had made sense and gone against the nice, neat, preconceived notion of the war I had wrapped in my mind.

Becky disappeared beneath us as we were ferried into a landing zone to its north. We went in cold. A scout ship had spotted movement in the area, three Vietnamese with bicycles carrying in supplies, so we were sent in to check it out.

The LZ was quiet, and as we moved into the tree line, Hue spotted a trench that paralleled the large grass field. Covering the South Vietnamese soldier, Beal and I watched as he slipped into the trench and scurried down the hole to the nearest fighting position, a gun emplacement just around a bend to our left. Moments later he returned obviously relieved.

"Old," he said, flashing the familiar smile. We radioed the finding back to Blue, told him what Hue had said, and then were told to keep moving.

We found the well-used trail less than fifteen minutes later. Two feet wide and covered from aerial observation by the thick, overhanging canopy of vegetation, the trail was concealed well. The path itself was packed clay, and in the heat of the dry season it didn't offer any clues as to when it was previously used. That is, at first glance. Hue had taught us a new trick when it came to reading trails. Go to the nearest bend and look again.

The North Vietnamese were using bicycles to carry in war freight, and since they had trouble keeping the wheels of the bikes on the path because of the huge loads, they left marks in the surrounding jungle. Sure enough, at the first bend we saw tracks that ran over the vegetation and left marks in the softer soil. If the scout observation helicopter had spotted three, then how many had it missed? From the looks of the soil, a number of bikes had been moving south.

After we called in our findings, Blue told us to work our way down the trail in the direction the bicycles had taken. I gave Hue a break and took the point. Beal served as my slack man, the man who covered the point man while the point man was busy studying the trail for signs of booby traps. Three hundred yards down the trail, I knelt pointing to our right. Ten yards or so off the trail was a bamboo screen of some sort, weaved into a tight pattern.

Beal saw what I was pointing at and knelt as well, motioning for the RTO to bring up the radio. While Hue and I moved in to check it out, Beal let the platoon know what was going on.

The weave was part of a hut wall, an aboveground storage facility covered from the front by two empty fighting positions. Brush had been cut and placed around the storage hut to keep it hidden from the trail that wound around its front. But whoever had placed the brush had neglected the exposed sides. Peering in the doorway, I aimed my rifle back and forth across the dark, empty hootch. Hue watched the fighting positions with interest, and when I cleared the hootch, I turned to cover him as he checked them out. Still leery from our last jungle battle, Hue moved cautiously, while I nervously fingered the stock of my rifle. Nothing! They were all empty. Judging from the wilted vegetation that had been cut and placed around the hut, whoever had been there had left perhaps the day before.

Our attention returned to the storage hootch. I felt around the doorway for wires or potential booby traps. It was clear. I eased the bamboo door open and stared at the hinges. The door opened quietly letting the twilight from the surrounding jungle into the dark but cool hut. Maybe twelve feet across by ten feet wide, the hut was empty with the exception of the large green cannisters that lay on the shelves on the walls. Antitank mines, Chinese by their appearance, the kind they showed us in Ranger training and said could blow an M-60 tank off its tracks. With a heavy sigh I counted eight of them from outside of the hut. Best not to take chances.

Ed called in the findings and sergeants Andreu and Burrows moved to get a look at the hootch.

"Damn thing's out of place out here," Andreu said. I nodded. "Have you been inside yet?"

I shook my head. "No, not yet. I was waiting to see what Blue wanted to do."

"He's talking to Apache Six now. Wait until you get an answer," he said, heading back to the lieutenant, while Burrows remained behind staring at the hut.

"What'cha got in there?" Burrows said.

"Looks like tank mines," I said, showing him the mines that rested on the shelves.

"Eight of them, huh?" he said, while I knelt in the doorway, facing out, as did Sergeant Hue. The fighting positions were empty, but still . . .

"What are we waiting for?" Burrows asked indifferently.

"To see what Six wants done with them, whether to blow them in place or bring them back with us."

Burrows nodded and when I turned back around I saw him lifting the first mine off of the shelf. I started to yell only to have him turn, holding the wheel-like mine smiling.

"That could've been booby-trapped!" I said, trying to maintain my composure. My heart was pounding.

"Yeah, but it wasn't!" he said, brushing by me with the mine. "What's the big deal?"

I wanted to tell him that the big deal was that the mine could've been booby-trapped to go off when someone nudged it, and the explosion could've sent his ass, along with Hue's and mine, into a hundred lifeless pieces through the jungle back toward the rest of our platoon. I wanted to yell at him and maybe beat him until he understood that I didn't want someone like him taking chances with my life, that I was taking enough stupid chances of my own, thank you! Instead I said, "Did you die again last night and come back as a dumb-ass new guy?"

"What's wrong, you losing your nerve?" he said, heading back toward his squad.

Was I losing my nerve? I'd been running on it too long, and it was frayed at the edges and was looking worn. Maybe I was losing my nerve, but I hadn't lost my common sense. I knew if I was to survive the war, it would be that common sense and not my nerve that would do it.

"What's with you? You look pissed." Beal said. He was carrying the rope he'd retrieved to remove the antitank mines from a reasonably safe distance.

"Burrows just pulled one off of the shelf."

"What?" Beal stared at the mines remaining on the shelves, his mouth dropping open slightly.

"He just lifted one off when my back was turned," I said.

"That silly son of a bitch!"

"Yeah," I said. Then I helped him tie the rope to the first mine and retreated behind a tree with the others. We cleared the mines one by one.

"Blue says Six wants us to bring them back if we can," Stephenson said, cradling the radio's handset to his ear.

"Tell Blue we're clearing them now. Tell him we have seven and that Burrows has the other one and he's waltzing it toward them. We'll need some time to clear the rest."

I knew Burrows believed in reincarnation, so I was hoping he'd come back again soon with a little more common sense. Like on the next mission.

"We'll be taking a CBS news crew on patrol with us," Blue said, studying our reactions during the mission briefing. He got the expected frowns.

"Why?" The question came from Braun, who seemed to be asking the collective question on everybody's minds.

"In the words of Walter Cronkite, 'That's the way it is,' " Hugele said. "There'll be three of them so that means three of us will remain behind while the news crew takes their places on the helicopters. The squad leaders will each pick someone to stay here, and we'll divide the CBS people into the squads. We'll be going back into the Dog's Head, and this time I want everyone to carry an extra hundred rounds for the 60 gunners. Squad leaders will run a weapons check in half an hour, and I want everyone ready on the flight line by 0900 hours. Any questions?" Lieutenant Hugele asked, knowing that with this group there'd have to be.

Beal spoke up first. "Why the Dog's Head?"

"Because that's where we had our dog fight with the NVA, and CBS'd like to get some action film, if they can. They've been flying with the scouts and gunships all week and haven't gotten anything, so I guess they want to round it out with some ground patrols, and that's where we come in. Gentlemen, I want you to take it slow and easy and safe. Sergeant Burrows's squad had point last time so, Sergeant Jorgenson, your squad will take it this time. CBS'll get their film, and we'll get back in one piece. Any more questions?''

"Yes, sir," Cortez said. "Do you think they can film my good side? After all, I have my fans to consider.''

Everyone laughed at the moment, but when the lieutenant dismissed us, the mood became more somber; our minds and imaginations turned to thoughts of the Dog's Head . . .

By 0900 the helicopters were lining upon the flight line, while a Pink Team took off on its customary lead mission. From the TOC, the captain was leading the news crew that would go out on patrol with us. There was one on-air personality, Richard Threlkeld, a cameraman, and one sound man. Blue saluted Funk, who returned it and then introduced the visitors to the lieutenant and the platoon sergeant.

While they were making the introductions, the rest of us saddled up and made our way to the awaiting helicopters. Squad 4-4 would take the point on the mission, which meant we'd also take the lead helicopter. Lead was our place in formation, and it had become something of a superstition with us. We knew it made no sense and that it really didn't mean a damn thing if we didn't do it, nevertheless we took our customary position.

We flew past Nui Ba Den on our right, past LZ Grant, beyond to Carolyn and then veered off toward the Dog's Head, which was flanked on three sides by Cambodia. We were being lifted in so CBS would have something for Walter Cronkite to show on his six o'clock evening news, and for the most part we were angry about it. We felt as though we were being used. Sorry, Walter, that's the way it is, too.

When we touched down, the cameraman was busy filming the landing, thinking that maybe he was immune to the war as he leaned further out of the opened helicopter to get a better shot with his shoulder-carried camera.

Taking the landing zone proved to be easy enough. There was no enemy fire, and when we raced to the tree line we were surprised that it had been so quiet. Of course, it was unnaturally quiet for a reason.

"They here," Hue said, studying the ground around us. The soft orange soil revealed numerous boot prints. A few feet into the tree line, the South Vietnamese soldier found some hastily dropped equipment. Off to the right an antiaircraft position, a deep pit with a mound in the center for the .52-caliber heavy machine gun, lay recently abandoned. Scattered machine-gun rounds in broken links lay around the pit, where an NVA soldier's pith helmet lay on its side.

"You think we'll find anything?" the photographer asked. Easygoing, he seemed indifferent to the obvious danger. But then, maybe it wasn't so obvious for him.

"Count on it," I said.

"Why?"

"Because he said so." I motioned to Hue.

"If it gets tense and we lose somebody, pick up his rifle and fire."

"But I'm a newsman," he said as though I'd said something wrong.

"Look, after the battle's over, the NVA will probably feel very sorry that they shot you, but chances are if we have enough fire power, we can keep that from happening."

The photographer nodded, not really convinced of my assessment, and off he headed toward Burrows's squad to get his pictures.

"Those folks think they're invincible?" Beal asked as he studied the CBS news crew. The three of them stood surveying the landing zone and running sound and lighting checks.

"I don't know. Seems that way."

Beal and I turned back to Hue, whose face registered concern. "They here," he said again nodding at his own assessment. "They here."

Hue took the point, while Beal and I had our people move slowly into the tree line behind him. We were halted even before we could enter the tree line as Hue came across a trench line that surrounded the landing zone. Unlike the last one we'd found, this one showed signs of recent use. The edges were falling in where NVA soldiers had pushed off to get farther into the forest only minutes before. Less than two miles from Cambodia, we wondered if they had fled back across the border or if they were trying to draw us in. A scout observation helicopter flew ahead of us to draw enemy fire. It also helped to drown out the noise we made as we moved. That had proved to be a useful tactic in the past, and we hoped it would serve us again now.

Fifteen minutes later Hue came across a trail we knew he'd sooner or later find. Braun said that Apache Six wanted us to follow it toward the border to see what we could find. Beal and I suggested we leave a blocking force just inside the tree line to keep any North Vietnamese Army soldiers who might be following us from blocking us in. Blue said it was a good idea but he turned us down. "If we hit it, I don't want us separated."

We knew he was right, but it didn't sit well with either of us. If we encountered an NVA force ahead of us, then those who were following would close the trap behind us. After an hour of moving along the trail, Stephenson brought the radio traffic to our attention. "The low bird says he has all kinds of movement up ahead of us. Six is asking for Blue's assessment of the ground situation. Here, listen. Sounds like we're turning around."

Stephenson passed the radio's handset to Beal who finally smiled. "We are. The old man and Blue don't think it's worth the risk. That's show biz, folks. Best to have the news folks film live soldiers than a Vietnamese reenactment of the Alamo."

"Good," I said. Hue nodded in agreement. I'd never seen him so nervous, and that bothered me. A question brought me out of my thoughts. It was Dennis Henderson, a spec four in another squad, who was given the task of walking point on the way out. "I was wondering if you'd give me a hand on point," he said.

"What's up?"

"I got a new guy as my slack man," he said, pointing to one of the platoon's new arrivals. "I'd feel better knowing I had someone I could rely on. I was wondering if you could help me out?" Henderson wasn't the type to ask for anything he didn't need. Point had become my specialty, and with Hue's help I was getting pretty good at it. Maybe good wasn't the right word. I was getting used to it, as was Beal, and we'd earned a reputation for walking point. The last firefight in the Dog's Head seemed to enhance it.

"Sure," I said to the soldier, who seemed relieved. Besides, I didn't like being in the middle of the platoon. I preferred the point because when something happened, you knew exactly what and where it was. You didn't have that helpless feeling of hearing the war going on around you and not knowing who or what you were fighting. I argued the merits of walking point with Braun one night while we pulled guard on a perimeter bunker. He wondered what I was trying to prove.

"I'm not trying to prove anything. Being on point makes me feel like I'm in control, like I have a say in all the crap that's going on around me."

"Bullshit! Your trouble is you got this good-guy mentality and for some silly-ass reason you try to come across as a nineteen-year-old Lone Ranger with Hue as your trusty Indian companion."

"Twenty. I turned twenty in February."

"Yeah, and you probably asked for a mask and silver bullets for

presents, too. Look," he said with frustration, "let some of the
other people pull their load. Even Hue's smart enough to give it a
rest sometimes."

I told him I would, and he left it at that. Until he saw me
moving up to the point. The big radioman shook his head and
frowned.

"I'm gonna help out on point, Blue," I said. "The lieutenant
told me to take it easy going back."

I said I would, smiled to Braun, and took the point. Henderson
and I would run a split point. He'd move along one side of the
trail, I'd work the other. Returning on the same trail went against
every principle the Rangers had drilled into my head, but I didn't
make policy, I just followed it. I did, however, decide to follow
my own pace, and that pace was slow.

Less than fifteen minutes into the return trek, I came across a
small side trail that had showed no signs of recent usage. I looked
down the small path, at the GI bootprints. Probably one of our
guys had taken a few steps down the path only to backtrack to the
main trail and follow it toward the border. GI bootprints with the
familiar track pattern of the jungle boot—only other tracks criss-
crossed them. Kneeling to get a better look, I heard an NVA
soldier scream in surprise. I looked up. He was standing less than
ten feet away, firing at me as he turned to run.

Something hit me in the right thigh driving me back and down
as though I'd been hit with a very hot baseball bat. My leg was
burning, and I returned fire as I fell, hitting the soldier in the side
and back as he turned. Then I saw the orange bursts of AK-47 fire
as another soldier behind him shot me again. The second hit felt
like someone had kicked me, and when I aimed to fire at him, I
managed to get off two shots before the magazine in my rifle was
empty. I turned to see if anyone was nearby to help me. No one.
Henderson hadn't yet cleared the bend in the trail, and when I was
shot, the rest of the platoon dived for cover. Close by there were
no large trees or anything else to hide behind. Lying on the trail,
I wondered if that was how it would end. As I fumbled for another
magazine, the NVA opened up on me again. I felt the dirt kicking
up around me and hits to my foot and side. My right front thigh
muscle had ballooned out in a bleeding surge. My left leg was
growing numb, and my back hurt. I knew I had to do something
soon or die, but before I could come up with anything reasonable
I saw a small Vietnamese soldier racing around the bend. It was
Hue, running and firing and jumping in front of me giving me the
time and protective fire I needed to crawl to safety. When I'd

finally made it behind the high roots of a tree, Hue came bounding back firing as he did. John Wayne Hue, all 120 pounds of him! Next to him was Henderson.

"You okay?" he said, while Porky came up to support us, tearing up the jungle with short bursts. North Vietnamese returned the small-arms fire. They were the blocking force but we hadn't given them time to set up their ambush.

Taking out my compress bandage, I tried to put it on the exposed muscle but the severed pieces pushed out the sides of the small bandage. Blood spilled through and down my fingers. The tissue was silly putty that wouldn't take shape anymore. No matter what I did the torn muscle wouldn't fit back into the skin.

Someone was yelling for a medic while I struggled with the bandage. When I finally realized it wouldn't be enough, I took off my shirt and tied it around the leg using the sleeves as ties. The flow of blood slowed from that wound. I was somewhat relieved. That wasn't so bad. But as I sat against the base of the tree the ground beneath me was filling up with a dark red ooze. Christ! It was my other leg, the left back thigh. I saw where the bullet hole had ripped through the pantleg. I ripped it open. When I did, the back of the leg fell out with it. Any sense of relief I'd been feeling fell with it.

"I'm gonna give you a shot of morphine," Doc Devalle said as he knelt beside me, inspecting the wounds. Then he hurriedly dug through his aid bag.

The firefight was still going on, and I saw the CBS cameraman bounding up to film the event only to be stopped by the heavy gunfire.

"Can you move?" Doc asked. I knew what he wanted to do. He wanted to try to help shoulder me back down the trail. I could hear Blue yelling over the noise of the small battle, "Get him back here if you can move him and remember to stop the bleeding!" Doc couldn't, but he slowed it and called for a medevac helicopter.

"Doc, there's no way you can carry me, and if you try we're both going to get shot! And I don't want to get shot again!" I said while he tried to argue, but Devalle knew I was right.

"You take off and I'll get back there, even if I have to crawl. Now, *go!*" I yelled. The morphine was beginning to kick in, and I could feel the pain being pushed back. Porky was giving me all of the cover fire I'd need to get back and Blue had the platoon create a wall of fire to help us move. But when I got to my feet and tried to run, I fell hard on my face. The legs refused to work.

Morphine's only good for the reduction of pain. It doesn't do anything for torn muscles. As I wildly clawed to get to safety, I felt two hands reach under my shoulder, pulling me up. It was Henderson helping me get to cover and supporting me as we moved. My legs were useless.

"God, I'm sorry," he said over and over again, while he exposed himself to the gunfire that was hitting the jungle around us. My left leg didn't offer any support but I used the right and my rifle as a crutch to awkwardly move along with his gait.

Henderson and Doc lowered me behind a fallen log while I tried to tell Blue what was going on. When Braun, Blue's RTO, saw who was wounded, he angrily shook his head and gave me an I-told-you-so look. I could also see there wasn't any satisfaction in it.

I was a mess. My legs were bloodied, my canteen had a bullet hole in it, and the heel of my jungle boot was missing a sizeable chunk where another NVA bullet had ripped it away.

"What's up there?" Blue asked.

"It—it was an NVA soldier . . . uniform, rucksack, helmet," I replied. "I think they were setting up an ambush, only they didn't have time to get it ready."

All the while the CBS soundman was sticking a microphone in my face. I swore at him, but that didn't stop him. He seemed determined to get the story, while the cameraman moved around to get different angles. Blue was getting reports from the other squad leaders over the radio, and he left Devalle to treat me.

"The medevac's twenty minutes out," Braun said to Blue, who nodded.

"There's no way we can get him back to the landing zone in time, so we'll set up a perimeter here. We'll request a jungle penetrater and lift him out," Blue said, and then to Sergeant Andreu he said, "We'll secure it here," leaving the platoon sergeant to carry out the plan.

Meanwhile the news crew were getting their story as the reporter carried out an impromptu interview. When he asked my full name, Braun said, "He's our resident hero. He's young and doesn't know any better."

During the interview the pain began to overcome the masking effects of the morphine. I could feel a burning sensation on my wounds, while the legs grew increasingly heavy and unresponsive. An exposed electric wire raced through my body to my mind where the current was pressing against my senses.

"Hang in there, Jorgy," a voice said as a hand rubbed my head.

Braun was also yelling into the handset, trying to find out where in the hell the medevac helicopter was.

Would I ever be able to take it easy again? My life didn't flash before my eyes, but a glimpse of my future did. I saw myself then as a cripple, then as a man with no legs. I saw the faces of my family and friends drop when they saw me. Incomplete, less than what they remembered. A cripple.

"It doesn't look like you broke any bones," Doc Devalle was saying.

"What?"

"It doesn't look that bad, Jorgy. Looks like you're going home."

I nodded and managed a thin smile. "Thanks, Doc."

More questions came from the news reporter, and I answered them in stride, the wounded warrior glib and in pain at the same time. Great copy! The stuff of Pulitzer prizes for them; the rest of us had nothing but the war.

The medevac helicopter hovered over the rain forest, lowering the metal wire that held the jungle penetrater hook. Doc Devalle tried to shoulder me over to the hook. When we stumbled and fell, Braun picked me up and carried me the rest of the way. As the helicopter swayed trying to remain in place, the platoon provided cover support. The big man guided the line until it was out of his reach. On the way up I was pulled through a tree. All of Doc Devalle's work was for nothing because the bandages were ripped away by the vines and branches. The faces of the medic and doorgunner on the helicopter registered worry, and as the medic pulled me aboard, he told me how lucky I was. Lucky? I didn't feel lucky.

"See that?" he said pointing to a hole in the deck. "That's a bullet hole. The fuckers tried to shoot us down! You're lucky. We're lucky," he said, examining the leg wounds and using one hand to stop the bleeding while he pulled out a large gauze to cover the left leg that was spilling over on the helicopter floor. A small stream of blood flowed around the bullet hole while the helicopter lowered its nose and raced off to the field hospital in Tay Ninh.

By the time we touched down on the helipad just outside the base camp's field hospital, the medic had much of the bleeding stopped and had managed to get an IV solution going. Loaded onto a stretcher, I was again raced into the emergency room. Nurses, medics, and a team of doctors cut away my remaining clothes, took X-rays, shaved my legs around the wounds, and then whisked me off to an operating room, where they closed off the ruptured veins and arteries then bandaged my legs with miles of gauze. I lost track of time, drifting in and out of vague dreams. I awoke startled and sweating, reaching for my rifle.

A duty nurse came to my side with a small white cup. The nurse was a big, comfortable blond with tired eyes.

"Here, take these," she said.

"What is it?"

She laughed a small laugh. "Aspirin. I'm afraid it's all you can have for now. The morphine hasn't worn off yet."

I wanted to argue the point but took the aspirin instead, hoping it would stop the constant pounding-throbbing of the legs, while the small electric wire in my mind was steadily increasing its intensity. I gripped the bed so tightly my knuckles whitened and my fingers hurt.

"When's my next shot of morphine?"

"You won't be receiving any more. I'm sorry, but you've already had two, and the policy is not to give you any more. I'm sorry," she said again. "I really am."

As she walked away, I got a good look at the empty surgical ward around me. I was its only occupant, the only patient in the long corridorlike ward with its smart, fresh beds. It was the first time I'd slept between sheets since being treated for malaria in Saigon, and they felt odd, not at all like I thought they would. The mattress, too, was softer than it should've been, or was it that I'd slept on too much ground or two many cots to view it any other way?

The headache was slowly receding, when there was a commotion at the desk, and the Blues came through the door and past the duty desk. Lieutenant Hugele led the way, while the others swarmed in around him.

Braun broke the ice. "Well, did they shoot your pecker off?"

"Fourteen inches of it," I said, "so that leaves me with only fourteen."

Braun smiled. "It's a shame they didn't hit you in the smartass. So how you doing, kid?"

"Fine," I lied. They'd come to see their buddy who was going home, and I saw no reason to make them feel any worse, especially Henderson, who stood at the end of the bed, looking guilty. "They're taking good care of me here, and the doctor says they'll be sending me to Japan soon."

"You didn't break any bones, that's good," Doc Devalle said, happy with his field diagnosis.

"We've boxed up your things, and supply will send them home for you," the lieutenant said. Beal nodded. "If there's anything you need before they ship you home, you just let us know, you hear?"

Burrows was there fidgeting. "Sorry about the Chinese mine thing," he said apologetically.

"I guess it wasn't my time, then," I said. Apology accepted.

"Do the nurses put out?" Manning asked, staring at the big, blond nurse behind the duty desk, his ebony face held a wry smile.

"Only for patients," I replied. Manning laughed, slapped me on the shoulder, and told me to get him some, too. One by one they said their good-byes. A few of the new guys who I really didn't know well drifted away until the only ones who remained were my buddies. Among whom was Henderson, who wasn't going to leave without absolution. I knew the feeling. I needed it from Torres and Zap, but they'd died, making it impossible. That had haunted me ever since.

"Thanks for your help today, Dennis," I said to the light-framed soldier. "If you hadn't picked me up, I wouldn't have made it back."

"Yeah, and if it wasn't for me, you wouldn't have gotten shot," he said apologetically.

"Are you kidding? I already have two Purple Hearts! Bullets seem to seek me out. Seriously, man, thanks for the help."

His deep set brown eyes searched mine for a minute and then relaxed when he saw that I meant it. "Take care, Jorgy," he said, tapping my bed.

When I turned back to Beal, he was slowly shaking his head. "I can't take you anywhere! Volunteering to take the point again! Did your momma drop you on your head as a baby a few times or what?"

"Look who's talking? You're on your second tour!"

"True, but you're leading in Purple Hearts. The news people called you a hero today."

"Is that right? Or did they just say that to fill in their story?"

The wiry North Carolinian shook his head. "Nope. Braun filled them in on your medals, so you're a bona fide hero."

I pushed back trying to get a better position against the pillows that held me in place. "I don't feel like a hero. I feel tired, Ed, like I've just been dragged through the mud and left out in the sun to dry. Those folks come over here looking for something that doesn't exist. I was so fucking scared when that NVA shot me. I couldn't think about anything other than trying to stop him from shooting me again. All I kept thinking was if the guy hadn't been so afraid himself and if he'd stayed there and aimed instead of trying to shoot at me while running, I'd be dead.''

"But you're not. You're alive and going home. Blue says that Doctor says you'll be okay. No serious damage, so take that as a sign, Jorgy. Go the hell home. You earned it, so do it. Look, I have to go. I'll be back tomorrow, so just take it easy. You hear me?"

I nodded, watching him go. Lieutenant Hugele appeared in the doorway and came down the hall at a formal gait. It was hard to take the military officer out of the man but Blue was trying. "Sergeant Jorgenson, the doctor tells me you're going to be fine," he said, while I wondered who this doctor was that told everyone how fine my ripped and throbbing legs had felt.

"Nothing serious, sir," I said.

"You probably kept us from walking into an ambush."

"Maybe. I dunno, sir."

"Well I do, and I appreciate it, so does the platoon. You've been an outstanding asset to us, and you'll be missed. You're a good soldier," he said, extending his hand. In the military, words like "outstanding" were used frequently by the officer corps; the extended hand offered the real sentiment. Your buddies and those who liked or respected you would extend their hands, linking the brotherhood bond. Others simply acknowledged your rank, keeping it impersonal and distant.

I shook the lieutenant's hand and added him to my list of buddies. After he left, the duty nurse returned to ask me if I wanted a cold soft drink. Even though the hospital ward was air conditioned, it was a field hospital, and the wards were only moderately cool.

When she returned with an ice-cold can of Dr. Pepper, she stayed and chatted awhile. After all, I was her only charge.

"It's nice that your friends came to see you," she said.

"Yeah, swell." My legs were pounding again. The pain was pushing up my back to my head.

"I'm always amazed how you infantry soldiers stay so close. It must be comforting."

"Could you spare me the pep talk." I'd cut her short.

She said if there was anything else I needed then just call. I felt like a bastard. She was just trying to be nice and help me pass the time by making me feel a little better. The trouble is I didn't want to feel better. I was too busy feeling miserable, thank you, too mired in self-pity to want to see the good side to any of this. Damn it! I deserved to go home, deserved to be treated kindly, and deserved the ice-cold Dr. Pepper! Who in hell did she think she was nosing in on my life anyway by trying to be nice? God, I was a jerk.

"Nurse?" I said as she looked up from her desk and then moved around to the counter and down the corridor to see what I wanted.

"Yes, Sergeant?" she said coolly.

"I'm sorry."

"For what?"

"For being an asshole. What you asked about earlier? Anyway, it is nice and comforting to have buddies like those. If it wasn't for them I wouldn't have made it out. They're good people."

"That seems to be the same with all you infantry types. A common bond."

"Maybe it's because it's the only real thing we have to believe in anymore. Most of us don't even know or care why we're here. All we know is that we are here. And maybe the only thing we really have is each other? I dunno . . . probably sounds stupid, huh?"

The big nurse shook her head. "I think it sounds admirable."

She had all kinds of questions for me, and I knew she was genuinely interested in what was really going on out there. Or maybe it was just verbal therapy. She stayed and talked. Maybe it was therapy for both of us. For the longest time we talked about everything and nothing at all. Late-night talk, not just to kill time but to keep the time and situation from killing us.

The morphine was wearing off and the pain pressing forward. She gave me what the doctor prescribed, which didn't seem to work at all. It was the conversation and Dr. Pepper that kept me from giving in to the burning gunshot wounds. We talked about the war, the hospital, the Rangers, Apache Troop, the dust and the endless process of trying to keep it out of the surgical wards. We laughed about shortages, absurdities, the excesses we'd experience when we got home, and when the laughter diminished along with the pain, we said goodnight.

"Try to get a good night's sleep," she said, helping me get comfortable amid the pillows. My legs were useless, and she helped me move by reaching back beneath my arms. When she started to walk back to her desk the big, comfortable blond nurse with the tired eyes stopped, turned back around, and smiled. "Thanks. I enjoyed our talk. I really did."

"Me, too," I said as she smiled again. I was thinking that

there is power in confession and a kindness as well. Watching her walk back to her duty station, I was touched by its healing process. The exposed wire of pain in my mind had been somehow lessened and the pounding-throbbing of my bandaged legs diminished to a slow, steady beat and a faint echo in sync with my heartbeat. I was bone-weary and restless, but I couldn't sleep. It would be days before I finally rested with any real or reasonable comfort, and then only briefly. A fire support base was hit several days later, and the ward began to fill with the wounded.

Although I tried, it was hard to feel sorry for myself when so many others around me had more serious injuries. Head wounds from bullets or shrapnel, bodies with limbs torn away in fractions of seconds, and nearly gutted soldiers were screaming, moaning, or crying throughout the hectic days and long, drawn-out nights.

Small, private battles were going on all around me; battles that could no longer be won, just refought with the same outcome over and over again: I was lucky and I knew it, but it was the kind of luck that offered little consolation.

I hated the surgical ward and the feeling it left with me; the feeling that my emotions were slowly being drained from my body, spilling from the jagged rips and wounds of those around me.

And maybe what really bothered me was that there was nothing I could do about it, nothing that might ease their hurt or pain. I wanted to run but didn't have the legs for it.

CHAPTER SIXTEEN

From the 45th Surgical Field Hospital in Tay Ninh, I was choppered out to the 25th Infantry Division's Hospital in Cu Chi and then immediately placed on another helicopter for the long ride to Long Binh. The hospital there was set up for surgery and would be the last stop before Camp Zama, Japan. The doctors in Tay Ninh said I'd be sent to Japan to recover and then home, but first they said I'd have to be operated on in Long Binh.

"I thought you guys already did that!" I said to a major who shook his head. He said all they did was close off the ruptured veins and arteries. Any real work would have to be done in Long Binh. Besides, I'd have to drain for seven days, he said, leave the wound open to reduce the risk of infection and of having to open me up a second time. Great. Just dandy.

In Long Binh I was placed on the surgical ward. Unlike the ward in Tay Ninh, this one was filled with the broken soldiers the field hospitals couldn't handle. Next to me lay a soldier who'd been shot six times in an ambush. He never spoke to any of us, and at night placed his face in his pillow and cried until he finally fell asleep. On the other side was a gangly doorgunner missing part of his right shoulder where a Viet Cong bullet hit under his armpit, changed directions on impact, and pushed upward and out the shoulder. The arm was held in place with wire and bandage. Three beds up a small, squat sergeant I knew from shake 'n' bake school at Fort Benning lay with a tube in his lungs, while a square bandage covered the entry wound where an exploding mortar round had torn his lungs and nearly killed him. Yellow-red fluid pushed out of the tube and into a large glass jar on the floor beside the bed; the type of jars that people back home were making terrariums out of. Robust and cocky during training, Nooks seemed smaller now, more subdued. Farther down, a soldier with a bandaged face lay breathing through a plastic insert in his throat. A bullet had destroyed his mouth and nose. To remain alive, he breathed through the plastic disc, short, raspy breaths. At night the faceless soldier tapped against his metal bed frame to a tune only he could hear.

Around the ward were only a small number of the war's casualties. We were the lucky ones; the sour smell from the burn ward told us how lucky we were. Still a gloom lingered over the ward. Two times a day we screamed and cried in succession while teams of medics and nurses cleaned out our wounds with a large plastic turkey baster filled with hydrogen peroxide. In the morning and then again late in the afternoon, the teams would go up and down the line, removing the bandages that clung to our wounds like tape. Then, using the baster the teams worked in the wounds, killing the germs and infections that inevitably tried to grow there. The teams worked quietly, apologizing with their eyes, while they performed the grisly task. No matter how hard we tried to be tough, to be macho and brave, we screamed or groaned, squeezing our eyes shut, as tears welled up and over the tightly closed eyes and streamed down our faces.

We would drain for a week, and then we'd be operated on, closing the wounds and slowly putting us back together.

On my seventh day, I was wheeled into surgery, given sodium pentathol and was unconscious in seconds. Moments later I awoke to the sound of a doctor telling me that I was okay. "Okay, so stop screaming, Sergeant. You're safe here. It's okay."

Apparently I'd been fighting a battle in my mind, and I was screaming until he calmed me down. But where was the operating room? What was I doing back in the ward? It was hours later, and the surgery was over, and finally I was awake. Looking around, I was embarrassed, while the others stared at me blankly.

Then the doorgunner broke the news to me. "Hey! It's you! You're a hero. The radio just said so. Hero: The sergeant who likes to walk point. On the news, man! Swear to God!"

"What?"

"You're on the news. You and your platoon. Let's see, they talked about someone named Blue—"

"My lieutenant," I said.

"Yeah, and someone named Bloor, and Del something, your medic . . ."

"Devalle."

"Yeah, right," he said excitedly. "But mostly about you and

hundreds of North Vietnamese soldiers. Man, you're a hero!''

I hadn't heard the news report, but later medics, nurses, and doctors came by to see me and talk to me about it. The next morning on rounds, my doctor smiled, saying I was going to Japan. "Oh yeah, was that really you on the news?"

"I don't know," I said, "I hadn't heard it."

"Damn right, Doc!" the doorgunner interrupted. "Jorgenson's a hero!"

"I heard it was you. Anyway, the XO here wants to present you with a Purple Heart tomorrow, so be prepared for it."

I said I would, thinking how crazy the war had become for me. I left the Rangers because I couldn't take the attention caused by the Silver Star, and now it was starting all over again. Where would I run to now? I was just happy to be leaving the country. I understood that part of the reasoning behind my going to the Blues was revenge. I wanted to get even with the North Vietnamese, to kill a few more for killing my friends, and that anger had kept my fear from overtaking me. Only now I wasn't angry anymore. I was tired of killing and tired of pretending that I wasn't afraid. It had all seemed so easy before I saw my first dead man or killed my first enemy. There was even a certain degree of fascination and excitement in the whole macabre business. Initially. But then, I slowly began to see what so many others had seen before me, that war is an expensive crapshoot, and no matter how well trained you are, it's still a random toss of the dice. Revenge wasn't a good enough motive anymore, nor was trying to live up to the childish image I had of what a hero should be. If I was a hero, then I was a frightened one, one who hadn't understood the cost of the action. I wanted to rest. I wanted to get away from the war but also knew that I never would. Like Sisyphus, I'd be forever condemned to pushing the rock back up the hill only to have it fall before I reached my goal.

Sergeant Hero was trembling again. I knew that it would only last a while or maybe the rest of my life.

The following morning, the division commander and his sergeant major came down the long bed-lined corridor, talking to the soldiers in his division while the division's senior enlisted man pinned Cav patches to our medical charts and asked us if there was anything we needed. Anything at all. When he came to my bed the sergeant major whispered something in the general's ear, and the general's face turned into a smile. A photographer stood idly nearby.

"So you're the sergeant I've heard so much about!" he said extending a hand. "A Troop, 1st of the 9th Cav, isn't it?"

"Yes, sir," I said, "Apache Troop Blues."

"Yes, uh-huh," he replied cryptically. "Well, you made a good impression on the news people, and it made the Cav look good. You did a fine job for us, troop, and if there's anything you need at all, you just let us know." When the general turned to leave, the sergeant major presented me with a Polaroid picture of the general's visit. Before he left too, I wondered aloud why the soldier next to me didn't get a picture as well.

"He's not in our division. He's with the 25th," the photographer said as he trailed behind the general officer.

I looked at the picture. The general was smiling and shaking my hand. I was wearing a stupid expression. In the background I could see the soldier who lay in the next bed, the 25th Infantry soldier who'd been shot six times. The general's visit was designed to help boost our morale, but it did little for those in the other beds who were from other units. I threw the picture away, thinking that somehow it didn't seem right. I was in a foul mood, so when the hospital's XO came down the corridor, wearing hospital whites and bearing a medal box, eight-by-ten certificate, and a fleshy handshake, I didn't give him the respect I should have.

"Congratulations, Sergeant. How does it feel to have your first Purple Heart?" A ward nurse, medic, and doctor on duty stood behind him smiling.

Shaking his hand, I read the name on the award certificate. Jorgensen. S-E-N.

"Well, it's my third Purple Heart, sir, and you spelled my name wrong."

The executive officer looked flustered, stared at the certificate, and then stormed off.

"You better watch it," the 25th Infantry Division soldier said, talking to me for the first time, "or they won't think you're grateful for the opportunity to be here."

I laughed for the first time since I'd been there and along with the others who'd heard what he said. The XO would never understand the punch line, but we laughed with everything we had.

After ten days I was informed by the doctor on duty that I wouldn't be going to Japan.

"We're going to send you to Cam Ranh Bay to recover. Then we'll send you back to your unit. Tomorrow we'll send you out," he said, as he made notations in my chart.

"I was told I would be going to Japan."

The doctor looked up from the chart. "No, you didn't break any bones. The bullets only ripped through muscle, and you're lucky, too, because had they hit the bone, you very well might have lost your legs."

"I don't feel lucky," I said. I could feel the anger building inside of me.

"What?"

"I said I don't feel so lucky, damn it! You want to send me to Cam Ranh Bay and then back to my unit!"

"That's right, you can relax on the beaches and go through physical therapy . . ."

"Fuck it! Send me back to my unit."

"No, no. You'll be going to Cam Ranh Bay first," he said in a tone that suggested he was doing me a favor.

"I want to go back to my unit tomorrow. What's the difference whether you send me back tomorrow or three weeks from tomorrow. I didn't break a bone anyway!"

"At ease, soldier!" he said, his tone abruptly changing.

"Go to hell," I said, while the argument spilled over the immediate area.

"He deserves to go to Japan, too! What's this shit you're trying to pull anyway?" the doorgunner yelled, while the 25th Infantry Division soldier in the bed next to me kept swearing at the doctor from his confined position.

"Fine. You want to go back to your unit and recover, that's all right by me. I just want to give you a few weeks on the beach to relax before—"

"Before what, Doc?" the gunner said, "Before he gets shot again. He's got three Purple Hearts now, for Christ's sake!" only the doctor wasn't listening, choosing instead to retreat under the barrage of insults those around me were throwing at him.

The next morning, the ward medic helped me get out of bed. My left leg was sewn together with metal wire to hold the torn muscles in place while the right thigh was closed with stitches. Covered in thick gauze wrapping, I hobbled down the corridor, saying my good-byes to my new-found friends, stopping at the duty desk to thank the nurses for their care and genuine concern.

"You really should go to Cam Ranh Bay," one said, mildly scolding me for my bullheaded stand. "It wasn't the doctor's policy, it's the army's," she added.

"I know," I said, "but he was the closest representative I could find. You'll have to forgive me but my attitude sucks these days."

"Take care, Sergeant," she said.

I said I would. What other choice was there?

CHAPTER SEVENTEEN

Clearing the Long Binh Hospital was easy and impersonal enough. The admin section cut me travel orders to my unit, and upon turning in my hospital-issue pajamas and bathrobe, I was issued a new set of jungle fatigues and, worst of all, new jungle boots! Half of the unofficial-official uniform were a grunt's boots. The older, more worn and rubbed white they were, the higher the soldier's status. The other half was the jungle fatigue uniform itself. New uniforms, like new boots, were painfully new. Bright green fatigues and rich, black and green boots were like neon signs reading, "I'm new! I'm new!"

My old uniform had been cut from me at the field hospital in Tay Ninh, as were my bloody boots. Fortunately, a nurse had managed to cut away my patches and nametag and put them in a small brown bag, along with my personal effects.

"Do you have a tailor's shop around here somewhere?" I asked the hospital's supply sergeant. He said there was one a few buildings down.

Tailor shops are a regular fixture on most military installations, and Vietnam was no exception. Patches had to be sewn on, uniforms tailored, and usually these tailoring services were found in conjunction with a base laundry.

Finding the tailor shop, I handed over my shirt and waited while an old Vietnamese woman, using a foot-pedaled machine, sewed me back into veteran status, my faded combat infantry badge, Cav patch, and Ranger scroll looking out of place on the new uniform. Sighing when it was handed over, I paid the old woman and then with a small degree of satisfaction went out to face the war again. A bus was leaving the hospital area for Bien Hao in a few hours, only I didn't want to hang around any longer. I wanted to get back to Tay Ninh as soon as possible and there, among friends, figure out my next course of action. I decided to hitchhike to Bien Hoa on one of the many military vehicles that departed the unusually large Long Binh facility. When I eventually made it to the air base I'd use the travel orders to hop a ride to Phuoc Vinh and then once again to get to Tay Ninh. The trouble was I couldn't walk very well. My leg muscles were rigid and tight, so I moved slowly at a stiff gait, a Charlie Chaplin waddle-walk, using my heels and toes to move instead of the muscles that would usually carry me with a healthy stride. I swore at myself thinking that maybe I shouldn't have been so quick to want to get back to Tay Ninh. I needed physical therapy, which I would've received at Cam Ranh Bay, only I blew that chance. The Tay Ninh field hospital had a physical therapy facility, which I knew I'd be spending some time at, and the sooner I got back to A Troop, the sooner I could recover.

After a quarter of a mile, my legs were screaming, the stitches and metal wire pulling on the skin, rubbing back and forth and sending a warm ooze into the gauze bandages that I knew would stick to the wound when they were replaced. I could see a gate leading out of the installation a block or so ahead, so standing beside the road I put a thumb out and waited. Two jeeps stopped with no luck. Neither was heading where I needed to go. Finally, a three-quarter-ton truck pulled over.

"Where you heading, Sarge?" a spec-five asked from the passenger's seat, while a PFC watched on with indifference.

"Tay Ninh eventually. Right now though I'm trying to get to Bien Hoa."

The spec-five smiled. "No problem," he said. "Hop on."

If walking proved to be a problem, then climbing into the high bed of a truck proved to be even more difficult. After a few minutes of trying to pull myself up, using my upper body strength, I managed to get my stomach on the tailgate, bending at the stomach and unable to swing my legs over.

"What the hell's wrong with you?" the spec-five asked, getting out to see what was taking me so long. "You look like a monkey fucking a football!"

"Can you give me a hand?" I asked.

"What for?"

"Because I just got out of the hospital. I got shot in both legs and I can't bend them very well."

The spec-five's expression changed from sarcasm to surprise, while the PFC's round freckled face registered shock. "You got shot!'' he said while the spec-five helped me over the tailgate, suddenly quiet.

"Yeah. I'm heading back to my unit now.''

"How come you're not in the hospital if you can't walk?'' the PFC asked. I decided not to go into it. Any way I explained it, I'd still sound like a fool.

"I can walk. I just can't walk that well yet.''

"Oh,'' the PFC said. He didn't really understand, but he knew that was the only answer he'd receive.

"Thanks,'' I said to the spec-five who only nodded. "Drive,'' he said to the PFC who turned back in the seat, shifted the truck in gear, and then headed for Bien Hoa. The PFC was easy to answer. It would be Beal and Braun whom I'd have trouble with.

Heading out the gate, we drove along the Long Binh installation's perimeter. Concrete bunkers and an intricate maze of barbed wire and antipersonnel mines provided a safe and comfortable buffer against any threat of assault, but if it hadn't been for the perimeter it would be difficult to tell Long Binh from any Stateside army installation. Surely, it was as comfortable—or more so— than Fort Polk, Louisiana, where I went through advanced infantry training! It even looked nicer, for that matter! Here soldiers would write home about the war in terms we wouldn't understand in Tay Ninh, but then I was reasonably certain that grunts in infantry companies would describe a different war from the one I knew as well.

Sitting in the back of the open truck, I knew I was heading back to my own version of the war, a smaller one than that of Long Binh and one a great deal more deadly.

Three Purple Hearts—and I'd been lucky! But I knew my luck was running out. Heading back to Tay Ninh, I felt like the people I'd seen hitchhiking out of Reno, luck and dreams exhausted and heading home with a new perception of reality.

The only consolation I had was knowing that the three Purple Hearts took me out of the field. At least I wouldn't have to go back out on patrol. That was a division policy. A soldier with three Purple Hearts merited a rear-area job, and after eight months in Vietnam, I finally felt I earned one.

From Bien Hao I caught a cargo flight to Tay Ninh, taking the flight out less than thirty minutes after I checked in at the air-base terminal. The trouble was when I landed at Tay Ninh, it was at the far end of the base camp. With my odd walk, I headed down the dirt road toward A Troop. Halfway there an MP patrol stopped me to say that the camp had been hit the night before and that they'd managed to stop an enemy sapper team that had infiltrated the camp. Of the eleven-man force, they'd managed to kill ten, but one was still unaccounted for.

"Keep your eyes open, Sarge," a spec four military policeman said. His spit-shined jungle boots reflected the bright glare from the late afternoon sun.

"I'll do that," I said, smothering a smile. Sure, I would. What the hell could I do anyway? I didn't have a weapon, and I couldn't walk very well. If I accidentally ran into him, he'd probably start laughing. Either that or he'd take a bead at this lame duck and fire.

A half hour later I waddled into the troop area, and as I passed the Blues area, heading for the unit's orderly room, Cortez, who was resting in a hammock, noticed me.

"I don't fucking believe it!" he said. He grinned. "What are you doing here?"

"They sent me back."

"You're kidding." Cortez looked me over. "What for? You ain't Superman, sport."

I shrugged. "Don't I know it. It was either here or Cam Ranh Bay to recover," I said.

"So you took here? Jorgy, what are we going to do with you! You're hopeless!" Cortez was from Southern California; it was unthinkable that I didn't select the beach! Cortez grinned. "Glad to see you're okay. Welcome back, anyway, shithead!"

I received the same greeting in the orderly room. But judging from First Sergeant Sparacino's expression, you'd have thought he had seen a ghost as I stepped through the orderly room door.

"What are you doing back here?"

"They sent me back, Top. Well, actually they were going to send me to Cam Ranh Bay for a few weeks first and then send me back. I just told them to hell with it, send me back to my unit. They did."

He stared at me, dumbfounded. "What am I supposed to do with you?"

"They want me to go through some physical therapy at the field hospital here."

"Jesus, I already sent your personal effects home. They told me you were going out to Japan!"

"They changed their minds."

The older sergeant was perplexed, uncertain really what to do with me. "Look, go back to your hootch and take it easy for a few days until we figure out what they want you to do. As for the troop, I'll tell you right now I don't know what to do with you. I'll see what kind of jobs we have back here, and I'll let you pick. It's the least we can do. Let Sergeant Andreu know you're back." And then when he sat back down behind his desk, he added, "Can you type?"

I shook my head no.

"That's too bad. Schwenke left yesterday, and I need a new company clerk. Well, think about it anyway. He couldn't type all that well, either."

Walking back to the squad's hootch, I opened the door to my sleeping area and found someone polishing his boots on my cot.

"Who are you?" He said. The room was rearranged, all my personal effects gone, and my military gear had been turned into unit supply. In their place the intruder had spread out his belongings. Jesus! It was another new guy shake 'n' bake.

"What are you doing here?"' I asked.

The new guy seemed surprised by my questions, but because he was new he was eager to answer.

"I'm the new assistant squad leader. The old one got greased," he said.

"I'm the old one. This is my room," I said, suddenly resenting the intrusion: *his*? Not mine! Greased was I?

The new-guy sergeant was apologetic as he scooped up his things, saying he'd be more than happy to find another room that wasn't in use. New guys were always eager to help or impress and the shake 'n' bake was doing his best to keep the tradition alive. "So, what's it like? I mean, getting shot and all? How does it feel?" asked the new-guy sergeant.

It was a stupid question, but he was only trying to be sociable. "It feels lousy," I said. "I'll tell you what, go ahead and keep your things here. I'll find a new room." Only the new-guy sergeant wouldn't hear of it.

"No, no. Stay. It's your room. It's okay, really," he said, moving his duffel bag out in the hallway.

"Hey, eh . . . where are you from?"

The new-guy sergeant suddenly smiled. "Pittsburgh," he said, hoping it would mean something.

"Seattle," I said. "How long you been in-country?"

"Two weeks. You?"

"A lifetime," I said. He didn't understand yet; he still had a long way to go.

Friends came and went with unusual frequency, and I spent a great deal of time going through the same information. "Yeah, I'm back. No, they didn't send me home. Yes, I agree it sucks," and so on, until Braun and Manning showed up in the doorway, the large RTO dwarfing the slender soldier.

"See, I told you!" Manning said to the big man, who only stood staring at me as though he still couldn't believe what he was seeing.

"Yeah, I see, but I still don't believe it. It looks like Jorgenson, but it can't be. He got shot, and we sent him home to stay. Judging from his uniform, this here's a new guy who happens to look like Jorgenson, which in itself is tough enough burden to carry, let alone being new to boot!"

"It's nice to be missed," I said, easing into the cot. I had to keep my legs straight. Even sitting had become a difficult task.

"So what are you really doing back here, and don't give me that crap about them sending you." Braun's tone said that if my answer wasn't right then he'd thump me. Jim Braun would've made a great grade-school teacher, a two-hundred-pound brooding bear of a teacher who even the most unruly kids would listen to.

"They wouldn't send me to Japan. It seems I didn't break any bones. Their policy is to keep those with flesh wounds in-country," I explained.

"A broken bone? Is that all?" he said to Manning. "Hold the boy down, and I'll break his knees! Seriously though, why did you come back early?"

"Because I was pissed off with them and the army and their stupid fucking policies. They weren't going to send me home, so I came back to the only other home I've known. I'm not happy about it, either, believe me." My explanation seemed good enough for him at the moment.

"So are you going to take a rear-area job now?" Manning asked. He knew the division's policy toward Purple Hearts as did everyone else in the platoon.

"You bet I will," I said.

"You better," Braun warned. "Here," he said, tossing a worn paperback on my cot. "It's for you. It's your autobiography."

I picked up the paperback: it was by Miguel de Cervantes.

"Don Quixote," I said, thumbing through the book.

"No kidding! I could've sworn it was you. Read it anyway. You two seem to have a lot in common. We'd like to stay and chat, but Manning here has a date with some scouts at the club where he gets to tell them all about his seven-day leave to Bangkok again and something about the benefits of what in legend is referred to as a basket trick. Hobble on over and join us when you can, Tiny Tim.'' The big man smiled, a bear with a friendly grin, before the two left to join the others.

I could recover there and I knew it. It was home or at least as close to one as I'd know in the army, and for the moment that seemed to be enough.

A short while later I heard a knock on my door, followed by the face of Tony Cortez who'd just come back from the orderly room.

"Got some mail for you, Jorgy." He handed me a packet of letters. "Looks like you're popular."

There were five letters in all. Each addressed to Sgt. "Hero" Jorgenson, some to the attention of CBS News, others with variations of the spelling of my name.

I opened the first and made it through the first paragraph before I looked back to see who it was addressed to. It couldn't be me! It had to be for someone else.

"You're a fascist baby killer!'' it read. "You prey on war and its victims. It's a shame you were only wounded and not killed! I hope you lose your legs!!!''

It was unsigned and carried a California postmark. Of the second letter, I only made it through the first paragraph before I stopped. It, too, was of the same nature, though this one held no wishes one way or another. It simply said the war was wrong. I was wrong and what I was doing was sinful. I opened another letter and it thanked me for killing Communists for Jesus. I took the remaining letters and dumped them in the garbage. I didn't kill babies. I didn't murder anyone. I was a soldier in a war, for Christ's sake! Couldn't those silly bastards see that! What did they think Vietnam was anyway? I knew people were protesting the war, marching in the streets, some carrying enemy flags, trying to stop the war. I also knew they got to go home after the marches, putting away their street uniforms and equipment, while we still had the war twenty-four hours a day. Their commitment was emotional, and at times convenient, while our only real commitment was to ourselves and our buddies. Our commitment was to survival. Our emotions were being stretched beyond their limits by war, day in and day out, as we lost more friends to it.

I wouldn't lose my legs, you son of a bitch! Just pieces of them, thank you! And what did it matter if the war was wrong, what did that mean to any of us who were stuck in it?

I laughed at the absurdity of it all and even louder the more I thought of it. From the troop's enlisted club nearby I could hear the sound of music and laughter. My buddies were listening to Manning describe his R&R in Bangkok. Struggling to get to my feet, I wanted to join them. I wanted to laugh with them because I knew we were the crew of the *Titanic*. The big ship was going down around us, and even though we were doing our jobs the best we could, there was nothing we could do to stop it.

In the end there'd be experts and critics to explain how we could have avoided it. There always were and there always would be, but it didn't matter. All that did matter was the laughter and the camaraderie. But limping over to the small building that housed the club, I knew they wouldn't last either.

The ship was sinking, and the band played on, and we were dancing as fast as we could.

CHAPTER EIGHTEEN

During my recovery I was put in charge of the club. I would be its manager, bookkeeper, barkeep, and bouncer, not that it was all that difficult. The club was a twelve-by-twenty-four-foot, single-room hootch—a hut, really—made of long, inch-thin, wooden planks slapped together over a basic frame and topped with corrugated tin roofing. A long bench had been set in place on one side of the room. A crude bar and makeshift tables with folding chairs gave the club its character. Any flavor came from the music and people who used it, primarily those enlisted men within the troop. Occasionally soldiers from other units would come in, but seeing it was a club with private overtones, they'd finish their drinks and depart quickly.

A tape deck provided music and GIs returning from R&R in Hong Kong, Taiwan, Australia, or Thailand brought back reels of their favorite music, which ran the spectrum from country and western to soul. Cultural gaps were jumped musically while the soldiers drank canned beer or warm whiskey.

Schwenke had run the club at night, and First Sergeant Sparacino turned it over to me after he left.

"You get your beer from the class-six yard and the ice down in Tay Ninh at the ice factory. It's $2.50 a block, though the guy in charge will tell you it's three, but he's willing to dicker. You plug in your lights and tape deck to the scouts' generator, and you open at last light. However, since this'll be your only job, you can open at noon and close by midnight," Top said, wiping the sweat from his brow. The afternoon heat was dripping down his round, florid face. The top sergeant had more than the fighting to handle.

"What about the records?"

"There's a ledger book inside the club. I have three hundred dollars in the safe that belongs to the club. You use it to buy the things you need, and use the money you make to go back into the club and keep it self-sustaining. Sergeant Jorgenson, it's all yours," he said, handing me the keys to the padlocks for the club's two doors.

The club smelled like the stale beer that had splattered the concrete floor. The garbage would have to be picked up, ashtrays emptied, and stock inventoried before I could open the doors. Sure enough the ledger was where Top Sparacino said it would be. There were five cases of Black Label beer on hand, a few badly battered mugs, and several half-filled bottles of whiskey and gin beneath the bar on a shelf. There were also ten or so boxes of tapes to choose from, so putting on one marked "Stones," I began my work. When I'd finished it still looked like a run-down dive, but at least it was clean. Signing out a jeep at the motor pool, I drove down to the 25th Infantry Division's class-six yard and purchased twelve cases of beer. Instead of ordering just Black Label, I mixed the order to include a decent supply of Budweiser. Later, with a pass from the orderly room, Manning and I drove into Tay Ninh, weaving in and out of the busy traffic toward the ice factory on the city's edge. Tay Ninh was the spiritual home of the Cao Dai religion, an obscure religion with an elaborate colorful temple within the western province's major city. An odd blend of Eastern and Western beliefs, the Cao Dai listed among their saints such figures as Jesus, Buddha, and the French writer Victor Hugo. The Cao Dai was also a very potent military force. They maintained their own standing army that sometimes fought against the government in Saigon as much as it did against the North Vietnamese.

The city itself was an odd mix of buildings and habitats, with open markets and stores selling a variety of produce and livestock, as well as anything the GIs would buy. Shops and services that never existed before the arrival of the Americans suddenly became thriving enterprises, such as military laundry services, steam baths, and open-front bars blaring a wide range of music, while Vietnamese bar girls smiled and shouted for soldiers to come on in.

When we'd stopped for directions, a bar girl wanted to provide us with more than a directional course.

"You want boom-boom?" she said, chewing gum while she flicked long black hair out of her eyes. Dressed in a short, red dress and sporting white high heels and big loop earrings, she looked out of place in the throng of people dressed more traditionally around us.

"No, just directions," I said. "You know where the ice factory is from here?"

"How about a blow job? Numbah one, you like."

As I laughed another bar girl came out to talk to Manning. "We don't have time today," I said. Manning was disappointed to see an MP jeep driving down the road toward us.

"Uh-oh," he said. The bar girls noticed the military policemen and fled back to the confines of the bar. The smart jeep pulled up beside us, blocking traffic behind it. A big sergeant who could've easily been a lineman for a Texas College football team hid behind dark aviator glasses and an indifferent face. A skinny black spec four, also wearing aviator glasses and a flat, expressionless face, studied us as well.

"What are you doing?" the lineman asked.

"Trying to find the ice factory," I said. "We stopped to get directions."

Still no expression. "Is that right," the lineman said while the skinny spec four looked over our jeep.

"You have any travel orders or a pass?" the lineman asked.

I took out the pass that Sparacino had signed, showed it to him, and he gave it back to us smiling.

"Here you'll get more than a piece of ice," he said, enjoying his pun. "I guarantee your dick will melt if you put it in one of these ladies. The whole block here is off-limits because of VD, so you'd be wise to get your ice and get back to base camp. The ice factory is two blocks down and a mile on the right," he said. "We don't want to find you here again on your way back."

"Don't worry, we'll hide better," Manning said, smiling back at the two MPs. He was pushing it.

"That's not what I meant. You trying to be a smart ass?" the lineman asked, shifting in his seat to show his size.

"No, are you trying to be a prick?"

"Just doing my job, Sergeant."

"And we're just doing ours." Manning wasn't backing down, and so far no laws had been broken. It was a verbal jousting match, and Manning felt right at home.

"You grunts think you're such hot shit," the MP lineman said, sneering while the black spec four broke into one as well.

"We are," Manning said. "You folks treat us like shit and it makes us hot."

"Just don't be here when we get back," the MP sergeant said as they took off. Moments later, when their jeep was out of sight,

Manning's bar girl returned carrying a lunchbag and gave it to him as he handed her a ten dollar MPC note.

"What's in there?"

"Dew," he said breaking into a wide grin, "Mary-G-Wanna."

"But—but the MPs! I mean you pissed them off and they'll probably be waiting for us at the main gate when we get back," I protested.

"I'm certain they will be, too," Manning said calmly, "only they won't check us. Not this time. They'll think we wouldn't dare try anything this time just because we pissed them off. Now, let's be off, my boy. Our ice is waiting!"

I stared at him, wondering if he was out of his mind, and then started the jeep and drove toward the ice factory.

The two MPs were waiting for us at the main gate on the return trip, the lineman sergeant looking over the jeep before we could pass into the base camp.

"I see you found your ice," he said to Manning. The long blocks of ice laid across the back of the jeep were already melting in the heat.

"I don't suppose you picked up anything else in town, did you?" he said, looming over Manning and leaning on the windshield.

"Yep, marijuana and a case of the clap!"

Jesus! He was out of his mind! I stared at him open-mouthed, while the big MP just shook his head.

"Boy, you are an asshole, you know that?" he said.

Manning nodded. "My mother's side of the family. She was a Texan."

The lineman MP stiffened with that but waved us through the gate.

"Get the fuck outta here! *Now*!"

Slipping the jeep in gear, we lurched forward, and when we were out of hearing distance, I tore into Manning.

"Are you out of your fucking mind?" I screamed. He just took it all good naturedly, smiling as I've never seen him smiling before.

"Just testing a theory, and it worked. You know, I bet we even had time to get laid!"

"There's an R&R allocation open for Hawaii. It's yours, if you want it," the first sergeant said as he stepped into the small club while I was cleaning up. As usual, the wooden bar was covered with spilled beer and crushed cans lay scattered on the floor. At 10

AM the burdening heat and heavy humidity were making the older soldier's life miserable. The army he could handle. The war he could handle. But Vietnam and its staggering temperatures he couldn't take, and it was a constant battle keeping his jungle fatigue shirts dry. Of all the people I'd known in Vietnam, Sparacino had the most difficulty with the temperature. But I was certain the first sergeant could handle subzero temperatures while many of us would slowly freeze to death.

"What you got cold?"

"Bud or Black Label, Top, but the ice is almost gone."

The first sergeant peered over the edge of the bar, staring into the muddled cooler that held a half-dozen or so brightly colored beer cans. A few small pieces of ice floated on top, puny remnants of the blocks purchased in Tay Ninh at the ice factory.

"Bud," he said. "There's not much else other than Hawaii. I know you've missed your chance at a few R&Rs already, so it's your decision."

I told him I'd think about it, thanking him for letting me know. After all that had happened, I'd put the R&Rs out of mind, secretly thinking that I wasn't destined to have one. Though I kept telling myself I wasn't superstitious, I couldn't rid myself of the feeling that signing up for another one might get me wounded again—or that I'd suffer a relapse of malaria. That was stupid, but I kept away from the orderly room and the R&R sign-up rosters anyway.

Top finished the beer and pulled out a ten-cent MPC note to pay for the drink, but I waved it off.

"No, no!" he protested. "You have to refill your inventory."

"No problem, so far we've made about six hundred dollars profit," I said smiling. I was proud of the way I kept the books and had operated the small club. We bought beer at ten cents a can and sold it for fifteen cents. A few pilots flew me in some hard liquor, so I sold shots as well. We'd done quite well, and I wanted to brag a little.

"Profit?" the first sergeant said in hushed, desperate tones. He looked as though he was suffering from heatstroke.

"Yeah, Top, six hundred dollars. Right here and the records are—"

"You're not supposed to make a profit! Jesus, you want me to go to jail?"

"No, I just—"

"Six hundred dollars profit! My God, that's what they nailed the Sergeant Major of the Army with. He's going to jail." Sparacino was pacing the floor wondering if he'd made a mistake by putting me in charge of the club. Then he stopped suddenly, realizing there was a way out of the dilemma. "Get rid of the books! Don't keep track of anything!"

"But how will you know I'm being honest?"

Top looked at me like a frustrated football coach trying to explain the rules of the game to his dumbest, but most enthusiastic player.

"Jergensen," he said, mispronouncing my name, as he always did, "I don't worry about you being honest. That's why I put you in charge in the first place! Get rid of the books and get rid of the money! You hear me!"

"How?"

"I don't know! Buy something for the club here, make it look like a club instead of the inside of an ammunition box. I don't care what you do with the money, only don't ever, *ever* tell me about it. You're not supposed to make a profit, you understand?"

I said I did, while the back of his fatigue shirt grew dark and damp.

"Good," he said as I pulled out the club's ledger, ripping the pages up in front of him. "That's better. That's better," he said, mumbling to himself as he left the club for the unit's orderly room just as Beal and Braun entered.

"What was that all about?" Beal asked while reaching over the bar to fish out a cool Bud for himself and a Black Label for Braun.

"The club's not supposed to make a profit, and so far we've pulled in roughly six hundred dollars."

Braun was reaching into his pocket for the Military Payment Certificates to pay for the beers and stopped short when he heard me explain the situation to Beal. "Woolerridge, Woodbridge or something like that. Command sergeant major or whatever, had made quite a bit of money skimming from some clubs and they sent him to jail," Braun said, opening his beer.

"Yeah, that's what he was talking about," I replied.

"So Top's afraid the same thing can happen to him—not that he has anything going here—but the army's out to make examples out of some of the enlisted honchos, so he doesn't want to take any chances. Six hundred dollars, huh?"

"Profit," I said nodding.

"In that case, I think I'll have another one, on the house!" the grinning bear said, doing what he did best.

That night Beal convinced me to take the Hawaii R&R. "Go to Hawaii," he said over the din of the music and the crowd of GIs in the club. No missions were planned for several days, and the troop was enjoying the chance to take it easy—"easy" in Vietnam meant drinking at the club or going outside to smoke a bowl of grass. Sometimes they did both while occasionally officers and senior NCOs patrolled the troop area looking for "dopers." Fortunately, the patrols tended to be sporadic and random. Beal laughed whenever he saw the two-man patrols eyeing the club and any group of GIs with suspicion.

"You know, one of the biggest problems I saw in the army in Germany was alcohol. Everyone thinks drugs are a problem over here, while all I see is some grunts smoking grass in the rear areas, while the officers and senior NCOs get blind drunk damn near every night on cheap booze!"

It was true or at least seemed that way. I'd heard rumors of heroin use in the troop, mostly by the rear-area maintenance soldiers who had the time and safety for it; those of us who went out in the jungle wouldn't risk it. But they were only rumors, and there was never any confirmation of use unless that information was being kept from us. Still, I knew that if it was a problem of major proportions, then Andreu our platoon sergeant, would let us know. The squat Puerto Rican, who sometimes seemed crabby and smartass, was in fact, well meaning and sincere, traits that earned him the respect that other NCOs couldn't even buy!

"White sand beaches," Beal said, taking a sip of his constant can of Budweiser beer.

"Pussy." Manning was sitting a few stools down the bar and was listening to the conversation.

"Cheeseburgers and ice cream," Beal added.

"And pussy!" Manning said again.

"Sun and surf, the land of the great PX, color TV, soft beds with sheets."

"And don't forget the pussy!"

Beal shot the smiling sergeant an agitated look. "Oh, yes, and pussy." Manning smiled.

"I dunno, I was kinda looking forward to Taipei or Bangkok," I said.

"There are no slots open. Besides, Hawaii is in the good old U.S. of A. You're combat trained, you can survive seven days anywhere without getting wounded," Braun said. "Take Hawaii."

"I knew a guy in B Troop who went to Hawaii and then flew home from there. He never came back." Manning said.

"What do you mean he never came back?" asked Braun.

"He just said 'fuck it' and went home. He had it with the war and the army."

"The army's not the Girl Scouts. You can't just quit," the RTO argued.

Manning shook off his objection. "He did."

"They'll catch up to him one day," Braun said.

"He knows that, only by then he figures the war will be over. To him jail is better than the jungle. There it is," Manning said, taking a drink.

"Don't worry, the war will still be here when you get back. Go to Hawaii, be a gimp, and let some blond, blue-eyed, bikini-clad wench comfort you. Then, come back and tell us all about it," Braun said. "It's a tradition."

"Yeah," Manning nodded in agreement. "Tell us about the round-eye pussy."

"The boy's gotta one-track mind," Beal said, staring at Manning.

Braun offered another view. "You're assuming the track's in working order and any train of thought is on schedule."

I signed up for Hawaii. To my surprise and relief I received it. I made arrangements to fly down to Camp Alpha, the division's R&R center in Bien Hoa. Several days later I was on a commercial charter flight to Honolulu with two hundred or so other smiling GIs. After an uneventful flight, we arrived at the Honolulu airport, a lifetime and several dimensions later. It seemed ridiculous that only hours earlier we'd left a country that was ravaged by war, where people were dying every day in hideous ways. Here we were, plucked up and removed to another setting where our mannerisms wouldn't be understood or appreciated.

As we taxied into the airport, we peered out the windows like little children, pointing out excitedly things that the island's inhabitants would have considered quite ordinary. When the door opened and an officer appeared in the aisle saying we were to board the buses for the R&R center at Fort DeRussey, where we could join our loved ones and families, I wondered what in the hell he was talking about. Once we pulled into the R&R center in the famed city's resort area, I understood. Crying wives cradling babies or GIs shouted greetings. Hawaii was a common meeting ground for married soldiers whose families flew from the States. As we filed from the bus, soldiers and families rushed and embraced, leaving those few of us who were unmarried and without families present to stand around idle, looking foolish. There were tears and laughter, frenzied hugs and kisses. I felt good for them. I also felt terribly alone as did the other unmarried soldiers. We quietly filed into the R&R center hall for a briefing, amid the laughter and gaiety around us, your standard military pep talk: do's and don'ts while on R&R, followed by a stern warning for those of us who were unaccompanied. "At no time will you leave the islands for the continental United States. Those soldiers caught trying to return to the continental United States without authorization will be subject to courts-martial. Is that understood?" the officer asked. It was the end of his short briefing.

"You bet it is!" whispered a black soldier next to me. "Don't get caught!"

"There it is!" I said, giving him five. He laughed and slapped his open palm against mine.

"Chicago, man. Where you going?"

"Seattle, Washington," I replied, realizing that I was going home, even if it was only for a short time. I'd surprise my family and friends, and they'd be excited to see me.

"We can share a cab back to the airport. I hear the airlines will only sell GIs round-trip tickets so we'll return. It's cool."

"Let's go," I said, heading to the center's locker room to change into a khaki uniform. Few of us had civilian clothes to wear, and the khakis were the most presentable dress we had. When I emerged from the locker room, an army major stopped me.

"Hold on there, soldier," he said, blocking my path.

"Yes, sir, what's up?"

"You have orders for those ribbons?" he asked, staring down at my chest at the three rows of medals I'd received in Vietnam. On the top row the Silver Star and the Bronze Star with V device rested over the two rows of brightly colored ribbons. The ribbons were a present from Cortez who purchased the bar holder at the PX and then had the new company clerk fill in the ribbons.

"Yes, sir, I do."

When I handed him the copy of the orders, his cynical eyes ran from the name on the orders to my name tag as he went from page to page. Top Sparacino had warned me about such incidents and told me to plan ahead. It seems that some GIs had decided to make themselves more acceptable to the public at large by purchasing a few ribbons from the post exchange and adding them to their uniforms. The major's eyes and hard stare softened, and he suddenly seemed more amiable.

"Looks like they're all yours," he said and then reached over to adjust the ribbons. "However, they're out of order. Here, let me help you." The officer rearranged the ribbons in the correct order then stood back to appraise his work.

"There! That looks better," he said. He held out his hand, "Congratulations, Sergeant. That's quite an impressive display. Enjoy your R&R."

I wanted to tell him about McIntyre, Beal, and a whole bunch of others who were equally well decorated, but I let it pass. The major was just trying to make amends. Besides, I think what really caught his eye were the three Purple Hearts. I looked too young and too healthy to have them. It was funny then because I thought most others had the same awards. It hadn't occurred to me that there were others who didn't, nor could I understand why anyone would want them. I was proud and embarrassed at the same time, and in the awkward moment he excused himself.

"What was that all about?" asked my traveling buddy from Chicago.

"My ribbons."

"What you do, buy out the PX? You must be a grunt or something?"

"Yeah, or something. What about you?"

"Tanks. I'm with the 11th ACR, one of Patton's soldiers." The soldier from Chicago was pleased with himself. "He's about as crazy as his old man, but he takes good care of us, and that's all that matters. There it is," he said.

And that was it. The bottom line when it came to company commanders or commanding officers in general. Some would go on to earn names and legends for their efforts; others would only ride the coattails of the soldiers they commanded.

At the airport we purchased our tickets and went our separate ways, saying we'd see each other again in five days back at DeRussey. A simple enough plan, providing we didn't get caught by the MPs or miss connecting flights. Or decided not to come back.

When I arrived at the Seattle-Tacoma International Airport, I caught a cab home, knowing that my mother would wonder who was getting out of the cab when we pulled up. But after paying the cab fare, I noticed no one was looking out the window. When I tried the door, I got no response. Nobody was home. In the backyard a six-month-old dog was barking at me, straining at the taut line at the strangely dressed interloper. I knew of him, but he didn't know one from a walking fire hydrant!

"Shut up, Rascal!" For a brief moment the dog cocked his head to the side, studying me, before deciding that I was indeed a stranger. Walking over to the neighbors' house, I asked if I could use their phone. I called my brother and discovered that my parents were at work and my sister was in school. There was a key in the doghouse if I wanted to get in the house. Great! Nobody home and a pissed-off puppy standing between me and my first real bath in months. I told my brother I'd see him soon, and when I hung up the phone, the neighbor asked me about the war.

"So, is it bad over there?" she said, asking the most obvious question.

It was also a dumb question, but she was only trying to be pleasant, so I didn't say what was on my mind which was, of course it's bad over there! It's a war, for crying out loud! People are getting blown up, shot, and burned for no apparent reason. And you want to know if it's bad?

"It's no picnic," I said, settling for a more diplomatic answer. I thanked her and left to confront the pissed-off puppy.

"Okay, Rascal, it's you and me, buddy. You fuck with me, and I'll take you back to Nam and hand you over to some Vietnamese friends of mine who'll look at you like a side of beef!" I said as I was walking slowly toward the barking dog. Inches away from the black mutt's snapping jaws, I stopped short knowing he couldn't pull any farther to get me, then I sat down.

"Easy boy, easy," I said soothingly, but he kept tugging at the line. A few minutes later, when he was tired, I put my hand out to him and he made a slow growl. Then, I turned my hand over, bringing my middle finger back to meet the thumb, and with a pop snapped him in the nose. Caught by surprise, the dog yelped and retreated. When he attacked again, the taut line stopped him, and a few minutes later I repeated the process. This time he didn't attack but pulled back to his doghouse. As I slowly moved closer, he left the doghouse, and I found the key. When I was out of his chain's reach again, Rascal charged, barking. I looked back and smiled.

"I know the feeling, puppy." False fronts seemed to go hand in hand with being young.

After five days in Seattle, I was looking forward to going back to Vietnam. Maybe not really looking forward to it, but I wasn't comfortable at home. Sure, it was *home* and *back in the world*, but something was missing. I couldn't define it. All I really knew was that I wanted to get back to Tay Ninh, back to my buddies.

My friends had done their best to show me a good time during the five days, but nothing seemed to take away the edge. I didn't sleep at night, I pulled guard, not knowing it was guard then but rather something that needed to be done. My girlfriend was feeling guilty about someone she was seeing from school and was uncomfortable around me. Why shouldn't she be? Hell, I was uncomfortable around her, around all of them. They had their own lives and went about them with casual ease, and for that I was suspicious of them. They were too comfortable, too much at ease.

At times I ran across friends from school who were surprised to see me. One was overjoyed that I was still alive, having heard that I was killed in the war. He said something about my death being on the evening news. Another friend was surprised to learn I was in the military, let alone in Vietnam. I was the only one from school that he knew that was actually over there. "Wow! Isn't that something?" he said, adding, "Man, you could've gotten out of it like the rest of us."

When I flew back to Hawaii, I was relieved. I was going back to my friends, back to something I could identify with if only reluctantly. Home wasn't home anymore. Restless, I didn't like believing that the war was all I had, or maybe I was just upset, knowing that the five days were not enough to really let my guard down, to really get comfortable. All I knew was that I would be on my way back to the war after a brief one-day rest in Hawaii, and that my R&R had been anything but rest or relaxation.

When we boarded the chartered flight for Vietnam the following day, we were a somber and quiet lot. Nobody had really wanted to go back. There was only one empty seat on the plane, which belonged to the black soldier from Chicago.

"Looks like there's one AWOL, sir," a bored NCO said to an officer who was cradling a clipboard in his arm. Applause began slowly and rolled into a loud cheer. Up front, where the senior NCOs and ranking officers sat, heads turned. They wondered what the cheering was for but soon joined in, apparently thinking that it was for the seven-day R&R or the idea of going back to the war.

Of course we were cheering for the soldier who'd gotten away.

CHAPTER NINETEEN

There were no missions scheduled for the Blues the day after I got back from R&R, and like volunteer firemen used to frenzied work only when the alarm went off, they used the free time to take care of chores. Some were in the CP learning how to read maps or cleaning weapons, others pulled day guard on the camp's perimeter, emptied trash, burned shit from the communal crappers, filled shower barrels, or slipped off to find an open bar, buy something at the PX, or get laid at the steam bath. So, when the warning siren wailed across the compound, Blues came running from myriad directions, grabbing at equipment and weapons from the connex storage containers and racing toward the flight line for the line of helicopters that would take them out in the jungle.

Standing in the doorway of the bar, I saw that there weren't enough Blues assembled. Cortez was yelling for others to hurry.

"Downed helicopter," Braun shouted, leaning into his radio handset, while hands busily checked weapons and ammunition. Twelve Blues were ready and I knew they couldn't field the full platoon of twenty-one. I ran over to the connex storage container and joined the others. Blue and Andreau nodded, but Braun frowned and shook his head.

"A scout helicopter was shot down. NVA are in the area, and the gunship is still on station, trying to cover the crash site. They don't know if there are any survivors," Blue said. "You'll take point 4-4," the lieutenant added. Beal nodded. He was the squad leader now. I was just visiting. My legs had scarred over, leaving deep scarlet lines where the bullets had torn me open. I walked with a noticeable limp but had regained use of much of the leg muscles.

As we splintered into small groups to load onto the helicopters, I took the seat next to Art Dockter, the crew chief. As the helicopter increased its shuddering and whine, we lifted up, the nose dipped, and we roared off to the crash site. I wondered what in the hell I was trying to prove. Braun's frown said it all, and as we flew deeper into the jungle, I wondered if maybe I should've stayed behind.

There was a mix-up in the landing pattern, and the lead helicopter landed much closer to the crash site than the other two helicopters. Because we were out to find one of their own, the pilots had brought us as close to the jungle's edge as the blades would allow.

"Yellow smoke!" Dockter yelled to me, pointing into the thick green and brown jungle wall. "They dropped a yellow smoke on the crash site, maybe seventy-five meters ahead."

Blue, Andreu, and Braun were emerging from the second helicopter while the other Blues followed. They were a good one hundred meters or more away but they could hear Dockter yelling over the radio that the downed helicopter was in a hundred pieces and that there had been a body in sight, moving! The downed crew was taking small-arms fire, and it would be a race to see who got to the crash site first, us or the NVA who'd shot them down.

"Oh, shit!" I said, squeezing the stock of my rifle and staring into the rain forest. Hue was looking at me strangely. But then he had a right to. I was stupid, foolish, and went against every operating rule the Rangers or the Blues lived by. I could smell smoke from the smoke grenade and caught a faint glimpse of it slowly billowing through the trees.

"Shit! Shit! Shit!" I said, racing toward it at a dead run. Devalle was hesitating, looking back at the rest of the platoon who were hurrying to catch up with the point squad. Beal looked at Hue and then took off after me.

"Fuck it!" Devalle said to himself. He indicated the direction to Blue and the others, then he led the rest of the squad into the jungle.

Sharp branches and wait-a-minute vines clawed and scratched at me as I ran. More smoke rose ahead of me, and I pushed harder to get past the jungle that blocked my way. Small abandoned fighting positions and old bunkers flew into sight after I passed them. Finally, I could make out the twisted path of wreckage from the downed loach. The small observation helicopter was just a light metal and fiberglass skin filled with highly explosive fuel and ammunition. Fortunately for the crew—if there was anything fortunate about getting shot down and crashing through thick jungle—the fuel had not ignited. The aircraft was so much litter in tree limbs and on the jungle floor. A twisted pile of splintered fiberglass and metal pushed out of the ground like an impressionistic sculpture. At its base, lying bent over backward was the observation helicopter's doorgunner. His left eye hung from its socket by a blue-white tendril, and an army of fire ants covered his body. Some were caught in the sticky fluid from the ruptured eye. Unable to move, the doorgunner was moaning.

I hastily scanned the immediate area and then focused back on the dangling eyeball and the ants. I could hear Beal breaking brush behind me and knew the others would only be a few minutes behind. Kneeling behind the doorgunner's head, I put down my rifle and brushed away the angry ants that had turned the doorgunner's exposed flesh into tiny, red welts.

Reaching under his arms, I gently began to pull him out of the wreckage, digging in with the heels of my boots to get more leverage. Only then did I notice the pistol aimed at my face from less than six feet away and the frightened face and the shaking hand of the man behind it.

"Don't shoot—Jesus, don't shoot," I said, sitting down with the wounded doorgunner now in my lap.

"I . . . thought, I thought you were the gooks. Oh, my god, I almost killed you!" The man holding the .38 pistol was the helicopter's pilot. He lowered the wavering hand, while he wiped away the blood that was dripping down his face with the other hand and began to cry. Seated against a tree that had been severed by the falling wreckage, he had waited for the NVA soldiers he knew would come. With his broken back there wasn't much else he could do.

"You're gonna be all right now," I said, only I wasn't so certain who I was really saying it to. The doorgunner opened his good eye and squeezed my arm. Not really knowing what to do with the damaged eye I bandaged it in place.

"Tha-thanks," he whispered. The pilot was still crying but now they were tears of joy and relief. My own eyes were burning, but I stifled my own tears as Hue's face brought immediate fear to the wounded pilot's face.

"He's one of us," I said. "You're okay now. We got you. We got you."

Seeing what was going on, Beal immediately provided protective cover and then motioned the others in around the crash site as they came into view. Stephenson was on the radio informing Blue that we had two survivors and that we'd have to look around for the third. The small observation helicopters usually carried a

three-man crew. As soon as Blue acknowledged the radio transmission, Beal had the squad begin the search.

Stephenson, the squad's RTO, waved him off. "They say it's
okay. There's only two."

Beal secured the perimeter and then moved over to help the
injured pilot.

"Jesus . . ." the wounded doorgunner said, trying to take his
mind off of the injuries he'd received. They'd been baiting the
NVA in the bunker complex, firing on the bunkers and fighting
positions to draw fire, when the North Vietnamese Army soldiers
opened up, hitting the loach in the engine and tail rotor, sending
it into a powerless, falling spin.

"Oh, God. Oh, God," he moaned as I sat there cradling him,
trying to comfort him with quiet tones, the way a father might do
for a child who woke up screaming from a nightmare. But the
doorgunner's nightmare wasn't really over. Like a father, I wanted
to tell him that everything was going to be okay and that there
weren't boogeymen out there trying to get him, but I couldn't; I
wasn't so certain anymore. Doc Devalle stood at my shoulder
trying to get at him.

"I'll take over," he said, laying down his aid bag. I pushed him
away.

"Leave him alone. I got him!" I said while Devalle looked on,
wondering what I was doing. "Get a medevac in here. We'll need
a stretcher," I said. Devalle nodded his approval.

"You're gonna be okay," I said over and over again to the doorgunner, as Beal attended the wounded pilot, occasionally looking
back at me with a concerned expression. By the time the rest of the
platoon was in place, Blue was in contact with the medevac helicopter, which was just a few minutes out. When the evacuation
helicopter finally arrived, hovering over the treetops and lowering
the stretcher down to us below, I was exhausted, physically and
emotionally drained, and it showed. I was losing it.

"You okay?" Ed asked after the doorgunner had been lifted up
to the medevac helicopter.

I told him I was, but I could see that he knew better. The threads
were showing.

"The pilot almost shot me," I said as Beal listened patiently.
"He had the gun leveled at my face, and all I could see was the
barrel of the pistol and his hand on the trigger. I don't want to get
shot again, and I don't want to go back to any hospital ever
again."

The North Carolinian nodded. There was nothing more to say. I'd finally understood what he'd tried to tell me but I hadn't been listening. I was invincible, for Christ's sake! One of the good guys fighting a war in some silly comic-book, Saturday matinee Hollywood fashion. Honor and glory just came naturally to the good guys, didn't they? Isn't that what I'd been reared on? Isn't that what I had to believe if any of this was going to make sense? You're damned right, it was! I was a Boy Scout in war, going after the merit badges and always trying to do the *right* thing, only the *right* thing had its price, and I had been paying for it on a dangerous installment plan.

Lieutenant Hugele thanked me for going out on the mission, saying it was good to see me as my old self again. Jim Braun and Beal both knew better, and so did I. I retired to the small club, settling in behind the wooden bar, knowing that the next time the siren wailed I'd let the others handle it. I'd pushed my luck to its limits, and there wasn't any more of me to give.

"What got into you today?" Beal asked as he settled down in a chair and stared at me. His face registered concern.

"I don't know. I just had to get to the helicopter before the gooks did."

"Hue said he couldn't keep up with you. You trying to get killed?"

"Not anymore. I'm done. I'm second string now, and I know it. It was stupid going out in the first place, stupid running in there like that. Stupid, almost getting my head blown off by a wounded pilot. Hell, I made more mistakes than a dumb-ass new guy. And the thing that bothers me is that it didn't matter. I didn't really care."

"Does it matter now?" the wiry North Carolinian asked.

"I'm so damned scared now I can't see straight. I'm gonna let Blue know."

Beal stared at me and then laughed. "Jesus, you looked like Jesse Owens out there. One minute you're there and the next you're off and running. When you tell Blue you ain't gonna go out no more, see if he'll let me stay back with you. It's time we turned this ballgame over to the rookies! Now, give me a cold beer, barkeep, and keep that help-wanted sign in the window!"

The last mission was viewed as a volunteer effort and Andreu respected the division's policy of pulling soldiers with three Purple Hearts out of the field. He couldn't understand why I went out in the first place. "How long you been in-country?" the Puerto Rican asked.

"Eight months."

"Eight months! Three doesn't even go into eight comfortably. You earned your job, so keep it," he said with a laughing finality. "I don't have a problem with that. You've done your share."

"Thanks," I said, pleased that he didn't have to push me to say that I was scared to go out anymore. How do you tell someone your luck has run out so that they'll really understand it? The old Puerto Rican saw it and recognized it and eased my fears with his comments.

The Platoon Sergeant understood—so maybe that's why he felt bad when he told me two weeks later that I had to go back out on patrol again.

"Why?"

"Because there's something coming up, something big, and the old man is trying to get as many people involved in it as he can."

"But the division's policy—"

Andreu shook his head sadly. "I know, and I'm sorry. I really am. I told the first sergeant and Blue that it isn't right, and even they stuck up for you only . . ." His voice faded. "I'm sorry," he said. I could see that he meant it. If he had tried to stick up for me, then I was certain it was in loud, swearing tones.

"Can I see the first sergeant?" I asked. Andreu nodded.

"Sure, but I don't think it'll do any good."

When I entered the orderly room, First Sergeant Sparacino took a look at me and then shook his head.

"Top—"

"I know, I know. Look, I can't tell you what's going on, but we're getting ready for something big—"

"Yeah, we're going into Cambodia," I said.

The first sergeant and the new company clerk were stunned. Their faces showed it.

"Where did you hear that?" Top said.

"The hootch maids have been asking us all week if we're going into Cambodia because of all the different units coming into the base camp." Over the last two weeks, a number of combat units, from army divisions not usually assigned or attached to the region, had filtered into the Tay Ninh base camp. They were readying for the inevitable push into nearby Cambodia.

"Oh, Christ!" he said, wiping his wet brow. "It's still top secret." Sparacino mumbled something to himself, then turned his attention back to the immediate problem. "Well, something's up, and we need all the people we have. It's Six's decision."

"Six doesn't have to go out there!" I argued while the veteran let me vent some steam.

"I'm sorry," he said. "There's nothing I can do."

Back at the club I found Beal tending bar while Henderson, Braun, and Art Dockter were playing hearts. Cortez sat with Bloor, laughing over something, wildly gesturing with his hands which caused Bloor to laugh even louder. I took a seat at the bar while Ed placed a cold Bud in front of me.

"How'd it go?"

"Lousy. Top says I have to go back out."

"Back out where?" Braun's growling question drowned out the taped music. A new guy at the far end of the bar shot Braun a hard look then quickly backed down when the bear returned it.

"In the bush," I said, taking a long drink. Outside, the evening sky held the humidity in place like a black wet sponge.

"That's bullshit!" he said, dropping his cards and joining us at the bar. "They can't do that!"

"Talk to the IG," Bloor said. The rest of the loosely assembled audience nodded and mumbled agreement. But even Braun knew that the division's inspector general, the army's omsbudsman, was in Phuoc Vinh, and we were light years away in Tay Ninh.

"You didn't volunteer, did you?" Braun asked.

I told him I hadn't.

"The problem is you've volunteered too much in the past. They expect it. What did they say when you brought up the division's policy about three Purple Hearts?"

"They said it didn't matter. Six has a plan." I took another drink, not really caring to go through it all again, but that wasn't the way problems worked in Vietnam. Everything was a communal effort, activity, or problem. My sense of outrage had given over to new voices.

"Fuck him!" Braun said flatly. "It's division policy."

"Yeah!" Manning piped in. "If he does it to you, then he'll do it to us!"

"Why don't you write a letter to your congressman?" Devalle suggested.

"Fuck the congressman!" Manning yelled. "Write to your senator! The bastards want to play games, then we'll play some games!"

"What're your senators' names?"

I shrugged. "One's "Scoop" Jackson. I don't know who the other one is."

"Scoop? What kind of name is Scoop?" Braun said while everyone smiled.

"I think it's Henry," I said.

"Don't need it anyway. We ain't exactly on a first name basis with him yet. But we will be. We will be."

So the great letter-writing campaign of 1970 began, and when the makeshift committee was satisfied with its contents, we dropped it in the outgoing mail.

We were helping to slingload a downed scout helicopter when the call come in.

"Sergeant Jorgenson?" Andreau yelled across the grass landing zone on the top of the small loach helicopter where I was busy trying to get the sling locked in place. After rescuing the crew and securing the landing zone, the only other thing left to do before we could get out of there was to get the salvageable aircraft out first. Usually troop maintenance personnel did the work needed to ready the aircraft for the sling load. At times we helped them.

"What's up?"

"I don't know," he said, cocking his helmet back to look up at me as we talked, "but a helicopter's coming in to take you back to Tay Ninh. It's a few minutes out, so get your things ready."

"Just me?"

The old Puerto Rican nodded. "Special delivery. Go on, Jorgy, we'll get this."

On the short ride back to the base camp, I wondered if maybe Six had changed his mind. But when we touched down on the air strip, First Sergeant Sparacino escorted me from that helicopter to another farther down the flight line.

"The battalion commander wants to talk to you ASAP. I don't know what you did, but whatever it is, I'm behind you," he said, wiping his sweat-filled brow. "Good luck."

When the helicopter finally arrived in Phuoc Vinh, the battalion sergeant major was there to greet me.

"You Jorgenson?"

I nodded.

"The old man wants to talk to you, but I wanted to talk to you first. How long you been in the army?"

"Eighteen months," I replied.

"That's long enough to know how to use your chain of command. You got a problem, you take it up your chain of command." The battalion's senior sergeant was giving me a mild chewing out, and judging by what he was saying, I knew it had something to do with the letter to my senator.

"I couldn't get past my troop commander," I said.

But the sergeant major wouldn't buy it. "You should've taken it up the chain anyway, and we could've handled it."

I would have been banging my head against a wall if I continued. I wanted to tell him about the difficulties of getting to talk to your troop commander, let alone anyone in a higher position, when you're out on patrol, but knew reality really didn't matter. In the army, you either followed the rules or you got chewed out, and since he wasn't screaming I saw no reason to push him to it. I wasn't angry with him or even pissed off at the army. I was angry at the troop commander because he'd changed the rules of the game by raising the stakes on me and then calling my hand. My ace in the hole was the letter to the senator. Judging from the response it was enough.

"All I'm saying is that when you have a problem keep it an army problem and use the chain of command. Hell, if you would've come to me in the first place, I could've handled it!" We walked on in silence toward battalion headquarters.

The meeting with the battalion commander was a copy of the talk with the sergeant major. Yes, I said, I should've used the chain of command. Yes, I was wrong taking it outside the army. And, yes, I would come to him next time. The battalion commander, though, wasn't without his own apologies. From their sincerity and concern, I could see that maybe I should've taken the problem to his staff. They said that the troop commander had been wrong and that they'd take care of it, which I was certain they would do. Senatorial inquiries required written replies, detailing the investigation to the inquiry and the action the army took to correct the situation. The battalion commander said I could catch the mail helicopter back to Tay Ninh and that there should be no further letters to the senator from me. The battalion staff would schedule a physical and mental evaluation for the report to the senator, and from that they would determine my status.

While I was recovering from the gunshot wounds in the hospital in Long Binh, I received a letter from my parents telling me that Senator Jackson had called after the CBS News report, saying that if there was anything he could do then to please let him know. My father thanked him for the call and the concern, saying the senator's attention wasn't necessary since I was coming home. The CBS News report had said as much, reporting that I was on the way to another Purple Heart and a one-way ticket out of the Vietnam war. So much for news reports.

When I returned to Tay Ninh, the news was all over the troop. GIs I hadn't known very well were suddenly coming up and shaking my hand. Those I had known well or who had taken part in the letter-writing campaign celebrated it as their own victory. There were, of course, exceptions. Most notably was Sergeant Burrows whom I'd heard say something about how it was funny someone could be a hero at one moment and a coward the next. When I heard it, I laughed, thinking about how Burrows still thought there was a difference between the two. I shook his attitude off. The war had a deeper impact. I was having trouble sleeping at night. I kept my rifle with a round chambered and web gear next to my cot. I took short naps in the day and pulled a quiet, restless, private guard at night.

When I was assigned additional duty as sergeant of the guard for the perimeter bunkers that were Apache Troop's base responsibility, I was secretly relieved. Now, at least, I had a legitimate excuse for staying awake until dawn, an official duty instead of an unofficial vigil. Since I knew that ground or sapper attacks by the NVA usually came in predawn raids, I wanted to be ready.

I wasn't afraid of dying in the war as much as I was frightened by the very real possibility of getting wounded again. Dying came easy; it was the survivors who had to carry the grief or the scars. I also knew that my next wound or injury might not be as forgiving as the previous ones, so I wasn't taking any chances. My M-16 was always within reach, and I slept with a loaded .45 automatic. At night I waited, uncertain whether I was paranoid or maybe just painfully aware of the possibilities.

The physical was easy enough. The doctors took a look at my health records and scars, nodding and making notes for their report. Shrapnel wounds, a concussion, malaria, and two bullet holes in the thighs in ten months. I'd been on a LRRP team that had been hit hard, and I had fifty-four missions as a pointman, which was enough to make one doctor laugh, shake his head, and ask, "Do you expect to live to twenty-one?"

"Yeah, I plan to."

"Not the way you're going."

The physical examination was performed in the base camp, but the mental evaluation had to be done in the rear support area, where a psychiatrist was available. After another long helicopter ride, I found the mental hygiene clinic that looked officious enough, if not clean and comfortable. A quiet reception area with several desks and one bored specialist gave way to several opened offices that displayed similar desks, several practical but uncomfortable-looking chairs, and an obligatory book shelf. The paint was olive drab.

The psychiatrist was a tall, thin-faced army officer who spoke in muted tones that went with the office. Dressed in loose but starched fatigues and polished jungle boots, he looked suspiciously military, the type of army officer who might remind you that your boots needed polish.

My attitude sucked, and I wasn't as much defensive as angry. I'd played by the rules only to have them changed by others during the game. I at least felt I deserved a say in the matter. And when I didn't get it, and the more I thought about it, I was ready to bellow and rave at the next opportunity I had. The psychiatrist had been unfortunate enough to have been in that position. However, he wasn't there to argue. He was simply there to talk, and while I'd been good at reading jungle trails, I was lousy at reading people. The doctor was about to give me a lesson.

"Have a seat, Sergeant," he said, closing the door and returning to his desk. "So, tell me why you're here?"

"Simple, Doc," I said. "I was ordered to show up, so it might save time if you told me why I'm here."

"Well, besides the obvious evaluation, I'd like to get an idea of where you're coming from."

While the jargon was hardly army and he seemed friendly enough, I still didn't see any compelling reason to tell him anything useful. Seeming sincerity was no reason to drop my guard or open up to him. After all, it was an official evaluation. Not a social call, and I didn't know him.

"Where I'm coming from is the war out there in the bush," I said, pointing to the wall, "the one beyond the snack bars and massage parlors. You'll have to forgive me, sir, but from beyond the barbed wire, it's light years away."

"I imagine it is. Care to tell me about it?"

"What's to tell?"

"How about the reasons why you don't want to be out there anymore."

I laughed a short, quick laugh. "How about three Purple Hearts. Division policy says it's enough."

"What do you think?"

"I think I'm tired—"

"And maybe afraid?"

"Yeah, that, too, I suppose." I was thinking back to the faceless soldier in the surgical ward—his blank eyes staring out of a depression covered by bandages—as he tapped his hand against the gray metal bed frame to the rhythm of the wheezing in and out of the disc implanted in his throat. "Sure, why not?"

The doctor went on to summarize my brief military career, asking me if I volunteered for everything along the way. You didn't get in the Rangers without volunteering, and you didn't stay on point unless you liked it.

"Yes, sir, I volunteered. The point is after I got shot in both legs I didn't volunteer to go back out. That's when someone did it for me—"

"And that makes you angry?"

"No shit, sir."

"Why? Are you angry with yourself for not volunteering or for being made afraid by what they've done?" The smiling, quiet doctor hit the nail on the head, and I was angry at that, too. He was opening me up in spite of myself.

"The guy that shot me was maybe less than fifteen feet away. He hit me in the right leg first and knocked me down before I returned fire and killed him. It wasn't until later that I noticed he'd shot my canteen, my boots, and had hit me twice. The doctors in Tay Ninh told me how lucky I was because if the bullets had hit my bones then I very probably would've lost the legs on the spot. I was lucky with the Rangers, too, and lucky again when we got overrun out in the bush. You know, when my buddies were dying, I couldn't do a damn thing to save them. You know how helpless that makes you feel? God, all I wanted to do was get back at the fucking NVA, and with the Blues I had my chance. In one firefight I killed five gooks, and you know what?"

"What?"

"It didn't feel as good as I thought it would. Shit! One of them even had a picture of his family in his dumb-ass wallet . . . "Oh, yes, sir, I'm afraid all right, afraid I'm going to do something stupid or careless that'll get somebody else fucked up. I don't feel lucky anymore. I just feel old."

"I see you have a number of decorations. How do you feel about those?" the psychiatrist asked.

I laughed again.

"Do they bother you?" It was difficult to justify a life or lives for small pieces of metal adorned with brightly colored ribbon, especially if the people who've died were friends.

"Yeah, Doc. They do. They're just reminders." I wasn't yelling anymore, but my adrenaline was pumping, and the office seemed too small and confining for me, and the doctor was too much in control.

"I have all the bad memories I care to have. I don't want any more," I said, suddenly tired. "Look, Doc, I don't really have much more to say. Maybe I've said too much already. Can I go now?"

He nodded. "I think we can wrap it up for now. But I'd like to see you again sometime if you'd like. If and when you feel like you want to talk, I'm here."

I said I would, if anything came up, knowing damn well I wouldn't. He'd hit too many exposed nerves, and that bothered me. More than that, I also felt slightly relieved. I'd always gone along with what people told me to do in the army without enough hesitation. It felt good to yell and complain, and when I told Sergeant Andreu what happened he smiled, saying, "Good soldiers always bitch and moan. It's the quiet ones I worry about."

Though I never heard the outcome of the report, I didn't have to go back out in the field again unless I volunteered for random missions. I had less than one hundred days to go. I was a *double-digit midget*, which meant that I was getting short. My tour of duty would be over soon.

The Tay Ninh base camp was filling with soldiers and equipment for the push into Cambodia. We knew it was coming, as did the Vietnamese. You couldn't have that many soldiers, let alone new tanks, armored personnel carriers, and helicopters flying in and landing everyday without something being in the wind. We knew Cambodia had to be the target since it was the closest target in the region. The Fish Hook, Parrot's Beak, and Angel's Wing were major infiltration routes into South Vietnam, and we were certain they'd be targeted in the push. Since we were under nightly enemy mortar and rocket attacks from those areas, it didn't bother us that they would be targets. When the push finally did come, taking the US forces twenty-four miles into Cambodia, the relief from the nightly attacks was well received. "Rocket City" became Tay Ninh base camp once more, a base camp we were beginning to abandon in order to move closer to the action.

In the initial drive into Cambodia, we'd lost several scout helicopters, the first getting shot down but able to land safely, where the Blues could pick up the crew. The second proved more costly; the scout helicopter took a direct hit from an RPG and fell in flames into the large bunker complex it had uncovered. The pilot and crew were killed instantly. Another scout doorgunner had died when he was dropping grenades on another bunker complex, when the white phosphorous grenade he was to drop blew up as he released it. The Blues hadn't encountered much contact, which made me feel better about staying behind.

Less than a week later Lieutenant Hugele, Blue, was knocking at my door. "Sergeant Jorgenson?"

I opened the door and found Blue looking troubled.

"A Ranger team from your old company is MIA, and we're looking for volunteers for a rescue mission. You interested?"

"Damn right, sir!" I said, reaching for my web gear and rifle, while he wondered aloud if I wanted to let Cortez and Beal know about it.

"Sure, Blue. When we going out?"

"ASAP, we're the closest Blue platoon to the LRRP team's last known position, and the Rangers are asking for our assistance. I thought you'd like to know."

I liked Blue. As a platoon leader the quiet Texan had the unique ability to be able to get the men in the unit to want to work for him without having to order them to. Andreu said he was probably the best officer he ever worked with. Beal agreed. "Usually they're so damn cocky and know-it-all that they don't care to listen to what any of us lowly enlisted men might have to say. Blue not only listens, he weighs the ideas and goes with the best one!"

We'd heard that Hugele was up for captain and a rear-area job in Phuoc Vinh. We hoped he'd get it.

My mind was racing with questions as I made my way over to the new bunker Bloor, Stephenson, Esquibel, and a few others had dug for added protection. Beal and Cortez were there as well.

"Jorgy, what's up?"

"There's a LRRP team missing in Cambodia. The company's looking for volunteers," I said. Cortez and Beal responded along with Duane Bloor.

"Which team?" Beal yelled.

I could only shrug. "I don't know. Blue's finding out more now. He wants volunteers over on the flight line as soon as possible.

"Let's go!" Beal said. I had my weapon and equipment, and while the others were racing to the connex container to retrieve theirs, I was busy looking for more volunteers. I only saw six or seven people on the flight line. We'd need more.

Art Dockter hurried toward a liftship following Mr. McIntosh— Minimac! The scout pilot, who some said had balls bigger than he was, was preparing once again for another mission. John Bartlett, a gunship pilot from Whitefisa, Montana, was heading toward a sleek Cobra gunship, nonchalantly whistling to himself. All volunteers, and each making me proud of the troop.

Cortez, who had recently been given a well-deserved rear-area job, was saddled up and ready to go as well. Like the rest of us former Blues, he couldn't quite ignore the siren's call, even though he wanted to. "Fuck it! I don't need that crap anymore! I'm a REMF now," Cortez used to say whenever anyone harassed him about going back out on patrol. But when the troop's siren wailed, calling the Blues to recover a downed helicopter, Tony was always there, seeing if the platoon had enough people to do the job—hoping there was, but ready to go it there wasn't. Cortez was a 60 gunner like Bloor and had earned a reputation as a solid one, so when Blue had asked for volunteers for the LRRP rescue mission, Tony was one of the first people I thought of. Cortez didn't have much time left to do on his tour.

"Hey, Tony! Hold up a minute," I said as he headed toward the TOC.

"Yeah?" Cortez said. He had been a boxer who managed to keep his nose from getting broken too many times. Small cuts lined his brow, and his hands were strong and fast. A Southern Californian by birth, he was a Californian by nature as well, laid back. Of course, I could tell that the former boxer wasn't someone I wanted to mess with.

"You're too short to go on this one. Why don't you sit it out?"

"You mean like you and Beal? Besides, we're all Ranger trained. It's in our blood. Don't worry about it."

A short time later we were ready to go. The Vietnamese evening was muggy and the dusk was hiding patches of ground fog. We'd managed to put together an eighteen-man force. Since the platoon usually operated with twenty-one men, eighteen was close enough to satisfy the lieutenant, who was coordinating his plans with Sergeant Andreu. Once that was done, he briefed the rest of us.

"A LRRP team was hit last night in Cambodia. One of the five Rangers managed to make it back to Fire Support Base David, saying that the team leader had decided to move after he called in their last night position. Nobody had any good reason to worry about them until this morning, when they couldn't be reached by radio. When the lone survivor got into David, he informed them that two Rangers are dead and that the other two are still out there, somewhere. That's where we come in—we're the closest Blue Team to the area," he explained. Beal's face showed his concern.

I knew what he was thinking. Whose team? Who are the dead and missing LRRPs?

"Why did they move after they called in their night position?" someone murmured. I just shrugged. It was dumb, but it didn't change anything. Two Rangers were still dead, and two were missing.

As Beal, Cortez, Bloor, Doc Devalle, and I boarded the lead helicopter, my mind fell back to Song Be when Zap and Torres had died. As the helicopter lifted up over the barbed-wire gaining altitude for the rescue flight I fought to climb out of what I was feeling.

We touched down on David a while later. Blue had time there to interview the surviving LRRP, a tall, black E-6 who looked worn out from the experience. After the team had been ambushed, the remaining three Rangers fell back firing. One had been shot several times and couldn't go much farther. The E-6 decided to "escape and evade" to get the alarm out to the company by making it to the nearby fire support base. The North Vietnamese Army unit that had ambushed the Rangers was doggedly searching for the survivors with flashlights. The E-6 escaped through the jungle, avoiding NVA patrols along the way, finally moving to just outside the small infantry and artillery outpost. He waited for morning before walking to the wire in plain sight, hands raised and yelling for the perimeter defense not to shoot.

Armed with the coordinates that the team had called in just before the ambush, and with the E-6's information, we boarded the helicopters for the short flight out. NVA were in the area, Blue told us, so we were to be ready but not fire blindly because of the two Rangers out there, maybe more, who needed our help.

Just before we left, we asked the E-6, whose name was Dwight Hancock, whose team had been hit. "Cochran's," he said wearily. Deverton Cochran was a friend, the kind of LRRP everyone wanted on his team because he never gave up. Even on the grueling five-mile run in the hot Vietnamese afternoon, when Cochran looked like he was about to pass out and the veteran Rangers were taunting him, Cochran pushed on. That was the kind of thing you expected of a good LRRP.

Nevertheless, critics said that Cochran had broken one of the patrol rules, a rule that I could still hear the training NCO emphasizing in the recesses of my mind. "After you've called in your day or night halt positions *never*, I say again, *never ever* move from that position. Gentlemen, if you don't move and something should happen to you then at least we'll know the coordinates in which to look!" But for one reason or another Cochran decided to move. Judging from what the survivor had said, the move had come after sunset, which complicated matters.

More than likely the answer had to be with radio communications. The rolling Cambodian hills and carpet-thick jungle could turn a working shoulder-carried PRC-25 radio into a useless piece of white noise. Without communication, a LRRP team was helpless. If he moved, then it was for a critical reason and not something to be second-guessed without all of the facts.

"Who else is out there?" I asked.

"Laker, Andrus," the staff sergeant said. He was bordering on exhaustion. I knew the feeling and left it at that. And Royce . . . Royce Clark."

"We gotta find them," Beal said to himself more than anyone else. We were making wide passes over the last known coordinates of the missing Ranger team. Far below in the rich green, golf-course-like open fields the patches of sunlight gave the quiet setting a haunted expression. Small patches of trees bordered the open fields and gradually joined into forests, where occasional coffee-color trails could be seen. After our third pass, we were getting ready to fly to yet another field when Beal noticed a muddied figure waving frantically. Art Dockter was the second person to see him and leveled his machine gun to get the man in his sights.

"No! No!" I yelled, hitting his arm and waving him off. "It's one of the Rangers. *Rangers!*" I said again. The veteran door-gunner nodded, speaking into his radioset while Mr. McIntosh strained, turning to see what Dockter had reported. The helicopter turned hurriedly and raced toward the soldier. Even before we touched down, Beal and I had raced out to grab him as Cortez and Dockter covered our run. The Ranger was one of the cherries. Unlike the smiling confident Ranger I remembered from the company, he looked worn and exhausted.

He was talking excitedly, gesturing toward the far wood line. If he wasn't in shock, then he was damn close to it. "He's over there! Shot in the knee. Jesus, we thought you were leaving. Over there!" The Ranger looked familiar, but I couldn't remember his name.

The second and third Blue helicopters were unloading the volunteer reaction force, and Blue was hurrying over to learn what he could from the second Ranger, as Sergeant Andreu spread the platoon out to cover any unexpected surprises.

"Where are the others?" Blue asked the tired Ranger.

"Back-back up in those woods. We must have walked into a

company-size force because when we entered the tree line, machine-gun fire came from everywhere. The gooks just kept firing into them. Clark was shot in the knee, and I took a round, too. We—we hid from them. All night.'' The MIA Ranger was talking excitedly. He said that Cochran and Laker were still up in the bunker complex and that we had to get them. We assured him we would, but first we had to get the second missing team member.

"If it wasn't for Hancock we wouldn't have known what happened," Beal said to the LRRP, whose name we learned was Andrus. Judging by his strained movements, he was in substantial pain.

"Is he okay?"

Beal nodded. "Cut and bruised and dead-ass tired. But alive enough to lead us back here," Beal said "We've been out since before first light."

It was true, and even though the weather was too fogged in to even attempt a rescue mission, Mr. McIntosh and Bartlett said to hell with it and cranked up their helicopters anyway. Time was the deciding factor. Bravery, too.

"Where'd you leave Clark?" Beal asked. The Ranger pointed toward a distant wood line. His blood loss had made his arm heavy.

"The NVA spent all night looking for us. They tried. They came close—I'm glad to see you guys." Then he started heading back to the hiding place. "Hold on," I said taking the point. Ed and Cortez followed at a safe interval. When we reached the edge of the woods line, I wondered where the Ranger had left the wounded man, when I heard a small cry from just a few feet away. The underbrush was carpet-thick and dense.

"Here . . . right here," the broken voice said. I knelt down to help him. Seconds later Doc Devalle was at my side, taking over. Blue had the platoon covering the far wood line where Andrus said they'd walked into the ambush. It was too quiet. I got an uneasy feeling. Hue felt it, too, and got down. Then Bloor spotted the NVA soldiers taking aim in the wood line opposite the kill zone. They had tried to outflank us. Yelling, Porky opened up and the rest of the platoon tore into the position before the NVA could return fire. Screaming and the din of small-arms fire replaced the awkward quiet.

Blue was on the radio calling in coordinates for the guns on FSB David. In minutes the first round *swoosh*ed over our heads and exploded near the target. Dust and debris were everywhere, the noise deafening.

"Roger Redleg, adjust seven-five mikes to your left and fire for effect," Blue yelled into the handset as the artillery rounds were falling over the enemy wood line. In the distance we could hear more Hueys ferrying in more troops. When the first few helicopters had touched down four hundred yards behind us on an empty green knoll, I could see the red, white, and black Ranger shoulder patches on some of the soldiers exiting the helicopters. Even from that distance I could make out the familiar gait of Johnny Rodriguez and a few other old friends. It wasn't the time for a reunion, though Rod nodded and smiled when he saw Beal and me. A new Ranger company commander was with them, and the burly captain was busily assessing the situation before talking with Blue. A grunt platoon from FSB David was on the next lift, and it looked as though it was going to be a while before we could check out the forest the artillery was raking.

Beal and I began moving into the previous evening's kill zone. Only a hundred meters away we spread out, running fast and low and keeping a careful eye on the tree line before us, while one of our machine gunners covered our every move. Just inside the wood line I found the first NVA fighting position and the blood-soaked ground where the others had fallen. A second and third bunker only a few feet apart lay quiet, just in front of the blood pool. When the NVA had opened up on the LRRP team, they did so at point-blank range. Cochran, carrying the backup radio, was hit outright, taking the brunt of the enemy's automatic gunfire. Laker was next to fall. Even if he had managed to leap out of the kill zone there had been no place for him to go. There were enemy bunkers to the left and the right. Straight ahead was the heavy gunfire. Perhaps he desperately tried to scramble backward. Andrus was the next soldier shot. Clark and Hancock could do little but scramble back, firing. When they did, the radio was shot up so there was no way to report what had happened to the mountain relay station.

Beal was checking out the bunker on the left. I took the fighting position to the front. Hue covered me, and Cortez watched after Hue. Both positions were empty, hastily abandoned. Pieces of Ranger equipment lay on the ground as well as some of the NVA equipment. It was the knife that caught Ed's attention. "Part of the team's," he whispered. I nodded.

I picked up a Chinese canteen, after checking it for wires or a trip release. There were no signs of the dead soldiers, and only a fool would've believed they'd somehow managed to survive. The pool of blood was deep and small pieces of flesh lay there as well. The NVA soldiers had moved the bodies. But where?

"They're moving out!" Cortez said, looking back to see the Blues, Rangers, and grunt platoon heading for the tree line where we'd received fire. The forest was burning from the exploding artillery rounds, and the air smelled of cordite, smoke, and congealed blood.

"We ought to check here," I said to Tony, who nodded. Beal checked yet another bunker only to find it empty.

"They're here, damn it! I know they are," Beal whispered angrily. But there was nothing we could do; the line of soldiers was moving away from us

"They want us back!" Cortez said as we carefully moved back out of the kill zone, moving in the direction of the others. The NVA might have buried the bodies or moved them, but we would never know. The war had moved again, and it was time to move with it. When the line of grunts on the far left got just inside the tree line that the artillery had hit, the surviving North Vietnamese soldiers opened up. A grunt fell clutching his face. The lower section of his jaw had been severed, and it dangled like a red and white ribbon beneath his head. His tongue had been splintered as well, and in shock, he held it and sobbed. A second grunt took a short burst in his right leg, and he lay screaming on the ground as everyone leaped for cover. Close to a shell hole, Beal and I jumped in and returned fire. Seconds later we were joined by Bloor and Cortez.

"Medic!" someone was yelling, while we stared up and over the shell hole rim toward the sound of the voice. A good seventy-five meters of open ground separated us from the wounded men.

The screaming soldier was crying, and the voice called desperately for the medic again. From our vantage point we could see that Doc Devalle couldn't hear the voice. He was busily attending the wounded Ranger.

"Cover me!" Cortez said, getting to his feet and leaving the cover of our position. Beal and I looked at each other in surprise and then quickly provided cover fire for him as he sprinted across the open ground, and retrieved the first wounded man. That done he raced back to help the second man. The former boxer moved with the grace and ease of a ring professional, slipping to the left and then back to the right, while the NVA rounds hit around him. He managed to drag-carry the second man, who still clutched the remains of his chin as Cortez led him to safety. A medevac helicopter had been called in, and when it lighted down, Cortez helped ferry the wounded soldiers over to it.

"Jesus Christ! Who's that? John Wayne?" Ranger Rodriguez clearly admired Cortez's actions.

"No, just Tony Cortez. One of our people," I said.

Rodriguez nodded. "Then you got some good people," he added. "That took balls."

Overhearing our conversation, an overweight NCO from the reaction force shrugged. "I don't see the big deal. I could've done that."

Rodriguez shook his head in disgust, studying the fat man the way a housewife might view a roach. "Could'ves and should'ves," Rod said sarcastically. "And oh, yeah, fuck you!"

"Besides, we can't all be heroes," I said, facing the fat man. "Somebody has to wave as the parade goes by. Welcome to the sidelines."

Seeing that he was outnumbered and unwanted in the shell hole, the NCO got up and moved to another covered site. Laughter followed him. "Fuck the critics," we all agreed. The NVA gunfire ceased as division gunships attacked the tree line with a vengeance. Minutes later Cortez came sprinting back to the shell hole.

"Did we bore you?" Beal said.

"They needed help," Tony said as though his actions were nothing.

"Way to go!" I said, slapping him on the back. Embarrassed, Cortez turned the conversation back to the missing and presumed dead Rangers. "Maybe we ought to check the bunker complex out again. Maybe they might still be alive."

It was wishful thinking, and everyone knew it. We knew the grunts would eventually go back in, scouring the patch of jungle until they found the bodies or gave up and officially declared Cochran and Laker "missing in action, presumed dead."

Rodriguez stared at Cortez momentarily and then turned back to study the kill zone. "I don't know . . ." he said finally. "It's a miracle the others got out." Rod's voice was hollow, breaking.

"I'm glad we found the two," Cortez said, causing the veteran Ranger to turn back to the well-intentioned soldier. "That's gotta count for something."

"It does, man. It does," he said as the Ranger captain was signaling his men to regroup. Blue was doing the same. We, the

Blue volunteer force, would go on one final search before being pulled out; a search that would prove fruitless. When we prepared to leave, it was with great reluctance but the area was still very much under enemy control. There wasn't much choice.

"Take it easy, you guys," Rodriguez said, making his good-byes. When he got to Cortez, he paused and said, "Thanks" before joining the other Rangers.

"What was that all about?" Cortez asked.

"LRRP team leaders tend to look upon their team members or ex–team members as family. You volunteered to help his family, and to him that means something," Beal said.

"Yeah, man. And a thank-you from Rod is like getting a virgin in a Bangkok whorehouse—rare and far between!"

Besides Rod Rodriguez a handful of Rangers we knew came over to thank us before we left. On the long flight back to Tay Ninh, I was proud of Tony and was proud of being in the Blues. We hadn't been able to find the two dead LRRPs, but we had been able to find and bring in the two missing in action and yes, damn it! That did count for something! Cortez made us all look good. I felt good, too, knowing that I didn't always have to be the hero and that there were enough heroics to go around. The burden was no longer as heavy as it had been. The nice thing about admitting you weren't Superman was occasionally finding out that you could still bend steel when you had no real intention of trying. Volunteering for the mission was bending steel, and as I stared at the other supermen in the open bay of the helicopter, I knew we were the good guys. It also gave me a new appreciation of the role crew chiefs and pilots played in the war. As a point man on the flights out for a combat insertion, too often my attention was focused on the jungle below. Then, the closer we came to landing, it turned to the tree line, with my eyes searching for anything out of the ordinary—any sudden enemy movement that would reveal an ambush. Later, after the mission, the adrenaline and fear would wreak havoc, and a burdening weariness would take over.

Dockter didn't have to volunteer, but he did. Just as McIntosh, Bartlett, and the others had. Always covering us and always ready to pull our asses out of the fire we so often seemed to find ourselves in.

Yeah, we were the good guys all right, and riding back toward Tay Ninh, the only thing missing was the proverbial sunset. I didn't complain. Some days you take what you can get.

When we finally landed in Tay Ninh, I was heading toward the platoon CP when Staff Sergeant Burrows caught up with me.

"I thought you were too afraid to go out anymore?"

"I am," I said. "I don't like this shit anymore."

"Yeah, but you went anyway."

"Dumb-ass relapse," I said, stopping and turning to face him. "Look. We needed volunteers, so I volunteered. I didn't do anything special. I was just there."

"Sometimes that's enough," the big NCO said, heading across the NCO hootch. "See ya in the morning."

Burrows was always an enigma to me. Just when I thought I had him figured out, he'd throw me off with a compliment or a curve ball. "You've convinced me about reincarnation," I yelled after him. "When I die I'm coming back as a REMF!"

"No, you won't," he said without turning back. "It's not who you are."

"Fuck you!" I added as Burrows laughed. *"It won't happen again!"*

"Sure. You bet," he said. "Until next time anyway."

CHAPTER TWENTY

The war was in constant change. The war that I saw when I arrived was not the war I knew at the end of my tour. The Vietnam War was many little wars, and over the many years it had been going on, it had evolved in terms of tactics, weapons, and equipment used, and the type of soldier, airman, Marine, or sailor who fought it. Carbines gave way to M-14s, which gave way to M-16s. Bulky transport helicopters gave way to modified gunships that gave way to sleek and powerful attack helicopters. The war that the American advisors met in the early 1960s was not the war of the draftee or volunteer GI in the late '60s. Change was inevitable, but in the late '60s the speed of that change accelerated. Troop ships that once carried whole units and took months to cross the ocean gave way to eighteen-hour flights by chartered jets flying regularly scheduled flights into the new war zone. So GIs in the latter stages of the war became casual replacements from steady pools. Landing zones and fire support bases opened and then shut down with a seemingly hectic pace as well.

On a routine aerial recon mission, a scout helicopter's observer noticed something odd in the forest. A space in the forest displayed odd-looking tree limbs, limbs that looked surprisingly like upside-down helicopter skids. On closer inspection it could be seen that it was indeed a downed helicopter. Although no one in the region had reported a missing aircraft, we were sent in to find out whose it was and see if we could locate any survivors.

On the insertion we quickly took the wood line, hurrying to get out of the open-field landing zone and not be exposed to any sudden ambush. While we waited the first few minutes, listening and looking for any signs of movement, Blue signaled for us to move out. Ed Beal and I took the point. Moving in the direction the scout helicopter had given us, we stepped into the crash site with quiet surprise. The downed aircraft was a Cobra gunship, an older model. Where the automatic minigun and automatic grenade launcher should've been, there was only a minigun. While we carefully moved around the upside-down aircraft, I wondered how the ant mound had built up inside the pilot's small confined area. Then, on closer inspection I saw that the ''anthill'' was a decaying body with ants moving in and around the partially exposed skull. A splintered tree grew through the pilot's back where he'd been impaled on impact. The second warrant officer, the weapons-control man or gunner had been thrown free. Bits and pieces of his uniform and flight helmet were scattered around the front of the aircraft, and there were only the pieces of uniform and bleached bones left to prove he ever existed.

''He probably lived, crawled out,'' Beal said, studying the human debris. The officer's rusted pistol was locked in a skeletal deathgrip.

From that, I imagined what had happened. The helicopter had crashed, and the pilot had been killed when the aircraft tumbled through the high treetops and then was impaled on the two-inch-wide tree. The gunner, injured, crawled away from the wreckage, clutching his pistol and knowing that help would soon be arriving. For his sake I'd hoped he passed out before the animals inched in to finish him off.

Then, I had my second surprise.

''We got a map and a wallet here!'' Cortez said, pulling out a plastic division wallet from the cockpit of the aircraft along with the plastic covered map. Going through the wallet for identification, Tony found a driver's license, some family photos of a young uniformed officer, sternly facing the camera in one frame, and then the same man in civilian dress, holding a small girl, while a proud wife stood next to him, smiling. The Military Payment Certificates were a vintage I didn't recognize. Since I'd been in Vietnam there had been two MPC changes, but this script dated from before my time and even that of Burrows, who was already on his six-month extension.

While Cortez was busy studying the wallet, I was looking over the map, startled by the green jungle region where I knew at least three fire support bases should've been.

''Jesus! How old's this thing?' I said. Beal, glancing over my shoulder, estimated maybe two years or so. There was nothing left to do but recover the fragments of the two, load them into rubber body bags, and send them to Graves Registration for identification. With the serial number from the pistol, the numbers on the helicopter, and of course, the wallet, identification wouldn't be difficult. The difficulty would come to the families of the dead pilots when any hope of their survival or possible capture would disappear with a telegram.

The war was changing again. Lieutenant Hugele was gone and so was Doc Devalle. Both reassigned to Phuoc Vinh. Many of the Rangers I knew from the LRRP company had left as well. When Hue stepped into the club looking depressed, I asked him why the down face.

"They're sending me to officer's school," the small Vietnamese soldier said quietly.

I remembered hearing something about Vietnamese Officer's Candidate School's requiring a ten-year obligation. I didn't know whether it was true or not, but judging from Hue's glum expression it appeared to be the case.

"Turn it down," I said. Braun nodded, handing the Vietnamese soldier a cold Budweiser, Braun's favorite beer.

"I can't. They no let me," he said.

"So when do you have to leave?" Beal asked.

"Sometime next week, maybe. They replace me." Hue drank the beer in silence. There was nothing we could say or do to change his spirits and that was frustrating. He'd already been fighting the war longer than anyone in our unit and more than likely longer than anyone in the division. Now he was committed to another ten years.

"Will the Pimp be picking you up?" Braun asked while Hue's moonfaced head nodded his reply.

The Pimp was Hue's commanding officer, a small, cocky, over-dressed captain who wore aviator sunglasses, a starched, finely tailored uniform that sported occasional flashes of gold braid and ego. The jeep he drove featured an unusual amount of chrome, and when he arrived each month to pay his sergeant, he'd chew out the more relaxed Hue and make him stand at attention while he officiously paraded around him, finding flaws in his uniform or person. It was on a second such visit while I was there that Braun and Cortez took to mocking the captain until the officer, angered by the act, said something angrily to Cortez who only smiled back, raising his right hand, flipping the captain off.

"You biet 'fuck you'?" Tony said, holding his middle finger inches in front of the Vietnamese Army captain, who angrily looked around for someone with authority to whom to report the incident. When he couldn't find anyone but indifferent enlisted men, he began to reach for his holstered .45, only to have Beal and a few others of us who knew and liked Sergeant Hue lock and load our M-16s with enough noise and cold indifference for the Vietnamese officer to get the point. Afterward, whenever he drove to the unit to deliver Hue's monthly pay, he hurriedly dropped it off and left.

It was Braun who nicknamed the captain the Pimp. When he showed up to take Hue away the Pimp didn't even offer to give the enlisted man a hand with his baggage. From the years he'd spent with the platoon, Hue had amassed a number of gifts and clothing items from members of the platoon. Besides his army gear, he had an electric fan, a tape recorder, radio, a beat-up guitar, a Levi-jean's jacket with matching pants, a pair of well-worn cowboy boots, and a dozen or so country and western albums.

The Pimp made it a point of berating Hue in front of us. When it was clear that the captain wasn't going to give him a hand Cortez and I moved forward. The Vietnamese captain quickly backed away.

"Take it easy, you little shit," Tony said, slapping him on the back while Hue said he would.

"You take care, Jorgy," he said to me in his lilting English. He offered his hand.

"You're the number one soldier," I said, shaking his hand. The compliment only made him smile. I was dead serious, and sad to see him leaving. "You're the best."

"No, I only have more practice. Thank you, my friend," he said, getting into the jeep. The captain wasn't about to leave time for long farewells. He quickly jumped in after Hue, starting the jeep and then hurriedly driving off. As they drove away, I felt sorry for Hue, disliking the pompous asses like the Pimp he had to serve. I'd heard so much about how lazy and worthless the ARVN soldiers were, but I wondered how we Americans would appear to others if we were forced to fight an endless war for those indifferent to our values? Nguyen Hue had taught me most of what I knew about surviving jungle warfare. He was the closest thing I'd ever seen to Daniel Boone, and I wondered how the platoon would fare without him. The platoon still had Tri, but Tri was useless as a scout or even as a soldier. Two weeks later, when the Cambodian mercenary Lam, who replaced Hue had shot Tri in the arm with a .45 for calling him an animal, the rest of us open-mouthed spectators could do little but watch on in surprise. The Cambodian replacement wasn't Hue, but he had pride and loyalty. Maybe we couldn't really ask for more.

Hue had spent five years in combat and since he was about to enter the Vietnamese officer's training program, it appeared as though he'd have to spend the remainder of the war in combat as well. For Hue and so many others in similar positions, it was a no-win situation, where his best bet might be in just breaking even, surviving the war. Hue was one of the reasons why I was in Vietnam, to help those like him, not those like the Pimp, who were making a profit on the war and taking advantage of the misery of others.

The Pimp dressed too well, wore fancy, highly shined boots that zipped up the sides, wore wraparound sunglasses, had a cigarette holder in the small pocket that was designed for a pen in his uniform shirt, and sported a thin mustache of the sort that General Ky wore. He was always a day or so late with Hue's pay, and rumor had it that he was into the black market, working with a supply sergeant in the 25th and selling military items to anyone who'd pay the going price. He wasn't selling weapons, the rumor went, but he was into blankets, C rations, and boots, and that was enough to keep the Pimp living comfortably in a bungalow in Tay Ninh. It was also rumored that the Pimp was a Cao Dai and that his rank had been purchased from a high-ranking Vietnamese officer for the going rate.

"Couldn't of been much," Cortez said when he heard the story. "The fucker's a real sleazeball."

The platoon would miss Hue, but we wouldn't miss Tri. After Lam shot him, our respect for the Cambodian grew. From the start he was up walking point with Ed and me, and for that much we were glad.

Point was the job you loved to hate, a drug that fed on itself and your imagination. Lam knew it and wanted to prove his worth by sharing the responsibility. The platoon knew the new scout would work out well.

The party, by party standards, was loud. Jim Braun and another Blue named Jack Miller were going home. Their ETS dates, estimated times of separation, were only a day apart so their orders came down from division together. They were to report to Bien Hoa to begin out-processing the following day. Then, after two to three days, they'd board an outgoing plane for *The World*.

To celebrate the occasion, ETS or *shortimer* parties were held, when time and the war permitted, and GIs reported into the out-processing centers drunk, hung over, stoned, or just smiling stupidly happy. For them the war was all but over, so their buddies threw a party.

Jack and Jim both drank so the party favor was alcohol of every sort, container, and size. Extra beer was obtained from the class-six yard, while pilots and crews provided vodka, gin, whiskey, and an occasional bottle of wine. Wine? Well, they meant well. The big radioman was singing the praises of us Blues while we, in turn, told him he could walk on water, piss into any wind without getting wet, and had brass balls that clanked when he walked. We all laughed, but the more Jim drank, the more maudlin he became.

"I'm going to miss you assholes," he said taking a drink of his twelfth Budweiser. "For the most part you're good people . . . for the most part."

"By the way, anybody want me to give my best to his wife or girlfriend when I get back?" Miller said, enjoying the party, only to be shouted down with a chorus of "Fuck yous!"

Beal had tended bar for a while and then gave it up to take a more active role in the festivities. "To hell with it!" he said, turning it over to Manning who, though mildly drunk, accepted the position, taking his payment out in drink.

"I'm really going to miss you guys," Braun said again. Manning was to take over his position as the platoon leader's radioman, and Braun seemed satisfied with that decision. Manning could handle a radio, and he wasn't intimidated by rank. He could just as easily tell a major to get the fuck off his radio net as he could give someone a time check. The old Blue, Lt. Hugele, had received the job as the battalion S-4 and would be going there as a captain, so that meant the platoon would receive another lieutenant to take over, another new-guy officer, gentleman, and dumbass to break-in. The first few weeks would be difficult. He'd probably want to do everything his way, the way the officer's training courses had taught him to do, only to find twenty-one or so frowning faces shaking their heads and wondering how long it would take the silly shit to realize that maybe they knew just as much about the war or maybe more than he did. A wise officer would realize this and utilize that experience, while a hard-nosed type might fight it as long as he could, unable to admit he didn't know everything. Braun hoped for the former, but told us to be prepared for the latter. Manning would help by being his RTO while the rest of us would have to help as well.

"Be gentle. Officers' egos are easy to crush. Let him think he can win the war by himself for a week. Then, help him out," Braun yelled before excusing himself to step outside to piss. Returning with a smile, he opened another beer.

"How many days you got left, Jorgy?" the bear said, standing behind me.

"Fifty and a wake-up," I said, turning in the stool.

"That leaves you less than two months to pick up three more Purple Hearts," he said with heavy sarcasm.

"I don't want anymore," I said.

"Good. Now, say it a few more times over and over again until you believe it. Kid, I'm going to miss your dumb-ass enthusiasm. You ever finish that book I gave you?"

I laughed along with him. I'd finished *Don Quixote* months before, occasionally picking it back up and rereading it. "Sure, you want it back?"

"Naw. It's yours. Hey," he said, taking his large hands and shaking my shoulders. "Don't do anything stupid, anything else, I mean. You done good, kid, so when your time is up, you go home. You hear me?"

I said I did, and then when he seemed satisfied with my answer, he went off to lecture Beal. Miller was doing pretty much the same thing with a few others in platoon. Mom and Dad were going away from home for a while so they wanted to make certain the kids knew what to do if anything came up. It seemed to be a trait common to many soldiers who were going home, a compulsion to tell us the things they felt we had to know to survive.

When much of the drinking and lecturing was over, thoughts turned to pranks. While there were some who resorted to real fraggings—that is, pulling the pin on a fragmentation grenade then throwing it at a person they wanted to frag—others were content to use psychological fraggings to get even. Urinating in the troop commander's private shower-storage tanks was one such method. Manning had tossed in a new psychological ploy on the troop commander by occasionally referring to him in radio transmissions as Apollo Six instead of Apache Six. Then some of the officers began to refer to Apache Six as Apollo Six, stifling laughter when they did.

But his success wasn't enough, so Manning called for the unveiling of a new weapon. "Powdered CS," he said with an evil grin. "Do we have any?" We did.

"Get me some, if you'll be so kind," Chuck Manning said. A new guy went to retrieve the powdered irritant. CS was a riot-control agent, developed to take over where the less irritating tear gas left off. The grenade form of the irritant would send billowing clouds into the air, causing even the most composed and committed rioter to cry and run blindly to get away from it.

During basic training at Fort Lewis, Washington, we were told to lie face down on the ground while training NCOs ignited two CS grenades.

"Keep your heads down and don't move!" the senior drill sergeant yelled as the two other sergeants pulled the pins on the CS grenades. With a slow hiss, a cloud spread over the ground where we were lying, covering the area like a stinging blanket. The soldiers who were closest to the grenades were gasping and crying. One was on his knees retching violently while others, who'd been unable to endure the gas, got to their feet and ran screaming, tripping over other soldiers. When the gas hit me, my eyes, nose, and lungs filled with sharp, hot needles. My groin and armpits were burning as well, and the pain was intense. I started to gag and then, using my hands, dug deep into the fresh earth, plunging my face into the cool ground, trying to take shallow breaths. When the cloud cleared only half of our original number was still on the ground, and they looked and felt much the same as I had.

Off to the side, wearing protective masks and chuckling, were the training NCOs and the senior drill instructor.

But powdered CS was designed to have a longer-lasting effect on the area where it was spread. As a powder, it could remain in an area longer. Powdered CS was dropped in fifty-five gallon drum barrels over bunker-complex areas where the powder would spread out on the wind. On several patrols we'd come across unexploded barrels and carefully set charges on them before hurriedly moving out of the area. Along the way, somehow, Beal and a few others had managed to store away several pounds of the fine powder in plastic bags for future use. One popular use was spreading out small amounts in the barbed wire strung in front of guard bunkers. Another use for the powder was locked in Manning's mind and soon to be revealed to the rest of us.

When the new guy returned with one of the plastic bags, Chuck smiled and walked out of the small bar as a few of us followed. He walked casually across the darkened compound heading towards the orderly room and then farther on toward the troop commander's hootch, then farther on to the small outhouse that was Apollo Six's private latrine. Doing a quick recon, Manning moved in spreading powder around the base of the small sandbag wall that ringed the inside of the one-man outhouse. When that was done, he loaded the remaining powder into a sandbag on the protective wall and removed another, setting it in its place.

"There!" he said when he joined us. "That should do the

trick.'' And it did, time and again, whenever the major used the latrine, unable to understand why his chest felt so tight and burned whenever he went to the bathroom, while the platoon chuckled at the private joke.

The morning after the going-away party, Miller and Braun boarded a helicopter for Bien Hoa as a number of us lined the runway for the traditional send-off. They waved, nodding and laughing as the helicopter took off. It made the wide circle for the pass and flyby. While the helicopter was making the turn Cortez, Beal, Manning, and a few of the latest new arrivals pulled the pins on the smoke grenades, and the smoke billowed up to the sky in colorful columns. Then it was our turn to holler and yell, applauding as the helicopter flew fast and low through the smoke. It was a small tribute to soldiers we cared about. Judging from the broad smiles, it was enough.

Over the course of the next month or so, we'd repeat the process for most of the other remaining veteran Blues. One by one they were going home. Among them some of the best members of the platoon, like Paul Engelbretsen, Dennis Henderson, Mark Esquibel, Bill Lugenbeal, Ken May, and Tony Cortez.

While some were casual friends, others were like family, and in addition to the technical skills the platoon was losing, we were losing a sense of trust and reliability as well. Those leaving were people we had relied on. Replacing them were a series of new faces, unknowns. Even their names seemed difficult to remember—''Get what's his face up here now? The new guy from back East somewhere . . . shit!''

Still, among them were men who were proving themselves, guys like Ricardo Socastro, Keith Weisse, Ron Swope, and Mike Toole. All of them were privates who'd give something back to the platoon by way of good soldiering skills.

With each rotation home, the parties held less impact or enthusiasm or real meaning. After all, the new guys couldn't really appreciate their significance. Their wars were still very much ahead of them, and that realization always seemed to loom over the proceedings. Their genuine friendships hadn't evolved yet. The combat missions, helicopter crashes, jungle firefights, and spent blood and emotions would create their bonds.

Until then they'd attend the parties, saying good-bye to veterans they didn't really know, and simply go along with the ritual.

It was a rite of passage, maybe the only real one any of us would find in the war.

* * *

We turned over our unit area to the Vietnamese and temporarily moved the headquarters to Phuoc Vinh and, later on, to the troop's new home at Fire Support Base Buttons in Song Be.

Buttons was little more than an extended fire support base but featured an airstrip, a dentist, a post exchange that consisted of several connex storage boxes, and closer access to the Cambodian sector the division had assigned us to cover. Song Be was also where Zap and Torres had died, and my last, vivid memory of the fire support base was of standing on the flight line staring at their lifeless, twisted bodies before the helicopter lifted off for Graves Registration and their eventual shipment home.

As we flew into Buttons and touched down, my thoughts flashed back to that time and feeling, and I was suddenly uncomfortable and trembling.

"Cold flight, huh?" a new guy said, a PFC who'd recently been assigned to the platoon.

"Huh?"

"I said it was cold up there. You'd think because it's hot down here that the helicopter flight would've been warmer. Strange," he said. He had no way of knowing why I was trembling. I was staring out into the wall of jungle but fighting the small battle over again in my mind. But it still ended the same way, no matter how much I wanted to change it.

The troop's new home was still under construction and though a number of Quonset-hutlike structures were in various stages of building, there was still a way to go. For the time being, we'd share the small slotlike, sandbagged sleeping areas that were large enough for a cot and maybe an ammo-box seat. There was no room to stand, and we had to hunch over or sit down as we entered. Three sandbagged walls and a corrugated metal roof, reinforced by more sandbags, rested over a plywood floor. Besides the grunts and various other personnel, the tiny hovels housed an army of rats.

The platoon met near the troop TOC, playing chess, reading or just talking during free time. While the engineers worked on the new troop facilities, the troop worked on creating a troop area. Latrines had to be dug, outdoor showers constructed, guard bunkers worked on, as well as the perimeter defense.

To add to matters, there was also a new lieutenant to break in, but then, that wasn't my concern. With only a month to go, I was, technically, no longer part of the platoon. When we arrived at Buttons, First Sergeant Sparacino turned over the responsibilities of perimeter security to Beal and me. Ed had three weeks to go, a week less than I did, so Sparacino wanted to give us something to do that would keep us busy and the troop reasonably safe while the perimeter wire and bunker network were completed. We were assigned four bunkers that faced twenty-five yards of deadman's land with one line of barbed red wire between the bunker and jungle. The engineers would eventually clear away a larger portion of the jungle, but for now our sector was the easiest access to the fire support base.

"Hell," Top said, looking at the incomplete perimeter, "Even the front gate when it's open is tougher to get through!"

He was right. It would be relatively easy for an enemy soldier to low-crawl through the one line of barbed wire and then quickly and quietly pass the bunkers and into the interior of the fire support base.

"We have some modifications to make," I said. Beal nodded. We set out claymores, trip flares, and trip wires, hung empty Coke cans with pebbles in them on the barbed wire. If the wire moved, the pebbles would rattle, and the guards in the bunkers would hear them. We cleared away brush in the deadman zone to provide better lines of fire from the bunkers, and then lay the last of the CS powder along the base of the barbed wire.

I remembered the ground attack that had hit Buttons in early November, recalling how the NVA hit the perimeter with line after line of attacks, the human wave approach, to overwhelm the bunkers and force a hole that would provide access into the base. The attack failed, but not before it caused considerable damage, wounding and killing a number of GIs. Having fought against several ground assaults without the aid of barbed wire or fortified bunkers, I didn't relish facing another with less than a month to go in Vietnam. And neither did Ed, who couldn't believe that the engineers were finishing the troop area before the perimeter was done.

"Fucked-up priorities," he mumbled. Though we were happy that Buttons didn't have the almost nightly incoming of Tay Ninh, the absence was quietly unnerving. Those who had become accustomed to the mortar and rocket attacks were visibly on edge in Song Be. It was too quiet. An MP on the back gate had been shot and killed by a sniper, so we knew the Viet Cong were still active, and when radar picked up troop movement in the nearby jungle we knew something was up. Helicopters were taking fire outside the fire support base, and the perimeter guard was put on red alert, off and on for a week. Those who had remembered the last ground attack on Buttons had reason to worry.

They had held off being overrun by coordinated use of gunships, artillery, and perimeter defense. If the perimeter defense was lost, then the other two might prove to be useless. But here was a gaping hole in the base protected by four partially completed bunkers and one strand of barbed wire. Time and again grunts would pass by the compound and remark on the situation.

"Aren't you gonna finish the perimeter?" became the standard question. The standard response to our replies was a casual sigh. The questioners knew that at least we would have to bear the brunt on any assault.

Eventually, the perimeter was completed without incident, much to the relief of those on Buttons. The new lieutenant was a West Pointer, I was told. A gung ho Airborne Ranger who was determined to correct the mistakes he'd immediately seen in the platoon.

"Another fucking dumb-ass new guy," Manning said. He sounded so much like Braun that Beal and I did a double take. "He's been here all of a week, and he knows exactly how he's going to win the war. They should tack on another hundred and ten dollars to his check for hazardous thinking pay!"

"Give him some time," I said, "be patient with him. He's only an officer."

"At least we don't have to break him in," Ed said when Manning had gone. I nodded, looking at my calendar. Thirty days were showing on the Julian calendar where I'd marked the days of the year off, one by one. The small day blocks seemed so little now. The war was all but over for us, and there was just a handful of veteran Blues left in the platoon. It didn't take much to notice the envious looks we'd received from those who knew we would soon be going home. There was a certain amount of satisfaction in it and emptiness, too, because we were damn glad to be leaving the war. Yet at the same time we felt some guilt for leaving the others behind. But then, Vietnam was many little wars, individualized and fragmented. It seemed to me that that was the division's and the army's big problem. The men at the top couldn't understand why soldiers found it difficult to take pride in their divisions or army when there was no sense of belonging to any real organization. Soldiers were merely replacements, brought in daily, part of a rotation system, to replace wounded, dead, or departed soldiers. Personnel rosters changed almost daily, so that buddies only looked after close buddies. New replacements simply became FNGs without names or faces. Platoons, troops, companies, battalions and divisions took on "Us and Them" qualities. But then, I wasn't in charge, nor could I see the whole picture. I only had my small piece of the war to deal with, and it was getting smaller everyday.

CHAPTER TWENTY-ONE

I was sent by the first sergeant to Phuoc Vinh to pick up some radio equipment for the troop. When I returned, a runner said Sparacino wanted to see me in the orderly room. The old top sergeant was going over an inventory list on his desk with the unit's supply sergeant, and as I entered Sparacino looked up.

"Good. This'll take care of one problem anyway. Sergeant Jergensen," he said, while I smiled, thinking that as long as I knew the man he'd always mispronounced my name.

"What's up, Top?"

"Sergeant Beal's been medevaced."

The news hit me hard. I'd seen Beal earlier that morning. He was still working on the perimeter and would probably still be working on it when I got back.

"Medevaced! Why? What happened?"

"Malaria," Sparacino said. "They've sent him down to Saigon, and from there he'll fly out to Japan. I know you're his buddy, so I was hoping you could take his rifle down to him. The paperwork's all filled out and signed, and I want to make sure he gets it."

The rifle was a Soviet SKS that he'd picked up after a firefight. It was an authorized war trophy and as such could be taken home, providing the paperwork was correct and proper. Many times in the past, pilots and officers seeing the weapon made him offers for the long rifle with the fine wood-grain stock, only to have Beal say it wasn't for sale. Ed was proud of his war trophy and had spent a great deal of time securing the paperwork to take it home. Now, with malaria, he would only be able to take what he could carry, while the rest of his things would be shipped home or be returned to the unit supply for redistribution.

"I'll give you a three-day pass to deliver it," the first sergeant said.

"I can get there tomorrow sometime," I said, knowing I could hitchhike at the airstrip, using the various transport helicopters to make my way back to Saigon. I had a reasonably good idea where the hospital was and knew that if I could get to Bien Hoa, then Saigon was just down the road.

"Take the three days just in case," he said, handing me the pass, along with Beal's Soviet rifle. "Thanks, Jergensen, I appreciate it."

The first sergeant made it sound as though I was doing him a favor when, in reality, he was doing me one. I knew Ed hadn't been feeling so well for the last two days, but in Vietnam that seemed to be the common condition. C rations, the heat, and the hard living conditions left people looking haggard and worn, so Ed's condition wasn't out of the ordinary. He had been scheduled to go home in less than two weeks. Now he wouldn't be going home until the doctors in Japan gave him the okay. When I got back to the hootch several squads of the platoon had moved into, I saw Ed's cot empty, his equipment gone. Wearing a frown, Manning came over.

"You heard about Beal?"

I nodded. "Yeah, Top wants me to take a few of his things down to him."

"I'm glad you are. Damn near everyone was drooling over the SKS when they carried it over to the orderly room. When you going?"

"Tomorrow morning."

Manning thought it over and said: "Would you tell him good-bye for me and, I dunno, keep in touch. He's good people, Jorgy."

I nodded.

Chuck was feeling the way I felt. Another part of the old platoon was gone, and though we should've been happy about Ed's leaving, we somehow weren't. Though many of us had talked about reunions and getting together Stateside, we knew it wouldn't happen, or that if it did, circumstances would be too different to keep the camaraderie alive. It was the *then* that counted, that mattered. Anything in the future wouldn't hold the same value.

From Song Be I caught a ride into Phuoc Vinh and was stuck there for three hours. While I waited for an outbound helicopter, I strolled on over to the Ranger company and watched it from behind the company's fence. Young, busy-looking Rangers were going about their daily functions, some checking and cleaning weapons, other practicing walking drills, while two more burned shit. Not seeing a familiar face, I walked back to the flight line, laughing at the thought that I was the Lone Ranger and my Trusted Indian Companion was in the hospital with malaria. No more masks, no silver bullets, or hardy hi-ho anythings. I was Don Quixote at last, realizing that it wasn't the valiant quest after all. But along the way I'd learned something about friendship, the kind where the Sancho Panzas stuck beside you, looking after your welfare. I didn't know too many who really believed in the cause anymore, but I knew a lot who believed in each other. And though I knew it had to seem laughable to people watching from a distance, there was a certain dignity and honorable air about that.

From Phuoc Vinh I caught a Chinook to Bien Hoa and then was lucky enough to hop another ride into Long Binh. By the time I got into Saigon, it was late afternoon, so with the Soviet rifle slung over my shoulder drawing strange looks, I knew it wouldn't be too long before the MPs stopped me. Less than ten minutes later an MP jeep going the other way in traffic did a U-turn and wheeled to a stop next to me.

"Hold it right there, Sergeant!" an officer said. I saluted and he returned it with a lackluster salute of his own. It always bothered me when officers wouldn't provide the same respect they demanded, and it annoyed even more when the mild sneer remained on his round face as he dramatically assessed the situation. The officer wore starched, tailored jungle fatigues and, of course, the standard aviator sunglasses. He wore a highly polished, painted helmet liner that displayed his rank and MP status the way a neon light might advertise a cheap bar. He wore Cochran jump boots instead of the standard-issue green and black jungle boots, and a government-issue pen stuck out of the top of his left shirt pocket. A .45 hung low on his hip, and he was the prime example of a Saigon Commando. The driver was a thin spec four dressed in the same uniform as the officer with, of course, the exception of the rank ensignia. To the officer I was the typical grunt and probable AWOL—and if I wasn't, then he'd at least give me the benefit of his authority. When he had finished his assessment, he said, "Your button is unbuttoned, soldier."

The top left button of my shirt pocket was undone, and he and the driver seemed to take satisfaction in my chore.

"Your boots look like they need some polish, too," he added smiling.

"Sorry, sir. We don't polish boots in the field. We don't have the luxuries of things like shoe polish or brushes," I said. If he wanted to push it, then I'd push back.

"Got a copy of your orders and ID card?"

"Yes, sir, I do," I said, producing the necessary documents for his inspection. His head bobbed from the name on my ID card to the nametag sewn on my jungle fatigues. He handed the documents back. "You have any paperwork on the rifle, Sergeant?"

"Yes, sir, I do," producing the war-trophy papers for the officer.

"The name here says Beal. What are you trying to pull?" The officer said in a tone that sounded as though he uncovered a major crime.

"That's right, sir. If you care to check with my unit, you'll see that I'm delivering the rifle to Sergeant Beal who's in the hospital down the road with malaria."

"Is that right?" he said, his tone suddenly changing. Maybe the crime wasn't a crime after all. "If he has malaria like you say, then they'll fly him out to Camp Zama, Japan, and if that's the case, he might not be able to carry the rifle with him. I don't suppose he'd like to sell it?"

"I wouldn't know, sir. It isn't mine. It's my buddy's."

"What do you say we check the serial number on the rifle just to make sure it's the one on the records," he said, holding out his hands while I reluctantly handed him the rifle. He took his time handling the long, sleek weapon, admiring the polished wooden stock and the rich, black barrel. He folded and unfolded the spike bayonet of the rifle after an awkward moment and then finally gave a cursory look at the rifle's serial numbers. Handing the rifle back to me, he took out a small green notebook from his uniform pocket and wrote something down on one of the pages, ripping it out and handing it to me as well.

"It's my name and unit. If Sergeant Beal wants to sell it, then tell him we can work something out." He returned the notebook to the pocket and then nodded to his driver to start the jeep. With the same casual indifference, he offered a tired salute. Returning it with a crisp one of my own, I smiled.

"By the way, sir," I said, turning to leave, "your button's unbuttoned." I grinned as his face grew red with rage.

What was it about some people who wore their rank like a god-given birthright? Military courtesy and regulations outlined the expected behavior, but how one administered it was something else entirely.

When I reached the hospital, I had to check the rifle in with the

MPs at the secured gate. Then, checking with the duty officer, I found out where Beal was—no great trick since I had been on the same ward six or seven months before. I followed the officer's directions and my memory down the hall and up the stairs until I came out on the polished corridor that led into the ward. I was hoping to see the blond nurse who had worked the ward when I was there. I couldn't remember her name, just her face and knowing she was the kind of nurse you wanted helping you when you were in the hospital. A dark-haired captain manned the duty desk, along with a florid enlisted medic in hospital whites.

"Yes, Sergeant, can I help you?" the captain said, while the medic was checking something on a clipboard.

"Yes, ma'am, I'm here to see Sergeant Edward Beal, A Troop, 1st of the 9th. He's my buddy, and my first sergeant sent me down to bring a few personal effects before he left."

"Which division?" she asked.

"The Cav," I replied while she checked a patient roster.

"I have a Robert Edward Beal with that unit who . . . oh, no," she said with a pained expression. "They flew him out to Japan late this morning. I don't know what to tell you. I'm sorry."

"There's nothing left to say, Ma'am. Thanks," I said, turning to leave and then wheeling about. "I don't suppose you have a blond lieutenant nurse who works this ward. Big eyes-and-smile type? Worked the ward last November?"

The dark-haired nurse stuck out her lower lip in a near pout. Bright blue eyes sighed with her. She must have been a heartbreaker at the officer's club. "I'm sorry," she said again, "I only arrived in-country in June."

The enlisted medic looked up from what he was doing. "I knew her, but she left about two months ago. Sarge, it ain't exactly your day."

"Don't I know it," I said, walking away. And I did know it, too. I knew it all too well. People came and went with too much frequency, and the war became an impersonal experience, communal only in its purpose and shared responsibilities. I remembered something Braun had once said about it after an incoming rocket had slammed into a parked helicopter, missing our barracks by a good hundred feet.

"We could've been hit!" I said, watching the burning helicopter. The big, burly man shook his head. "Naw, the gooks were aiming at the helicopter because they know if they hit us, the army will only send more troops to replace us. However, helicopters cost big bucks, and if enough of them are destroyed, then the taxpayers will scream to Congress, threatening to vote them out of office. That's when they'll seriously think about ending the war. When the price gets too high for anyone to bear. Until then, we'll just come and go because in terms of dollar value we don't matter.''

"Bullshit!" I said while the big bear of a man shook his head again. "We matter!"

"Maybe to each other we do, but you're arguing the emotional aspect of the war, and that's not the bottom line.''

"Which is what?"

"Which is that we're simply an acceptable loss," he said.

Acceptable loss was a military term I'd heard but never fully understood, and when that became evident by the expression on my face, Braun continued. "The 'acceptable loss' is the predetermined casualty figure the policy makers deem expendable prior to committing forces into combat. In short, it's the number of injured or killed an army is willing to sustain in order to achieve its objective. Like it or not, we're the acceptable loss. Congress has its own acceptable loss figure, too, only it's in dollars and cents—and until they reach that amount, until it's no longer acceptable, then we won't matter.''

I didn't like the concept or really understand it then, but making my way back to Song Be from Bien Hoa it had finally settled in. Soldiers seldom do matter.

Less than two weeks later my own orders came down from division. I was going home. Handing me my orders, the first sergeant also added something more.

"What's this?" I said, looking at the small, dark blue presentation box.

"It's a Bronze Star for Meritorious Service. You earned it.''

"I thought the old man wasn't too thrilled with me?"

"He isn't, but this has nothing to do with that. You're a damn good soldier, and that's all that matters. Well," he added smiling, "maybe to me, anyway, and you're one of my people. Take care, Jorgy, and by the way, the next time I tell you to take three days to run an errand for me. Take the three days. Now, go pack your things and go home."

I said I would.

"Good. There's an outbound helicopter going to Bien Hoa tomorrow. Be on it. Oh, by the way. You have three days to report to the out-processing station. Enjoy them." First Sergeant Sparacino extended his hand, and I shook it.

That night I partied with a few of the Blues while going through the ritual of the farewell process, which was smiling stupidly at everything and giving away the things I'd be leaving behind—the empty grenade box for my personal things, paperbacks, and assorted odds and ends that the average junk dealer would find useless but the combat infantryman valued highly.

The Blues were pulling a mission the following morning, and other than a few who were needed back in the fire support base, the war was going on well without us. Manning was pulling radio duty in the TOC and took a few minutes to say good-bye before someone yelled that he was needed on the radio.

Duffel bag in one hand and rifle in the other, I walked across the seemingly deserted compound area toward the flight line. I'd said my good-byes to Burrows and a few of the other vets the evening before, although there weren't all that many faces I knew well. Burrows was the only permanent resident, it seemed.

"You going to stay in the army?" Burrows asked. "I mean, you're not a bad squad leader, for a shake 'n' bake." His grin was the first I'd seen from the unsmiling professional.

"So how did you find out?"

"At first I thought that maybe you got your stripes with the Silver Star and Purple Heart you picked up with the Rangers . . ."

"And then?" I asked, taking the bait. He wasn't about to let me off of the hook, and I knew it.

"Two things," he said matter of factly, "First, you seemed more worried about acne than you did the NVA, which told me how young you were, and, second, I took a look at your records in the orderly room. Take care, kid," he said, offering a handshake that, like the owner, was forceful and to the point. "You're okay."

Then, the career NCO dismissed the conversation and went back to other matters at hand. In this case it was von Clausewitz on war.

Staring out over the new troop compound, I saw that nothing was the same, but then the war had always been transitional. Beal, Cortez, Henderson, Braun, and so many other of the Blues were gone. Their tours completed. So, too, were the majority of the scouts and doorgunners like Terry "Mugsy" Delorme, Mr. McIntosh, Art Dockter, and those I was just beginning to know. Captain Funk had given way to the new troop leader, and Lt. Jack Hugele, Blue, had left for Phuoc Vinh just as Doc Devalle had. And Hue, well, with his years of combat experience he had been reassigned to wherever the South Vietnamese Army could best utilize his skills.

One by one they'd left before me. The staggered tours of duty and differing job responsibilities eliminated any real sense of joy when it came time to leave; it was always an awkward parting, where the person leaving was troubled by wanting to get the hell out of the war zone while leaving his buddies behind to fight.

Sitting on the flight line, leaning against my duffel bag, while waiting for the helicopter that would ferry me back to the division's rear-area base camp, I had time to think about my tour of duty as well as what Braun had said about the war. Maybe when the bottom line was tallied, when it was all over, maybe our casualties were all just someone's acceptable loss. But not mine. I could see the waxen, bloated face of the dead grunt I helped carry through the night, still smell the jungle swamp's muck and mire mixing with the dried blood and decomposing body that had begun to emit its pungent odor and gases.

I could still see Dave Torres smiling and laughing the day before he died, Zap's stunned and dying eyes when the bullet entered his face, and remember the crashed and burning helicopters with their dead or wounded crews. It was more than the morning mist that made me shiver. So if it was all so damned acceptable, then why was I trembling? Maybe it was the thought of the surgical ward and the human debris I saw there. I expected to learn fear in jungle combat but found it instead in the pristine field hospital. I wouldn't forget the ward or the terrible sobs or screams I heard there. It wasn't acceptable. I wouldn't dismiss it that easily. Although it might've lacked significance in Congress, it had its impact on me.

From the pilot's area, I saw a cluster-fuck of warrant officers walking toward the flight line, laughing and ribbing one of their bunch. A lift-ship pilot, whose face I recognized but didn't really know, was also leaving, and the group was there to give him a proper send-off. While they held smoke grenades in their hands, the out-going pilot would get a flyby. After the helicopter had become airborne, it would circle the fire support base and then fly in, fast and low over the runway, through billowing clouds of red, yellow, green, and purple smoke that would rise in tribute to the officer.

He and I were the only out-going passengers and, climbing in, we stored our bags and personal effects in the open bay before us. With the familiar shudder and high, piercing whine the helicopter lumbered up a few feet from the ground, did a slow, lazy turn, and ambled toward the flight line. Then, cleared by the flight line tower and in a revving running start, it dipped its rounded nose and sped out and over the barbed-wire perimeter.

The war was growing smaller behind me as Vietnam turned into patches and shades of green and brown far below. Climbing high, we circled the fire support base and then, when we received the go-ahead from the tower, the helicopter roared back down toward the smoke grenades' fruit-mix of colored smoke that the pilots on the ground had extended in salute.

"Aw-right!" yelled the outgoing warrant officer above the noise, nodding to me while pointing to the smoke. He also pointed out the plumes billowing from the TOC area and orderly room. Next to the source of the smoke Manning, the first sergeant, and Mike Toole were yelling, laughing, and waving along with the others.

It was a small, silly ritual that meant nothing at all and everything in the world.

EPILOGUE

Initially, I suppose I viewed myself as a hot dog; someone with steel balls that clanked when I walked; taking big steps in a land of giants.

I was naive.

Over the course of the war I learned a great deal. During my time with Hotel Company Rangers and Apache Troop, I learned something about real heroism—and the bone-chilling fear one has to get beyond to help others when they desperately need that help.

I saw professionalism in nineteen-, twenty-, and twenty-one-year-old faces, kids' faces really, kids doing jobs that no one else wanted or could do. The Ranger/LRRPS I knew were unique soldiers. Elite by any army's standards. Not movie heroes but the real flesh-and-blood kind whose own stories seldom get told but deserve to be heard.

As for the men of Apache Troop, they were always in the forefront of combat. The pilots, doorgunners, infantry Blues, and everyone else involved took great risks and suffered greatly to achieve their goals. Inscribed on their unit patch were the words, 'The boldest cavalry the world has ever known.' During my time with the troop, I saw nothing to convince me otherwise.

It was Aristotle who said that dignity comes from deserving honors, not in possessing them.

The 1st Cav's Rangers, and Apache Troop, the 1st of the 9th Cav, possessed that dignity, as well as a certain nobility that can only come from combat.

Yeah, I was a hot dog in the beginning, a genuine Oscar fucking Meyer, only I didn't have steel balls. Nobody did. But I sure as hell knew more than a few giants.

AFTERMATH AND FOLLOW-UP

SSgt. Roberts Payton Burrows, Apache Troop's reincarnated warrior and likable pain in the ass was killed in action in October 1970. If there is such a thing as reincarnation, then it'll be nice to see Burrows coming back as a soldier when we need him again. He was a professional soldier.

Doc Devalle, the Blue Platoon medic, as well as Ranger Johnny Rodriguez have died since their return from the war. They're missed by all those who knew them.

Capt. Paul Funk, the Apache Troop commander, is now a major general in the army. This doesn't come as a surprise to those of us who had the pleasure of serving with him.

Lt. Jack Hugele, Blue, is a successful banker in Houston, Texas, where he resides with his family.

Jim Braun and his family live just outside of St. Louis. He's a successful businessman.

Duane "Porky" Bloor and his family live in Wisconsin.

Lt. Michael Brennan, the former Ranger company platoon leader, today is an army doctor. On his return to the United States, Brennan decided to enter medical school, and the army is better for it. At present he holds the rank of lieutenant colonel.

Tony Cortez is also a career soldier. An Airborne Ranger who's also Special Forces qualified, Tony is a sergeant first class stationed at Fort Ord, California. One final note concerning Tony—almost twenty years went by before the army officially recognized his act of heroism in Cambodia when he literally saved the lives of two wounded soldiers under intense gunfire. After nearly five years of tracking down eyewitnesses and taking statements, several of the Blues and I, with the assistance of Paul Funk, lobbied to correct the army's oversight. Hopefully, by the time this book is published Tony Cortez will have received a Silver Star for gallantry in action.

Robert Edward Beal, my best friend from the war is a successful businessman in Greensboro, North Carolina, and is active in veterans' affairs. By the way, Beal finally did get his SKS rifle. However, it was eventually stolen from his home. Last year I replaced it. It was the least I could do, seeing how he saved my butt more than a few times during the war. We see each other from time to time and talk frequently.

Chuck Manning is a fictitious name for a soldier who prefers to remain anonymous, for any number of reasons, the foremost being his Thai R&R "basket trick," which he says might be difficult to explain to a few important women in his life.

In the summer of 1988, Art Dockter, former Apache Troop doorgunner and probably the best protective cover man any of us Blues had during helicopter insertions or extractions, coordinated and hosted the first Apache Troop reunion in his hometown of Fargo, North Dakota. Thanks to Art's prodding and effort, the town opened its doors to the veterans. For many it was more than just a reunion. As Jim Braun said, "It was wonderful. My only regret is that I wish I would've gotten to know the pilots and crews a little better during the war." His sentiments were shared by many in attendance. During the war it seemed we were all involved in our own little worlds. The reunion changed all that.

I never learned what happened to Nguyen Hue, and although initially I heard he became a combat officer, there was little information to go along with it. I'd like to think he somehow survived the war and its aftermath. He deserved that much and more.

In July, 1990, the town of Hacketstown, New Jersey, along with a local VFW Post, erected a memorial to honor Julius Zaporozec and named a playing field in his honor. In attendance were fifteen members of Hotel Company Rangers, foremost among them Jim McIntyre, Zap's former team leader. McIntyre was the finest Ranger I ever knew.

Finally, there are so many others I served with during my time in Vietnam whom I didn't mention or praise. For that, I apologize by saying that *Acceptable Loss* wasn't meant to be a definitive account of the units I served with or the people involved. This book was little more than a personal account of what it was like to have been a point man in combat. Now, as then, the complete picture was always obscured by the immediate one.

On a personal note, I never did marry my high school girlfriend, although when I eventually did get married, it later ended in divorce. That's a common characteristic of Vietnam combat veterans, I'm told. There are no Purple Hearts in real life; there should be. Casualties turn up in some surprising places, with wounds that aren't easily defined.

My own wounds came back to haunt me—in a way—years later while completing an army physical. A doctor asked me why I hadn't told him anything about my hip fracture.

"What hip fracture?" I asked while he just gave me his best *you gotta be kidding me?* expression.

"This one. Here!" he said, pointing to the X rays they had taken to get a better look at a piece of shrapnel in my lower back.

I wasn't a radiologist and shrugged at the jagged line he was pointing to. "I didn't know I had one," I said.

"How is it that you didn't know, for God's sake? It had to hurt at the time!"

"Well, I suppose it probably would have had I known."

The doctor called in an orthopedic surgeon, and, after a brief consultation, they asked me to show them where I had been shot in the thighs. Afterward, nodding in understanding, they informed me that more than likely the first bullet had also fractured the right thigh when it knocked me down.

"Well then, how did they miss it in Vietnam?" I asked.

"Chances are the doctors were more worried about you bleeding to death or they might've figured since you wouldn't be walking for a while anyway the fracture would heal on its own . . ."

"Or they might have just missed it," I said, thinking that Japan might have been nice to visit.

"That's a possibility," the doctor agreed.

I laughed. There was little else I could do.

But that's the downside, and everybody has problems, so I'm not going to whine about mine. For the most part, life beyond the war has been good. No. Better than that. Since the war I've been fortunate enough to have been a fire fighter, a selling hack writer, a karate instructor, a law enforcement officer, and a sometime technical advisor to Terrence Knox for the television series, *Tour of Duty*.

There is life beyond the war. It just takes some time to see through the dust of the past. The view's not that bad.